Chicken Soup
for the Soul®

Teens Talk
GETTING IN...
TO COLLEGE

Chicken Soup for the Soul®:
Teens Talk Getting In... to College; 101 True Stories from Kids Who Have Lived Through It
by Jack Canfield, Mark Victor Hansen & Amy Newmark
Published by Chicken Soup for the Soul Publishing, LLC   www.chickensoup.com

The publisher gratefully acknowledges the many publishers and individuals who
granted Chicken Soup for the Soul permission to reprint the cited material.

Front cover photo courtesy of iStockPhoto.com/jorgeantonio. Back cover photo courtesy of
Jupiter Images/Photos.com. Interior illustrations courtesy of iStockPhoto.com/©Oleksander
Bondarenko(Alex_Bond), and /Cimmerian.

Cover and Interior Design & Layout by Pneuma Books, LLC
For more info on Pneuma Books, visit www.pneumabooks.com

Distributed to the booktrade by Simon & Schuster. SAN: 200-2442

Publisher's Cataloging-in-Publication Data
(Prepared by The Donohue Group)

Chicken soup for the soul : teens talk getting in-- to college : 101 true
  stories from kids who have lived through it / [compiled by] Jack Canfield,
  Mark Victor Hansen [and] Amy Newmark.

    p. ; cm.

  ISBN-13: 978-1-935096-27-6
  ISBN-10: 1-935096-27-3

  1. High school students--Literary collections. 2. College applications--United States-
  -Anecdotes. 3. Teenagers--Literary collections. 4. Teenagers' writings. 5. Teenagers-
  -Conduct of life--Anecdotes. I. Canfield, Jack, 1944- II. Hansen, Mark Victor. III.
  Newmark, Amy. IV. Title: Teens talk getting in-- to college

PN6071.C67 C45 2008
810.8/02/09283   2008935940

PRINTED IN THE UNITED STATES OF AMERICA
on acid∞free paper
16 15 14 13 12 10 09 08   01 02 03 04 05 06 07 08

See what other readers had to say about
Chicken Soup for the Soul:

Teens Talk GETTING IN...
TO COLLEGE

Admissions how-to books abound, yet *Chicken Soup for the Soul: Teens Talk Getting In... to College* reminds us that the best counsel of all comes from reading the real stories of those who have known first-hand the anxiety and uncertainty of the college application process. This reassuring collection shows high school students and their parents that there is no single right approach or perfect school and that it's the "who" that counts the most, not the "how" ... or "where."

~*Sally Rubenstone, Senior Advisor,*
College Confidential (*collegeconfidential.com*)

Finally, a resource that focuses on the process and experience of applying to college instead of on how to get in. Authentic, emotive, and entertaining — a necessary read for all college bound students.

~*Ryan Chang, Founder & CEO, Ivy Consulting Group*

What a valuable addition to that big stack of SAT, ACT, and college guides! *Chicken Soup for the Soul: Teens Talk Getting In... to College* really puts the whole college application process in perspective. Insight can make the unknown a very fun and rewarding experience, and that's exactly what this book will give you.

~*Kent Healy, co-author of* The Success Principles for T~~~~
"Cool Stuff" Th~~ ~~

Withdrawn

Chicken Soup for the Soul

Teens Talk
GETTING IN...
TO COLLEGE

101 True Stories from
Kids Who Have Lived Through It

Jack Canfield
Mark Victor Hansen
Amy Newmark

Chicken Soup for the Soul Publishing, LLC
Cos Cob, CT

Chicken Soup for the Soul

DEDICATION

This book is dedicated to all the nervous high school students and parents going through the college application process. We share your pain... and your excitement.

Contents

❹

~Parental Pressure and Support~

❺

~Road Trips~

❻

~Placing Your Bets~

7
~Essays, Interviews, Auditions, and Self-Doubt~

8
~Getting the Letter~

9
~The Waiting List~

⑩
~Now It's Our Turn to Decide~

⑪
~Disappointments and Silver Linings~

⑫
~Hey, I Totally Changed My Mind~

⑬
~Gap Years and Other Alternative Paths~

⓮
~A Few Words from the People Who Pay the Bills~

⓯
~See Ya...~

Foreword

If there's a book you really want to read,
but it hasn't been written yet, then you must write it.
~Toni Morrison

This book was created in response to a real need—a book that provides emotional support to high school students and their parents as they navigate the college application process. This is the most traumatic episode in many kids' lives, and in the lives of the parents suffering alongside them. Record numbers of high school students are graduating this year, and applying to colleges, which are sorting through double, even triple, the number of applications they received just a few years ago, for the same number of slots.

My teenage daughter, my teenage neighbor, our high school intern, my friends... have all asked for this book. It is not a how-to book. It's a book to support you as you go through this painful process. You are not alone, and the stories in this book open a window into the experiences of other high school students as they prepare to apply to college, go through the application process, wait for the answers, and grapple with their choices.

My kids would have benefited from this book while they were applying to college, and that is why we made it for you. Last year, my eighteen-year-old daughter, a college freshman, asked me to please create this book for the kids behind her. As the Toni Morrison quote above says, if there's a book you want to read, but it hasn't been written yet, then go ahead and write it—or ask your mother to do it!

That's the beauty of Chicken Soup for the Soul — we saw a need and we have responded.

I really wanted to vent in this foreword. We had mixed results in my household — my daughter and all her best friends got into their early decision or early action schools in December of their senior year. On the other hand, my son and many of his friends suffered major disappointments despite stellar test scores, grades, and accomplishments. And neither of my children was accepted by my alma mater, which was quite upsetting for a loyal alumna. Last winter, I seriously considered chopping up my wood Harvard chair and throwing it in the fireplace.

The college admissions process is inherently unfair, random, and inexplicable. I felt a bit like an admissions officer in reviewing the stories that were submitted to us for this book. We picked 101 great stories and poems, and we regretfully passed on dozens of additional great stories. Random, unfair, and inexplicable — I apologize.

We have included a few stories from around the world — from kids applying to schools in Australia, Canada, England, and Scotland. Since you are all students of grammar, I just want to point out that we have deliberately retained British spelling in stories from contributors outside the United States.

Enjoy this book. I hope it relieves your stress a little. The good news is that there are millions of other kids going through the same process, but of course that is the bad news too. Anyway — good luck. You will live through this.

~Amy Newmark
Publisher, Chicken Soup for the Soul

Chapter
1

Teens Talk
GETTING IN...
TO COLLEGE

Planning...
and Having a Life

Judge your success by what you had to give up in order to get it.
~Author Unknown

Four Years of Stress: A Cautionary Tale

Carpe diem!
Rejoice while you are alive; enjoy the day;
live life to the fullest; make the most of what you have.
It is later than you think.
~Horace

I had been stressing about getting into college from my first year of high school. I remember sitting in my freshman biology class, learning about evolution, genetics, and fruit flies, thinking, "I better do well on next week's test if I want to get into college."

It was ridiculous, I know. Starting ninth grade, there are about one million other things I should have been worrying about, like friends and boys and teachers. To a freshman, college hovers promisingly—albeit distantly—at the end of a long and fun road filled with proms, crushes, friends, and youth. But in my mind, the admission process lurked from a preset date in the future that each passing day was counting down to. I couldn't escape it; I could only prepare for it and hope that my fears about not being accepted anywhere, and therefore living a poor, sad, lonely life as punishment would not come true.

To be honest, I can't really identify what was making me feel such silly pressure. Perhaps it was partly my family, who had worked hard to send me to a private high school and expected me, as "the brains" in my family, to go to a great college, do well, and thusly live a fabulous life (as going to Harvard would automatically usher me into heaven on earth).

On the other hand, perhaps it was my previous experience applying to private high schools that made me so anxious: just as for college admissions, there had been essays to write, transcripts to produce, and interviews to ace. The only difference was that I wasn't applying to college, I was applying to high school, and I was only thirteen and overwhelmingly unsure. It had been a grueling, upsetting process, and maybe I thought that by preparing far in advance, I would somehow make the next time I had to apply for schools easier and less upsetting.

In the end, perhaps it was just my own disposition working against me. I am a planner, I am a worrier, and I am an over-preparer. Mix those traits with the demonized image of college applications lurking four years on the horizon and you get one very obsessive, very stressed Nacie.

The result was that I planned my entire high school experience around what would look good on my high school resume. I made sure I got into the advanced placement classes for history and English, my strong subjects. I tried to mask my weakness in math by carefully maneuvering into lower level classes, thinking a higher grade in an easy class would look better than a poor grade in a moderate level class. To round out my transcript, I overloaded on extracurricular activities, and spent most nights and weekends during high school in the theater, the photography dark room, or the astronomy observatory. Every opportunity that came my way was scrutinized by how involvement would help or hurt the way I looked to colleges. It was totally foolish.

So the years of high school passed by, each in their own unique and challenging way. With the approach of each summer vacation, my anxiety grew: one more year finished, one step close to college applications. At the end of my sophomore year, I started really obsessing over it, and by Christmas vacation of my junior year, I was in full-blown panic mode. People started talking about visiting colleges in the spring, my mom began to collect potential college brochures, and my dad started to prep me for my admission interviews over dinner.

Then it all started in earnest. There were applications sent to favorite schools for early decision, missed classes to go to interviews, and a sudden interest in anything that came in the mail bearing a college seal.

I felt sick with stress. I realized that the past three years had been filled with the displaced dread experienced upon waiting to board a huge rollercoaster. Suddenly, it felt like I was being locked into my plastic seat and launched full throttle into the air. The train had left the station, the momentum had started, and I realized with horror that all the worry I had carefully nurtured since the start of high school was meaningless and could do nothing to protect me from the loops, turns, and twists senior year would throw me.

And it did throw me. It was stressful, scary, intimidating, intense, and sometimes heart wrenching. The worst was hearing someone else got into the school you wanted and you were denied or, worse, relegated to that purgatory known as the waitlist. I got into several schools, but was rejected by several more. Each rejection stung and smacked with the feeling that if I had only tried a little harder, done a little more, it would have been an acceptance.

But before I knew it, the year was over, everyone had found a destination for the fall, and I was graduating from high school wearing a white dress and crying a single tear for the four years of memories I was too busy worrying to make.

It is true what they say: college is wonderful, a life changing experience. However, if someone asked me if it was worth all the drama and panic it caused in my life, I would have to say no. In fact, at this point I believe there aren't many things in life that merit that type of worry. Thankfully.

Looking back on the way I tortured and stressed myself over those years I cringe and wish more than anything I could tell myself not too. High school is an amazing time in life, when you are old enough to become your own person, but young enough to make mistakes without regret. I think back to so many of those carefree afternoons and Saturdays when, instead of enjoying the freedom and frivolity of being sixteen, I had my nose buried in a book about the top ranked colleges that year.

It is true that you need to work hard and stay focused to get into a good school, but there comes a point where you have done all you can and the only thing that is left is to cross your fingers and hope for the best. Worry, stress, and anxiety do nothing to help any situation, and college admissions are no different. I learned the hard way that the real skill in the admissions process is not earning a stellar GPA or accumulating hundreds of hours of extracurriculars or fretting about an uncertain future. If you spend every minute wishing for or dreading the future, then you will never see how wonderful and special it is to be where you are right now, in this moment. The real skill is preparing and applying, all while still living your life, devouring every experience, and waking up each day being excited and grateful for the present.

~Nacie Carson

5

The Waiting
Is the Hardest Part

Purpose serves as a principle around which to organize our lives.
~Unknown Author

I've been waiting since the fifth grade. At the age of ten, I decided that Yale was the college for me, and anyone who disagreed wasn't even worth talking to. When someone asked me what I was going to do when I grew up, I would smile and reply that I was going to Yale. "Oh!" they'd exclaim, "That's a very good school. What do you want to study?" That question always stumped me. "I don't know," I would reply, "But I'm going to Yale anyway."

I don't have a clue what sparked my infatuation with the college; maybe I overheard the name, or perhaps I read about it somewhere. But once I started learning more about the school, my enthusiasm continued to grow until just the utterance of that beautiful word could make my heart beat faster. Eventually though, just like all good relationships, my bond with Yale became more than just a love-at-first-sight sort of thing.

During middle school, my best friend developed similar feelings about Harvard, and we became, essentially, Ivy League groupies. We talked for hours on end, about GPAs and double majors and roommates. As we researched further and learned even more about our dream schools, I began to realize that somehow, as a naïve little ten-year-old, I had gotten it right. Yale truly was my dream school, and it still is today.

I've spent seven years daydreaming about Yale; picturing the moment when my acceptance letter comes, imagining myself walking to my first ever class, meeting the perfect Yale Man, graduating, getting married, having a perfect life, et cetera, et cetera. There's nothing wrong with dreaming, right? Now, as a junior in high school, I'm slightly more knowledgeable than I was back in elementary school, and I realize that my chances of getting into Yale are even narrower than my worldview was back in fifth grade.

That doesn't really mean anything to me, believe it or not. I've grown up a lot since the time when I first fell in love with Yale, and since then, I've realized that there are many other amazing colleges out there, and quite a few that could be (almost) as dreamy as Yale. I know that I'm going to major in journalism, and that I want to travel to the East Coast. And surprisingly enough, there are schools besides Yale that fit perfectly into those criteria.

No matter where I go to college, I owe Yale a lot. My dream of going there has driven me to work a lot harder than I ever would have normally. I know that colleges want people who are good at everything; or at least people who strive to be. So I've tried things, like swim team and water polo, that normally I wouldn't have done, and the experiences have been fantastic. I push myself academically, in the hopes of impressing the admissions board at Yale; enrolling in the toughest honors program there is, and taking extra classes beyond that. If I didn't have my goal of making it into Yale, I would never push myself so hard, because there would be no need. It's come as a surprise, but all the hard work has been fun, in an exhaustingly gratifying sort of way. I've spent all this time waiting for my chance at Yale, but my dreams don't allow me to just sit around and twiddle my thumbs.

I care a lot more about my grades than I ever could have imagined. I'll never forget my first A minus. The year was 2006; the class Honors Chemistry, and I felt like a complete and total failure at life. I'll never forget the surge of disappointment that coursed through me as I stared down at my first semester report card; it was as if someone had dumped a bucket of freezing cold water over my head and left me standing there, spluttering and gasping for air. To say I was devastated would be an understatement; to suggest I was overreacting would be completely true.

Even though that moment occurred less than two years ago, I can already look back at it and smile wryly, and shake my head at how high-strung I was. After I failed so horrifically in that first semester of Chemistry, I made certain such a catastrophe would never happen again. So I studied for hours on end before each test and quiz; I convinced my teacher to create extra credit opportunities, and I panicked whenever I made an error. Stressful? Obviously. Over the top? Of course. Kind of ridiculous? Perhaps. But I was successful; I got all As that next semester and I figured it had all been worth it.

Now though, I look back and I'm not so sure. I know that it's important to care about grades, and there's no doubt that it's great to get all As. But Yale wants students with amazingly interesting and busy lives, and because that's what they want, while waiting for my chance to take my shot at Yale, I've made my life more interesting and busier than I ever thought possible,

Applying for college is all about waiting, but not just the wait for an acceptance letter. It's also about the maddeningly long wait for a chance to even apply. I've been waiting for years to write my application to Yale, and my chance is coming soon. As I near the end of this wait, I've come to see that no matter how horribly long and seemingly unbearable waiting is, it can change lives for the better. The same goes for college. Even if the college of my dreams denies me, I'll have an amazing experience at whatever college I go to, and I believe that this can be true for all my college-bound peers out there. It all depends on what you do—with your wait, and with your life.

~Tress Klassen

A Worthy Goal

The only people with whom you should try to get even are those who have helped you.

~John E. Southard

When I was a baby I was abandoned in an orphanage. Thankfully, I don't remember, but the pictures I've seen tell a heart wrenching story. Most children left in Romanian orphanages are forgotten and it doesn't take long for their muscles to deteriorate.

I was no exception. The first year of my life I wasn't given any food. I sustained minimal existence on week chamomile tea and occasional diluted formula. There were no toys to stimulate my development, no one to talk to me, hold or love me. It was a cold, dark and bleak environment. The only good thing that happened to me during the first year of my life is that I was chosen to be one of the six lucky infants to be adopted into an American family in 1993.

When I look at the tiny passport photo my parents used to bring me into the United States, I wonder what they were thinking. How did my parents have the courage to spend borrowed money to bring such a sickly-looking child into their home? My skinny arms and legs were useless. I couldn't even clap my hands!

My parents believed in me. Mom quit her job and worked relentlessly with scores of therapists. I considered myself special because of countless "play" sessions I had each day. I didn't know it was work. I eagerly anticipated the myriad of therapists who entered my home every day to entertain me with their bags of tricks and treasures. I remember crying when the "play ladies" had to leave for the day, but Mom gladly "carried over" where they left off. Dad converted the basement into a giant play land where my sister and I could roller skate, swing or swim in a pool of Styrofoam peanuts. We had the coolest house on the block.

When I entered kindergarten, my therapy stopped. My parents continued to work with me especially during times of regression, which inevitably came after each surgery I had. Today there are no visible signs that I had such a rough start to my life. Yes, I had devoted parents who taught me the depths of my own courage and strength. But equally important were the therapists who worked with me each day. They were the unsung heroes.

In sifting through the childhood photographs that mark the progress of my growth and development, I'm in awe. I overcame every obstacle no matter how great it was or how many I had. But I didn't do it alone. I accomplished enormous goals because of the dedicated team of therapists who had nerves of steal and patience of a saint.

Why was I selected from the thousands of orphans to leave Romania in 1993? I truly believe God chose me because I have very important work to do with my life. I had to learn first hand what it's like to struggle through the quagmire of therapies, overcome those obstacles, and understand the importance of it all so that I can help others.

I want to be a "play lady" that some anxious child waits for, peering out the window of his or her home as I once did. I want to be a physical therapist so that I can devote the rest of my life to coaching people to work through the physical challenges they face. I want to be a cheerleader to them. And my greatest reward will be to watch them leave as a "whole" and "healed" person.

I want to be that unsung hero, and in order to get it, I must reach deep within and muster the courage to go to school each day. I need to get the highest possible grades in order to be accepted into the best college for physical therapy. Education is the key to my success.

Without it, I will be an ordinary girl blending into the crowded halls of my high school. I am lucky. I know what I need to do. My life may have started out poorly, but I have found a way to ensure the rest of my days will be positive. Going to school may be boring to some, for me it's the only way.

~Andrea C. Canale

Product Design

Children require guidance and sympathy far more than instruction.
~Annie Sullivan

It seems like the day I started high school, every single teacher I had said that it was important to get good grades because then we'd have high GPAs, and then we'd be able to go to college. None of the teachers actually came right out and said it, but the unspoken message was that if you messed up even ONE SINGLE TIME, your entire life would be ruined. The pressure to look ahead to the future seemed to start the first day of high school.

I did okay in the first half of ninth grade. I took all the classes I was supposed to take and got mainly Bs with a few As tossed in. For electives, I had classes that I liked, a few I didn't, and some I couldn't wait to get through. But I passed them and that was all that mattered. I was always thinking about that stupid GPA and the fact that I had to keep it at least at a B average if I ever wanted to do something with my life other than collect aluminum cans from the side of the road.

Then came the second semester and an elective I took called Product Design. For some reason, I thought that this would be a class about designing things like labels or cereal box covers. I like to draw and I figured Product Design would be an easy A. How hard could it be to come up with a new design for a pop can?

It took about three seconds into the first hour of Product Design to figure out that I should have read the course description a whole lot more carefully. Product Design had nothing to do with logos or pop cans or cereal boxes. It was about using things like drills and lathes and welders. It was basically a metal shop class that I belonged in about as much as a candy bar belongs on the dashboard of a car on a ninety-degree day.

To make everything even worse, the teacher was one of those I'm-telling-you-this-for-your-own-good types. Only he wasn't only just telling us things for our own good—he liked being nasty when he told us we stunk at welding or drilling or whatever he had us do.

Looking back, I should have dropped Product Design after the first week. But I didn't. I kept waiting, thinking it would get better or I'd somehow miraculously get better at doing things I'd never done before. I also didn't drop because of my GPA. I wanted to keep it high and I was sure I could at least score a B in Product Design.

That was the longest semester of my life. Every single project I did was a nightmare. And everything took me two times longer to do than it did for the rest of the class. From January to May, my grade hovered around a C, and that was only with staying after school four days out of five to work on whatever the latest project was.

The stress was getting to me. At night I dreamed about welding. I woke up positive that I was going to weld my fingers together or go blind from the flame on the arc welder. I felt like I was going to throw up every time I stepped into the Product Design room. All I wanted was for the year to end.

But I didn't want to flunk. What would an F do to my GPA? I'd already decided that I wanted to go to college someday and I was pretty sure that I'd need a scholarship. So how could I get a scholarship if I got an F in Product Design?

And what about my parents? I'd never flunked anything before. They'd freak out if I brought home an F on my report card. I stopped having nightmares about welding because I stopped sleeping. All I could think about was why I didn't drop that stupid class when I had the chance.

Finally, after I messed up the last assignment and knew that I'd never be able to pull my grade up above a D, I told my mom. I figured that it would be better for her to know what was coming instead of being blindsided when report cards arrived.

She listened, nodded her head, and shrugged her shoulders. "Don't worry about it," she said.

I stared at her. She must not have been listening as closely as I thought she was. "I'm getting a D or an F in Product Design," I repeated.

"That happens," she said. "It's not the end of the world."

"But I might not be able to get into college!"

Mom looked at me. "Who told you that?"

"Everyone tells me that. The teachers, the guidance counselor—they all say you have to get all As and Bs if you want to go to college."

Mom hugged me. "Honey, you're a freshman in high school. Why are you worrying about college now? I didn't even think about college until I was a junior."

"It's different now."

"Not in this house," she told me. "You have plenty of time to get your GPA up. Tell me one thing: did you learn anything in Product Design?"

"Yeah. The teacher was a jerk."

"Did you learn anything about welding and metal work and all that other stuff?"

"Yes," I admitted. "But I suck at all of them."

"The point is, you know more now than you did going in. Isn't that what really counts?"

"I guess so."

"Then don't sweat it. And next year when you sign up for electives, you might want to know what you're taking first."

"Believe me, I will."

Mom hugged me again. I felt better. Not great, but better. And the more I thought about it, the more I decided she was probably right. I had three more years to take classes and get decent grades. I wasn't going to sweat it.

And I was definitely going to know what I was taking in every single class for the rest of my life.

~Hank Musolf

A Black Mark

Worry is a thin stream of fear trickling through the mind.
If encouraged, it cuts a channel into which all other thoughts are drained.
~Arthur Somers Roche

Everyone has something that they wish they could change but are forced to lay bare when applying for the college of their dreams. For some, it's the overall grade point average, or SAT scores, or extracurricular activities that they didn't do, or sports that they did but didn't stand out in. For me, it was a single grade in a single class in a single semester.

The class was Advanced Placement Biology. The grade was a C.

I received an A in all of my other honors and advanced placement courses. But the C grade for AP Biology jumped out at me, screaming, from a column of As.

I received a C through a simple yet baffling combination of teenage angst and drama that occurred right before the final exam. The exam was worth 30% of my grade, and I was unprepared, physically and mentally drained. My poor performance slashed my A grade to a C. If my class grade prior to the exam had been a little bit lower, I would have failed the class.

That was little comfort to someone who was previously a straight A student. I was out of the running for valedictorian, since there was little room for error in my competitive class. But even worse, I immediately believed that it seriously took away my changes for getting into my top choice for college.

Friends and family shrugged my worries off with truth and logic. "Why are you worrying? Even with the C, your overall GPA is just fine. You'll get into whatever college you really want to go to."

But against all reason, I could not stop worrying about the one thing that I could not change. "I got a C in AP Biology." I could not stop repeating it over and over to myself. A or B would have been understandable, but a C?

It was like an ugly pimple that I couldn't see myself, but I knew everyone else could. In my mind the black mark on my transcript and on my face grew larger and larger until it was the first, last and only thing I could imagine anyone noticing about myself on my application or in person.

I imagined the responses of the admissions committee at various universities.

"This girl must be a slacker."

"Whatever happened to her in the spring semester of junior year in AP Biology shows that she's not worth our time."

"Clearly, she has issues, and her issues do not belong at our university."

From November, when I submitted my applications, until March when I received notices of acceptance and rejection, I stressed, I worried and I overanalyzed. I wasted more energy and emotion than should ever be spent on something that couldn't be changed and could not have the power to control my fate.

My dad remarked, "I think what you're doing is not necessary," but when I insisted on applying to a lesser-known university because I was so worried that other choices would reject me, he wrote the check for the application fee.

As the application process drew to a close, I told fewer and fewer people of my worries. My friends no longer had a sympathetic ear to lend, and my family was tired of the grueling marathon. I kept my paranoia to myself, as the stress grew silently and disproportionately from what was reasonable.

The single grade in my past had become linked to success in college, my future and thus my overall happiness for the rest of my life.

I was frightened into thinking that because of it, I would be rejected from all desirable colleges, never have a good career, and therefore be doomed.

The applications process blinded me, distorted my logic, and prevented me from accepting the truth that others repeatedly told me: admissions committees do not accept or reject someone based on one grade, and a single college's acceptance or rejection does not ensure feelings of happiness or failure forever.

I have made many more mistakes in my life since then, but that was the only one that led to months of obsession, paranoia and stress. Yet I would not change that one black mark at all — the events that led up to it. I have no lingering regrets about the colleges that accepted me or rejected me and none about the college that I chose to attend.

All I regret is allowing something so small to corrode my insides for so long, when the future is determined not by mistakes that we all make at some time, but how we move on after they've been made.

~Joan Hyun Lee

Enjoy the Drive

Life is what happens to you while you're busy making other plans.
~John Lennon

When I was in third grade, someone told me that I could go to any college I wanted if I played the French horn. The next year, I told the band teacher about my new passion for the French horn, but ended up with a trumpet in my hand, because the teacher wanted me to start with the simpler instrument. I played trumpet for five years, but stopped before high school, when I would have switched to French horn, because band would have conflicted with soccer, which was going to be my college sport.

So I gave up the French horn for soccer, the sport that I loved, and I made the JV team as a sophomore. But I thought that I would never make the varsity team senior year, so soccer wasn't going to get me into college. Then, someone told me that I could become a rower and get recruited to any college that I wanted.

I gave up soccer and switched to crew in spring of my sophomore year. But I was too small to row and ended up as a coxswain. I coxed the boys' crew team for the next two years. We spent hours on the water in the mornings and afternoons but it was worth it. And after all, how many five-foot-tall girls get to tell eight six-foot-plus guys what to do, and have them listen? Senior year we came in fifth in a national regatta.

Finally, I had found something to get me into college and several crew coaches at top schools were interested in recruiting me.

Ironically, I decided that I didn't want to make a four-year commitment to a coach that I wasn't sure I would keep. So I didn't use my coxing to get into college either.

Early in high school someone had also told me that I needed to start a club in order to get into college. I started a political club and then spent an unreasonable number of hours organizing students and hitting the campaign trail, spending more time on campaigning and helping candidates than on schoolwork. I was planning to be a government major, so this was the perfect way to start down the path to my ultimate career in government and policy-making.

I never played the French horn, I didn't row, and I spent more time campaigning than doing my homework, in preparation for my political career. I didn't use band, soccer, or crew to get into college even after countless hours devoted to those "recruitable" activities. And I haven't taken a single government course in college.

It seems that I botched all of my get-into-college plans, but what I ended up with were amazing high school experiences. In addition, I could talk about them passionately and sincerely throughout the college application process.

And one of my high school passions, being a volunteer EMT, has actually continued, and today I am still an EMT on my college campus, as well as a pre-medical student, which I guess is where I was headed all along.

High school should not be viewed as just an entrance ramp to college; it should be its own journey.

~Ella Damiano

Turning "I Can't" into "How Can I?"

Optimism is the foundation of courage.
~Nicholas Murray Butler

Because I was born with severe cerebral palsy, my parents—eager to find help for my condition—moved us from Iran to the United States when I was only eighteen months old. And if that were not challenge enough, I would later discover that for most of my life, I had been stalked by two killers. But first, some background.

I grew up attending schools where having a handicapped student was novel, but that never proved to be a problem for me. I always felt accepted by my classmates and everyone at school. From my wheelchair vantage point, going through grade school and high school was fun and fulfilling.

Growing up, I assumed I could never move out of my parents' supportive home and have the kind of college experience most teens do. You see, I'd always relied on my parents for the most basic of tasks. Every morning, they would help me get out of bed and stumble to the bathroom, then assist me with showering, brushing my teeth, and so on. Then they'd help me get dressed and ease me into my ever-present wheelchair—not to mention feed me, gather my books, and get me off to school.

Doing things teenagers normally do—rebelling, demanding

freedom, taking risks—was a wistful, daunting proposition for me, because I depended on my parents so much. I believed nobody else would help me. So I ignored and suppressed my desire to go off to university. After I completed two years at a nearby community college, I thought I'd have to attend a university within driving distance of my parents' house, get dropped off for classes, picked up afterwards—the same old drill. What choice did I have?

As I watched my classmates finish community college and move on, I felt empty inside. And angry. I wanted to be moving on with them. Sure, I should be happy making the Dean's List and getting good grades. But countless times, I got stuck in the thought, "If I weren't handicapped, I'd be living on my own and creating a great life at college like my peers."

Then one day, my humanities professor at the community college suggested I move out of the house and apply to the University of Southern California. "You're nuts," I wanted to tell him. "How could you possibly understand the effort and intricacy it takes for me to meet my basic needs every day—let alone live away from home?"

But I must admit, because someone else could see the possibility, I was inspired. Why should I weigh myself down with limited thinking? Why stop my creative mind from exploring possibilities and solving challenges that living on campus would present? In asking these questions, I realized the powerful difference between saying "I can't" and asking "how can I?"

By saying "I can't," I was already beaten; by asking "how can I?" my brain would automatically churn out possible solutions. I figured that since my brain is just like any other muscle, the more I used it, the stronger it would get. So when my professor planted the thought that I really could achieve my dream of living independently on campus, my desire came alive.

Don't get me wrong. My deciding to go to USC wasn't as simple as packing my bags, telling Mom and Dad to "just send money," and wheeling myself out the door. It became a long, grueling journey fueled by research, sacrifice, and problem-solving along the way. I had to explore all kinds of things, such as getting assistants to help me, not only with attending classes and taking tests, but also with meals and getting me ready in the morning and at night. Could I possibly find one person to do all of this? Could I chop up the tasks among several people? What could I realistically handle on my own without assistance? Simply asking questions helped me formulate solutions short of requiring my parents to drive back and forth every day to help me. That would defeat the whole purpose.

Not long after starting my search, I found a roommate willing to help me in the mornings and at night, so I got that part covered. Then, in my classes, I figured out that by making friends, I could ask for assistance with issues that came up like helping me type papers. I had to arrange taking tests with staff members in the office of disability; they would provide me with someone to fill in my answers on the tests. On a regular basis, I'd have to meet a friend or hire an assistant to help me at lunch and dinner. Getting these arrangements set up meant I could enjoy a fabulous new experience—living on campus for two years.

If orchestrating all of this seems like a big chore, believe me, it was. Imagine having to coordinate every "mundane" task around the schedules of several other people. No way can I say having to jump through so many hoops was "fair." But long before this, I had decided I could sit back with a "life's not fair" attitude and wallow in "being right," or I could accept my situation and figure out ways to even the playing field going forward.

Yes, it sounds corny to say it out loud, but I truly believe life is what we make of it. I'm proud to say I relied on my positive thinking and made living on my own at university happen. No, my disability didn't go away. I didn't "overcome" cerebral palsy. I can assure you I still have it. But I discovered the identity of those two killers I mentioned, the ones who had been dogging me, and so many other people. They're dream killers—negative thinking and reduced expectations. They add a highly destructive element to the world. Yet no one has to accept these deal breakers, no matter what disability comes with the package.

Sure, it may be okay for some to settle for a "safe" job with a "decent" mate and say they're happy because they're "secure" in this world. But like negative thinking, reduced expectations and safe choices destroy the essence of life.

Don't get me wrong. I don't suggest rashly rushing into new things. On the contrary, having cerebral palsy has given me the ability to patiently assess situations before ever moving forward. That's how I methodically and sensibly achieved my dream of living on campus while earning a marketing degree.

Today, I run my own business as a professional speaker, business consultant, and award-winning author. And what keeps me going is constantly asking—and answering—these two questions: How can I do what seems impossible? And how can I love my life just the way it is?

~Sourena Vasseghi

Chapter
2

Teens Talk

GETTING IN...
TO COLLEGE

Playing Catch Up

*If you have made mistakes, even serious ones,
there is always another chance for you.
What we call failure is not the falling down but the staying down.*
~Mary Pickford

From Maybe to MBA

Just don't give up trying to do what you really want to do.
Where there is love and inspiration,
I don't think you can go wrong.
~Ella Fitzgerald

I'm about to receive a BA from Florida Atlantic University, and I was recently accepted into the MBA program at the University of North Carolina. Not bad for someone who almost failed high school, right?

For as long as I can remember, I've had a burning desire to become the biggest success my family has ever seen. I am the youngest of three girls, and like many "babies," I fought for my parents' attention. You see, although I come from a great family, with strong bonds, we were, at best, an average, middle-class family. Mom and Dad were always working, and my sisters made just enough trouble to keep my parents' attention. Because I really was a good kid, my sisters—and their escapades—made it very easy for me. My parents were so preoccupied with my sisters, they didn't notice when I began struggling in school. After all, as the good kid, I'd never needed them to notice before. But that "goodness" didn't give me immunity from the poor choices that put me on track to fail high school.

It wasn't until my first year of high school that I realized how much courage it would take to succeed as a teenager. As soon as freshman year rolled around, all of my friends were suddenly consumed with alcohol and drugs. Few were concerned with their grades or excelling in much of anything at that point. Of course, I tried to be the good example. For a long time, my friends used me as the "go-to" person when they got in trouble—sort of a teenaged Dear Abby. But before long, my own grades—and interest in my own success—dwindled and disappeared. I went from being an A student to earning mostly Bs, and before I knew it, merely passing became my goal.

I'm not sure exactly what hit me, but I remember waking up one morning thinking "who is this person I've become?" That thought was immediately followed by another: "This needs to change, and it needs to change right now." That was my epiphany. Suddenly I began focusing only on my schoolwork, convinced that if I let myself fail, I would continue to fail for the rest of my life. And that was my biggest fear.

Almost immediately, my crowd of friends changed, my grades improved, and I assumed the attitude of a positive and determined student. By the end of the second semester I had raised my grades from Cs and Ds to all As (again). I worked hard to get into honors classes and, in my sophomore year, I was officially invited to be a part of the honors committee. From the beginning of my sophomore year until the end of my senior year, I was an honors student, earning almost all As. In my senior year I looked around and realized that all of the people I had surrounded myself with during my freshman year were gone. At some point, they had all dropped out. Some were in jail, others on probation, and the rest were still trying to "live life in the fast lane." None of them had realistic goals. I still, to this day, cannot express the triumph I felt the day when I realized that I had finally "made it."

I excelled academically in my last three years of high school, and I graduated with a 3.7 GPA — just five one-hundredths of a point away from graduating with honors. I worked hard to graduate in January rather than June, and I was awarded a scholarship that paid for 75% of my undergrad tuition.

My high school GPA and my financial situation chose my college for me: I attended the community college close to home and earned my Associates degree two years later. Once again, I felt like I really "made it." I entered Florida Atlantic University, a state university close to home. What can I say? I guess I was comfortable at home. Now I'm living in another state, but I'm finishing my undergraduate degree through distance learning, and the end is in sight. I've applied for and, contingent on attaining my undergrad degree on time, have been accepted to the MBA program at the University of North Carolina. I've "made it," once again!

I'm on my way to becoming what I want to be, but I almost settled for what I could have been. I realize now that there is no limit to what I can do when I set my mind to it. It is true, after all, that there are no limits to personal success, and that dreams can come true—with hard work and determination!

~Marie Franqui

Class Act
for a Major Clown

It takes a long time to bring excellence to maturity.
~Publilius Syrus

My son strutted proudly from his third grade classroom side-by-side with his teacher. "I'm going to the Air Force Academy," Dan announced in such a cocky tone, it caught me off guard. Then he confidently added, "Someday, I'll fly jets."

"Oh, good!" Mrs. Brent commented as she flashed me a grin.

Because he was only eight years old, neither of us took him seriously.

But the kid was serious! As he got older, he became more determined. So, my husband, John, began doing research on what it would take for Dan to be considered by the Air Force Academy. Dan would only need to have near perfect grades and be a sports hero, a community service leader, a polished public speaker, an Eagle Scout, an officer in his class at school, and receive a Congressional nomination. Easy? Not for most kids, but especially not for Dan.

He was very intelligent. But he thought school was a time for recreation... not a time for learning. He spent his days entertaining the other kids by clowning around.

The teachers at Dan's small Christian school were constantly frustrated by his carelessness about class work. His actual intelligence wasn't reflected in his mediocre grades. Dan didn't see the need to get class work in on time, write down assignments, or do homework.

By the time our son advanced to middle school, John and I were tearing out our hair trying to convince this brilliant child he couldn't make it into the Academy without hard work. We tried everything, but the kid was oblivious to our suggestions.

When Dan transitioned to the high school level, his English teacher was a young woman who'd assisted in his fifth grade class. She knew our son all too well. Though Mrs. Harris had to confess there were times Dan's antics had her breaking into laughter, she'd been exasperated for years with his attitude toward schoolwork. So, after Dan had joked his way through fall quarter of freshman English, Mrs. Harris gave him an "F" in the class. Because of missed assignments and late papers, it was the grade he deserved.

"No-o-o-o!" Dan cried when he saw his grade. "I can't get an F. I have to get perfect grades. I'm going to the Air Force Academy!" But he had a great deal of respect for Mrs. Harris, so he didn't argue with his teacher. Instead, the class clown suddenly got serious.

The change in Dan was shocking! He made up for the "F" by retaking English during summer school. After that, his grades became nearly perfect. He began excelling in tennis. He went through the scouting program from "Cub" to "Eagle" in an unprecedented eighteen months! Dan took on pubic speaking by becoming the Master of Ceremonies at many high school functions. Because of his keen sense of humor, he made every event fun. Finally, he was elected senior class president. In that last year of high school, John and I were overwhelmed by the multitude of honors and accolades Dan received for school performance and community service.

As high school graduation neared, we watched in stunned silence as our local congressmen and senator fought over the opportunity to nominate Dan as the ideal candidate for the Air Force Academy. Then, six weeks after high school graduation, John and I waved a tearful farewell as our son departed for Colorado Springs to begin his basic cadet training at the Academy.

While it was hard to let go of our son, for years we'd watched

Dan's dreams become reality as God led Dan away from his undisciplined habits. God had even assigned one stubborn teacher to point Dan in the right direction. Thank God for Mrs. Harris!

According to Dan, God is the reason he not only made it to the Academy, but the reason he made it through their grueling four year program, through flight school, through deployments to two wars, and beyond.

Our son's commanding officers now say he ranks among "the best of the best," though you'd never know it to meet Dan. He's just a humble guy, still clowning around whenever he can get away with it.

On a recent training exercise in Roswell, New Mexico, he bought a three-foot tall, fluorescent green, inflatable alien, whom he named "Dave." Dan strapped Dave into the passenger seat of his rental car and took the alien everywhere with him—a simple gesture to keep his guys laughing during their difficult training sessions.

At a recent promotion ceremony, I had the honor of pinning Dan with the designations marking him as a major in the United States Air Force. Interestingly, the official event took place on Halloween. The officer who conducted the "pinning" ceremony began by saying, "The only thing scarier than this being Halloween, is Dan becoming a major!" The entire crowd roared with laughter... well, except for Dave the alien. He just sat in the third row taking it all in through his giant, alien eyes.

~Laura L. Bradford

The Application Blues

If it weren't for the last minute,
I wouldn't get anything done.
~Author Unknown

I n March of my senior year, my friends were starting to get their acceptance letters—one was going to Caltech, another to Columbia, and two to George Washington University.

I was still trying to decide whether to finish an application to the University of Colorado at Colorado Springs—the campus was about two miles from my mom's house, and I didn't know of a single applicant who hadn't gotten in. It had been a rough year for me, and although my grades and test scores practically guaranteed my entrance to most schools, I had entirely failed to complete an application to anywhere.

Mr. Christian, my college counselor, had noticed that I was the only kid in my classes not begging for letters of reference. He called me into his office and had a little chat—he knew about the problems I was having at home.

"You need to go away to school—at least to Boulder or Ft. Collins," he told me. "UCCS will take you, but you're a smart girl. You can do better things."

I protested, of course. It was too late; I didn't have any money; I wasn't going to get any financial help from my parents.

Mr. Christian played his trump card. "You're a National Merit

Scholar. I can name three schools that will give you full rides even this late in the application process."

I grumbled, and then grumbled some more. Mr. Christian managed to get me to promise to complete an application for the University of Colorado at Boulder before I escaped his office.

That evening, I printed out the Boulder application and got a pen. I made it through the first page but started getting frustrated once again. All those questions about financial aid—I still had no idea how I was going to pay for school.

I set down my pen and stared off into space. There I sat for who knows how long. I didn't move until the phone started ringing. It took me a minute but I answered it.

The voice on the phone asked for me and said, "I'm calling from the University of Tulsa. We were wondering if you've decided on a school yet."

"Um... I haven't made a decision yet."

"Well, then, we'd like you to consider attending TU."

"Okay..." I was a little confused.

"We're able to offer you a full ride, on the basis of your test scores."

That got my attention. "What would I need to do to apply?"

"If you could just fill out the first page of our application online, you'll be all set. I have your test scores and your other paperwork already."

I thanked her, filled out the paperwork and sent it in that evening. The next morning, I stopped by Mr. Christian's office. He just grinned at me and told me to get to class.

~Thursday Bram

My Fortunately Unfortunate Grades

I can accept failure, but I can't accept not trying.
~Michael Jordan

A. B. B+. B. C+. That's usually what my high school report cards looked like.

Call it laziness. Call it a serious case of denial. Up until first semester junior year, I refused to believe that my grades were in any way related to an acceptance letter. College seemed so far away—I mean, really, me, going to college? Freshman year... sophomore year... I hadn't even had my first kiss yet! I had priorities. And trust me, college definitely came after getting asked to Homecoming.

Much of my cavalier attitude about grades stemmed from the fact that nearly everything that surrounded me up until high school seemed to glow with a golden aura. At my all-girl middle school... well, not to toot my own horn, but I won the science fair, wrote essays I was sure deserved Pulitzer Prizes, and tossed A tests in the recycling bin knowing I was one period away from another A. I played on every team, had a role in every play, and spent my lunch period meeting with the other student council officers.

Naturally, I chose to attend a high school where being "the best" is a prerequisite for enrollment. That, and you must be the proud owner of several thousand collared shirts.

Mr. Off's World History class was the first indication that

hominids and Mesopotamians would have to compete for my attention with a far more interesting species: boys. During roll call on my very first day of high school, my pen dropped to the ground when I heard his name. He was a boy I had been hearing stories about for the last two years. A fourteen-year-old Chicago legend, he already had a reputation for taking girls on dates to the Lincoln Park Zoo and throwing parties with beer in his condo. Oh, how I loved him. Every time he smiled, I thought about how cute he looked with braces. Once, I bought a pack of Cert mints with the sole intention of being able to offer him one.

He was the reason I settled for a B+ in a class in which I could easily have managed an A.

Math, on the other hand, has never been a subject near and dear to my heart. I worked with tutors, spent my lunch period with my teacher — and I could never manage more than a B-. I wanted a good grade because I was the type of student who got good grades, but as it became clear that new material built upon material I had never mastered in the first place (I still don't understand factoring), I grew apathetic and convinced myself that real life doesn't involve as many "x's" and "y's" as Mr. Owen would have me believe.

As teacher after teacher patiently doodled parabolas and the quadratic formula on overhead projector slides, I penned elaborate, dizzying notes to my best friend, rigorously detailing the exact stitching on a pale yellow Marc Jacobs bag and in the same breath denouncing algebra as an evil precursor to my future, math-less life in New York City as a writer. "Honestly, the only thing parabolas are good for is making a purse handle. By the way, have you thought of your Halloween costume yet?"

Then there was Ms. Porter, who most students disliked. I couldn't blame them. She was young, but serious looking. Her personality was stern. She was uncharacteristically harsh for a woman in her twenties, and even when she was supposed to be excited or think something was funny, her forced smiles and laughs were almost more painful to endure than if she had remained straight-faced. I loved her. She was a puzzle I wanted to solve.

One day, I brought her a book I thought she would like in hopes of breaking her tough exterior. She thanked me and we began trading books, but it was all business. I was never able to decipher her code. What did she want out of life? Why did she always seem so unhappy? I finally settled on the idea that, like many writers and lovers of books, Ms. Porter wasn't sad, but enjoyed characters and the intensified, beautiful book version of what love and life and happiness could be, more than she enjoyed real life. Ms. Porter was a modern-day Emily Dickinson, choosing to observe rather than participate.

Her reluctance to cheapen English by making it a throwaway class made her a great teacher, and I worked very hard. Accordingly, I always got an A. Other kids were sent to summer school—she was probably the only English teacher to do this.

My tendency to pour myself into whatever class piqued my interest—English, AP Comparative Government, French—and ignore everything else—was reflected by my grades. It wasn't until I saw my transcript at the end of junior year that I realized I wasn't such a red-hot prodigy after all. Bs were everywhere, and a B on a high school grade report is the kiss of death in college admissions. Bye-bye Harvard!

Sophomore year, the year I had gotten a C- in religion class, was by far the worst. I had a GPA of 2.7 one semester, a secret I considered asking the FBI to guard. At my high school, you got a C- and considered dropping out of society.

No one would have believed my grades. I was very involved in extremely... okay, dorky, extracurricular activities. I held positions on both our award-winning Model United Nations team and on the Forensics (speech) team. I was an editor of both the yearbook and newspaper. I entered national writing contests. I wrote letters to the editor of *People* magazine in my spare time.

But I was no star student.

The grade report woke me from my coma, and I managed a 3.8 GPA for the first semester of my senior year—the final semester that counts. I ended up applying to colleges with my cumulative GPA hovering around a 3.2. A respectable, above average number, but nowhere near what I needed to gain admission to the University of Pennsylvania, where I applied early decision.

If you had asked me senior year, amidst sobs and confusion about where I would attend college, I would have said I seriously regretted my high school grades. I regretted them because I didn't get to choose between Stanford and Duke, Princeton and Harvard. I wanted choices, not heartbreak.

However, I now realize that if I had been able to choose between Princeton and Boston University, my current school, I would have made the wrong choice. I would have chosen Princeton for the same reason someone would choose a five-star restaurant over a three-star restaurant: name, prestige, and bragging rights. Never mind that all my friends are at the three-star restaurant, or that its menu has all my favorite foods. In a pinch, most people choose five-stars without considering the finer points.

Getting good grades is something everyone should strive for, but trying your hardest is more important. I didn't try my hardest in every class in high school, and that is what I regret.

But do I think about that B- in geometry when I'm cheering on Boston Marathon runners or enjoying lobster night in the dining hall? Not a chance.

~Molly Fedick

A Student Teacher Who Made a Difference

A teacher affects eternity.
~Henry Adams

At the beginning of my senior year in high school, I had no intention of applying to college. Honestly, I thought that people like me didn't attend college, for many reasons. I am a Mexican American who was born and raised in an "under-served" urban community with limited educational resources. I attended the local community high school where college wasn't encouraged for the average student like me. The scholarships and college-related events were offered to the honor students.

The only contact that I had with my high school counselor was to choose my courses. As far as family, no one had ever attended college, and I had no idea where to start, and if I could even afford it. My thought process was that I would graduate from high school and get a job. My father had suffered a back injury while working in a factory and was unemployed for many years.

I felt that it was my responsibility to help provide for my family and contribute financially to the household. Besides, I could never envision myself as a college student completing a degree. It just wasn't for me.

Although I viewed myself as just an average student with average grades, I never realized that some key people at my school did notice my potential. I clearly remember the day that my psychology teacher abruptly interrupted my English class with some interesting news. She was excited about sharing some news with the English instructor as well as the entire class. She had just graded a research paper from one of her classes. Before she began reading it to the class, she stated, "I want to share a brief passage from this well-written paper that has college material written all over it."

It took me a while to realize that the paper she was reading belonged to me. Me, college material? No way. I blushed in front of my peers as she recognized my work. Of course, after a while I thought to myself, I got lucky. Although I enjoyed expressing myself through writing, I never thought that I was actually good at it.

The first semester was coming to an end and I heard many of the honor students talking about being admitted into the college of their choice as well as scholarships that they had received. I knew it was too late for me to start anything. I figured there was no point since I was so far behind.

It's funny how fate works, because all it took was one ordinary day, that became the turning point in my academic life. It was a Friday morning during my English class. Our student teacher invited the entire class to attend a youth expo at Navy Pier. The expo would take place the next day, which was a Saturday. I took a permission slip home and had my father's permission to attend. The plan was to meet my student teacher at the train station and go from there.

When I arrived at the train station that Saturday morning I noticed that my student teacher was waiting by herself, and no other students were in sight. She greeted me and we chatted for a while as we waited. Fifteen minutes passed, and no one showed up. We decided to go anyway. Throughout the train ride and the field trip my teacher talked to me about her college experience and how she was excited that I would soon experience college too.

I told her that I was too late and that I would not attend. She was genuinely surprised and disappointed. She was completing her Education degree at the University of Illinois at Chicago and she mentioned that I should apply. I didn't know much about this university but I gave it some thought. She also mentioned that she felt that I was a good writer and that I would do very well in college. I enjoyed hearing these words very much.

On Monday morning, I built up the courage to pay a visit to my guidance counselor to inquire about the whole college process. I remember feeling very nervous about the whole thing, but thinking it was something I had to do. I walked into my counselor's office and asked about applying to UIC. My counselor looked at me and handed me the application with no further explanation. The meeting was over. Being that I was a very timid student, I didn't bother to ask additional questions.

I decided to approach another guidance counselor about the application process. The next counselor took the time to sit with me, and basically informed me that UIC was too much of a school for me and that I should apply to a city college instead. She looked at my ACT score and warned me that the university would not be a fit for someone like me. I can still recall the warm feeling rushing through my face and my heart pounding in my chest. I felt rejected and like a failure.

I informed my student teacher about my experiences with both guidance counselors. She brushed it off and said to me, "Don't worry about it, I will help you out." She helped me with the application and registration process. A few months later I proudly informed her that I was accepted to the university and received financial aid to cover tuition and fees. I also decided to apply for several scholarships that I can proudly say I received. I obtained one for four years consecutively. At one point, upon receipt of a scholarship, I was invited to read my scholarship essay during the recipient ceremony, in front of over 300 people.

Overall, college was such a great experience and I learned the value of perseverance and self-confidence. I decided to take on a new challenge and completed a Master's Degree in Educational Leadership. I am currently in the process of applying to a doctoral program in Policy Studies in Urban Education at UIC. These achievements are still surreal to me.

As I reflect on my educational journey, I am grateful to that one individual who not only believed in me, but guided me through a crucial point during my senior year in high school. Thanks for everything, Ms. Tracie.

~Elizabeth Herrera

I Wish I Took More Time to Decide

*Planning is bringing the future into the present so that
you can do something about it now.*
~Alan Lakein

During my high school years, the most important thing was
what I was wearing to the Friday night dance and who I
was taking to prom. Although college was talked about
and our guidance counselors generally inquired about it, college was
the least of my worries. The football games, the cheerleading rou-
tines, the class council fundraisers... my high school years consisted
of one event after the next.

When I was graduating eighth grade and starting high school,
my older brother was graduating twelfth grade and going onto college. For my graduation, he gave me a card in which he wrote, "Enjoy
your four years... they go by fast." I remember not believing him
then, but looking back... boy was he right. Those four years shaped
who I was as a person, pushed me to my limit and encouraged me to
become an adult. I wouldn't change a thing about that time. However,
if I could go back I might have spent a little more time considering
college.

I was so engulfed in my junior and senior years of high school,
that when someone spoke of college I brushed it off. I wasn't ready
to leave my comfort zone of having all of my closest friends together

and knowing what every single day was going to be like. I wanted to live in the moment, and those moments consisted of cheerleading practices and school plays. Studying was something I did only AFTER I nailed my half-time dance routine. I knew my parents wanted me to go to college so I told them I would go to community college and I didn't worry about my SAT scores, college placement exams or campus tours.

When my senior year passed and everyone graduated and went off to their own colleges, I started to wish I had done the same. My friends were living away, meeting new people, discovering new places, and I was living at home and driving to and from class every day. It seemed exactly like high school. I hated it! I thought college was supposed to be different! Why didn't I take more time to research colleges and do the same?

Eventually, I did my two years at the community college and transferred to a four year school. But you don't develop the same kind of relationships you do when you start a four year school as a freshman. Luckily I knew a few people on campus and made my friends that way, but I have heard some horror stories about people who transferred who ended up going back home and finishing their degree where they knew people. I ended up loving college and wishing I had four years to enjoy the campus atmosphere instead of two.

My advice to anyone thinking about attending college is to think about it very seriously and explore all of your options well ahead of time. Even though your senior year might be packed, squeeze in those college tours and take the time to make a good decision. My college years are over now and I am working full time and I would do anything to go back to my college days!

~Kristin Abrams

What Are You Made For?

*Feelings of worth can flourish only in an atmosphere where
individual differences are appreciated, mistakes are tolerated,
communication is open, and rules are flexible—
the kind of atmosphere that is found in a nurturing family.*
~Virginia Satir

My older sister filled out thirteen college applications. She sent them all around the country—to Seattle, Chicago, Philadelphia, Houston. Then she sat back and waited for the replies, for the big fat envelopes, confident in her perfect GPA and her valedictorian's cap.

Three years later, my own applications sat before me. They were all terrifyingly blank. I didn't know what to say.

"What do you do in a typical day?" one question asked. How could I answer? The truth was that I stayed home all day. After my mom dropped me off at school I would pretend to go inside, then sneak back out across the soccer fields, catch the subway, and either go home or to the bookstore across the street. There I'd stay until my parents came home. When they asked if I wanted to go out, I'd tell them I'd had a busy day and was too tired. Forget extracurriculars. All I did was sleep, and when I couldn't sleep, read.

"What do you see in your future?" asked another question. But I didn't see anything.

"You should apply to as many schools as you can," said my dad. "Keep your options open."

He couldn't know that all of my options were closed. There was no way any college would accept me, no matter how smart I was, with weeks of school skipped and failing grades. Of course, I couldn't tell my dad that. I'd been lying to him—and everyone else—for months. I hid my report cards in a dark corner of my closet and deleted the concerned messages from my teachers off the phone.

So I took all of the applications and carefully put each one, mostly still blank, into an envelope. Sealed them, addressed them, and showed them to my father. Thirteen applications, just like his other perfect daughter. We mailed them together.

One day, about a month later, I snuck home early from school, only to find my parents sitting on the couch with sad, serious looks on their faces. "We're worried about you," they said. "We know there's something wrong. The school called and said you haven't been there since last week."

I started to cry. "I'm sorry," I said. "I can't do it anymore. I used to like school—I still like learning—but I just can't do it anymore."

"Do what?"

"Get up in the morning. I can't stand being up before the sun rises; I feel like a ghost. I fall asleep in all my classes. Not that it matters—not that they teach me anything I want to know. They won't let me write stories or talk about politics or anything else I might actually want to do. How do you expect me to get up every morning for that?"

My parents brought me to a psychiatrist, who said I was depressed. I could have told him that. But when he said it, suddenly no one was angry anymore. My teachers all told me they would help me catch up with my work. The principal told me I wouldn't be disciplined for skipping weeks of school.

So I went back to school, and it was just about bearable. At least I didn't feel so guilty about lying to everyone all the time.

But I couldn't stop thinking about those blank applications. Did it matter if I finished high school, if I wasn't even going to college? What was the point?

I was just about to give up again when I got a phone call.

"Hello, this is Susan. I'm calling from the admissions office at Hampshire College."

Hampshire College? I remembered the name. It was the only college I had even bothered trying to fill out the form for.

"We were wondering about your application," she continued. "Your SAT scores are very high, as are your grades until this year. But it looks like last semester you failed three classes, and the application itself was only half filled out. What's going on?"

"I've been depressed," I said, and then, before I could stop myself: "I couldn't stand school anymore. I couldn't take one more test. I'm not a robot, I'm not made like that."

I expected her to hang up on me. But instead she just asked, "What are you made for?"

So I told her about the stories and the poems that I wrote, how I loved politics and had twice interned with a local congressman, how I liked to read books about psychology and evolution and the beginning of the universe. I told her that I was made to learn, not to take tests or be told what to think. I told her that I was getting treatment for depression, but if college was anything like high school, I didn't want to go.

"Some colleges may be like that," she said, "but not Hampshire. We believe that every student should get to choose what they want to learn, to define their own education. It takes a special kind of student to succeed at Hampshire, and we think you're one of them."

"You do?" I asked.

"This is unofficial," she replied, "but I just wanted you to know that in a few weeks you're going to get a letter offering you admission to Hampshire."

It wasn't like my depression disappeared with those words. But to suddenly have a future again—to be told that a college wanted me in spite of my failing high school—maybe even because I couldn't succeed at a regular high school or college—because I was different, independent, special... that was enough to get me to finally fight against my depression, to love and believe in myself and, years later, to be happy.

~Alexandra May

Chapter
3

Teens Talk
GETTING IN...
TO COLLEGE

Standardized Testing
Madness

*The chief pang of most trials is not so much the actual suffering itself
as our own spirit of resistance to it.*
~Jean Nicholas Grou

Just Getting By

By "guts" I mean
grace under pressure.
~Ernest Hemingway

I don't think the word "college" meant anything to me until I took the SAT. Before then, it was just some abstraction, an empty word with no teeth to it. I feel the same way even now about power words such as "job" and "marriage."

I have always been the kind of person who tries to stay just a half pivot ahead of whatever's coming my way. To do less is to leave yourself in danger of being run over by life. And, as I like to say, if you worry about the next big thing too far in advance, you run the risk of overlooking all the small struggles that come your way before!

So, this might go some way to explaining how I found myself pulling an all-nighter on the eve of the SATs. I procrastinated buying the study materials for weeks. When friends discussed the classes they were taking to prepare, I tuned them out or changed the subject. When my parents mentioned the test, I lied and said I'd been studying with friends.

When I finally succumbed to the need to buy the infamous Kaplan study guides, I tried (and failed) several times to make a dent in them. I forfeited sifting through the fat deck of vocab cards in favor of playing solitaire on my computer. But on the night of the test that would determine the rest of my teenage years, my fear overwhelmed me.

I happen to be a naturally bright person who seems to do better on exams than I feel is warranted by the little amount of time I spend studying for them. For this reason, I am always fearful that my good grades are the result of nothing but good luck. And luck, as we all know, is limited. So before every test, whether it's an AP French exam or a mock-quiz about what happened on last night's episode of *Friends*, I fear failing. My only consolation for the SAT was that I knew it was impossible to get an F.

Instructors tell you to get a good night's sleep before the exam, to spend the night thinking about something else, relaxing, taking stock in the knowledge that you are as well prepared as you can be. Instead I found myself lying on my bedroom floor at three in the morning with bloodshot eyes trying to commit the word "obstreperous" to memory. Little did I know then that this is the real preparation for college — of course you can prosper in college without memorizing the quadratic equation or speaking in SAT words, but no one survives college without pulling an all-nighter during which you imagine your whole life is on the line.

I must have passed out sometime around 4 A.M. My mom woke me up in the morning and seemed discouraged to see me sleeping on a heap of vocab cards and unsharpened pencils. She asked if I wanted to skip the test and I grumbled that I did not. The last thing I wanted, in fact, was to endure another night of stressful anticipation. It's tempting to imagine that in putting off the test, I would take more time to study for it properly. But I knew myself and knew I would only repeat my mistakes.

My parents dropped me off at the test location and I marched in like a soldier already wounded before the battle. I found a group of people I knew from school and listened as they frantically tested one another. Someone said "cantankerous" and I realized I was walking into my own grave.

Finally, we entered the gymnasium and took our seats. If the adrenaline hadn't kept me awake, the discomfort of the old wooden and steel desks certainly would have. We had to sit in silence for many minutes before the tests were distributed. I started to unpeel the banana my mom had given me, when a proctor came and snatched it away from me. "No eating in the room," she said. It's always the small things that make a tough experience tougher.

The SAT is a series of quick twenty-minute sections. It feels like you're being drilled. No sooner have you survived one section than you are forced to endure the next. On every page of the test, there seemed to be at least one question I had to make a not-so educated guess at. Though they tell you not to answer ones you're entirely unsure of, it's hard to undo the conditioning of eleven years of school that taught us to act otherwise.

During the test's sole intermission, I met up with the same group of people I knew from school and listened as they commented on the test. "Not so bad." "Thought it would be worse." "That last math section was a joke." I remained silent and prayed for my luck to return. It did, somewhat. I "passed" the SAT and received a grade good enough to get into some fine schools.

But something more significant happened in the immediate aftermath of the test. Suddenly, the word "college" gained meaning for me. It was only after preparing for the test and enduring the experience, that I became invested in the idea of college. And once you complete the SAT, there is very little standing between you and the next stage after high school. So, I went home that afternoon and started to research schools, to better understand the weight of the SAT at different universities and at the same time to determine which college fit me uniquely.

Despite exclamations to the contrary, there really is no grade so bad it ruins your life. Even those friends of mine who weren't so lucky on their SATs retook them and eventually ended up at decent schools. The truth is that any exam, at its best, is a chance to demonstrate just how much you've learned. And in the case of the SAT, the most important thing you learn is how to handle yourself under enormous pressure. That's a truly valuable lesson.

~Seth Fiegerman

Gaining a Competitive Edge

I play to win, whether during practice or a real game.
And I will not let anything get in the way of me and my
competitive enthusiasm to win.
~Michael Jordan

It was never a choice whether I would go to college or not, it was expected that I would. I remember my grandfather picking me up from school one afternoon during my sophomore year of high school. As I climbed into his big Buick, he said, "Natalie, it's about time you start looking into different colleges that you might be interested in." My heart skipped a beat. College? I'm just getting the hang of high school!

A few months later, when I was completely consumed with preparing for my driving test, a copy of *US News and World Report's* college guide showed up in my bedroom. I flipped through it for a bit but it was so giant and overwhelming that I decided to concentrate on more interesting things like who had plans for that weekend instead.

As summer rolled into fall and junior year began, I noticed something different in the air—a vibe. Everyone seemed a bit anxious, a bit on edge. And then it started. At first it was just a quiet grumbling in the halls. It was a few people whispering where they were taking their SAT. Then there were more open discussions, about registering for the SAT and what scores were needed for which colleges. It rapidly escalated to what SAT-prep programs and tutors were best and how you had to have at least one to be "competitive."

I came home one day and asked my mom what college plans she had for me. "Well I thought I'd have Mrs. Schmidt over and you two could discuss where you see yourself."

"Umm, okay."

Mrs. Schmidt? She's my mom's friend. What does she even know about college other than the fact that she's sent four children away to various schools?

Mrs. Schmidt came over to meet with me later that month and asked me all kinds of questions that I was not equipped to answer. "Do you see yourself at a small school or a big Division-I university?" "How were your PSAT scores?" "When are you taking SAT prep?" "What do you want to major in?" "Have you thought about Greek life?"

I just stared at her dumbfounded. I don't know what is small and what is not. I can't comprehend what "40,000 students" means. And test scores? Majors? Am I one of the only ones who hasn't even begun to think about the SAT? I can't possibly figure out what to study in school! I am really expected to decide what I want to be when I grow up right now? At my kitchen table? At sixteen years old?

I felt like someone had dropped a one hundred pound weight on my chest. There was no way I could possibly answer any of these questions. I was overwhelmed, scared, and frustrated. Why couldn't my parents just make these decisions for me?!

When I asked my parents about taking an SAT prep course to gain a "competitive edge," I felt another crushing weight drop on my chest. "Natalie, I'm not going to pay for you to take a course. I don't believe in them. The score you get on the SAT should be reflective of your intelligence, not on different testing strategies you've learned. And anyway, you attend a college preparatory school. That's an edge in its self."

"But Mom! Everyone else is getting a tutor or at least taking a class!! You don't want me to end up at a bad school, do you?!"

My mom looked at me with great compassion in her eyes and said, "You will not end up at a bad school. You are a smart girl. How about I buy you a practice question book and you can study on your own that way?"

"Ugh. Fine."

So I studied on my own a little bit. I did some practice questions so that I knew what to expect on the test, and I worked on my vocabulary and analogy pairings. Then the big day came. My mom made me a huge brain-food breakfast and I drove myself to the testing site. I walked in and right away I realized something. I was calm. I was confident. I was simply taking a test.

Yes, it was a test that could potentially influence the rest of my life, but I didn't see it that way. Maybe it was because I didn't have all the strategy and the practice hours and the pressure and the money put into preparing for it, or maybe it was because I knew that I could always take it again, but I walked into that classroom knowing that I was going to do my best and that that was all that was expected of me. And you know what? That was the biggest "competitive edge" of all.

~Natalie Embrey Hikel

SATs —
Subjective Aggravating Torture System

In examinations, the foolish ask questions the wise cannot answer.
~Oscar Wilde

Sprawled across my giant, cozy living room couch, I stared at the images on the television screen. To my parents and younger brothers, it probably seemed as though I was deeply concerned about the fate of the players on the show *Survivor* as I gazed in their direction, but in reality I was far away from *Survivor* and far away from my living room. I was standing at the edge of a cliff waiting to either fall or make my way to paradise.

Now, of course I wasn't literally standing at a cliff's edge, but as I thought about taking the SATs the next morning, I might as well have been. In one morning, after one test, my entire fate would be decided for me. Would I go to college or would I jump straight into work without a degree? Would I go to Harvard or Princeton, or a local school that was not nearly as prestigious? Would I be able to become a lawyer as I dreamed, or work somewhere that didn't require a degree? Tomorrow morning would set the pathway leading to the next four years of my life, or even forever.

My mom's voice interrupted my thoughts. "Courtney, maybe

you should go to sleep early. You have to wake up early tomorrow morning for the SATs. Did you forget?"

Oh sure, I completely forgot. It must have slipped my mind that tomorrow I would never see the light again.

"I know. I'm waiting for *Survivor* to end." I replied.

"It ended about ten minutes ago. You're out of it," she replied.

"Oh right," I quickly answered. "I just, uh, dozed off for a minute or two. Okay, goodnight. Wake me up at 7:00!"

But that night I couldn't sleep. I tried counting sheep. The clock read 11:42. I tried repeating the alphabet over and over again. The clock read 12:36. I tried repeating S-L-E-E-P over and over in my head. The clock read 2:30. In four hours and thirty minutes I would be awake again, only to again, anxiously await my doom.

I watched the digital clock across my bedroom slowly change. Minutes seemed as long as hours. I felt like the victim of some crazy torture scheme. Time was nothing more than a subjective system manipulated by the will of an all powerful jerk, and tomorrow he would strangle me with calculus questions I couldn't answer and vocabulary words I never knew existed. With knots in my stomach and fear in my head, I finally fell asleep.

And woke up one minute later. Or at least, it felt like one minute later when my mom called me from downstairs.

"Courtney, hurry up! You can't be late. I made you pancakes for good luck. Dad's waiting in the car to drop you off. Come on already!" she yelled.

With my eyes purposely and dramatically half closed, I got ready quickly and ran downstairs. At least my last meal was pancakes. If I died of stress in the middle of the SATs, I'd have had my favorite breakfast. As soon as I finished, I was out the door.

Pale and anxious, I arrived. I looked around, saw my friends and other students in my grade, and realized I'm not the only one in this condition. Everyone felt nervous. What was the point of feeling this way? I was going to take the SATs, whether I liked it or not, and although I disagreed with the Subjective Aggravation Torture system,

I couldn't fight it. The only things I could do were calm down and do the best I could, striving for a perfect score.

Two and a half hours later, it was over. I sat on a bench waiting outside the building for my dad to come pick me up, basking in the sunlight with a smile on my face. All that stress and fear were completely unnecessary, I thought. The test was completely fair and not at all that difficult. My scores would come soon, and if they weren't what I had wanted, I could always take the test again, or even a third time.

A few weeks later I checked my scores online. A smile spread across my face and I thought back to the time when I felt nervous about the SATs. That day I was a new girl—smarter, more confident, and ready to attend a prestigious college with my impressive SAT scores.

~Courtney Starr Sohn

The SAT Meltdown

Every kid has at least one meltdown during the college application process. My son was no different.

Michael first took the SAT on a Saturday in March of his junior year. The SAT was not being given in our hometown, so that Friday I called him out sick from school, and we drove to the neighboring town where the SAT was being administered so that he would have no trouble finding the unfamiliar school the next morning. We then shopped for a stopwatch, replaced the battery in his calculator, secured a "back up" calculator, checked his pencils for suitability, and made sure he had his admission ticket, ID, and other paperwork. We even carefully planned a nutritious carb and protein breakfast — being a wrestler, Mike knew exactly which breakfast foods would set him up for the morning's ordeal. If it sounds like we were over-planning, we were. But when you are in the throes of testing, applying, interviewing, essay-writing, etc., you over-plan everything!

Mike came home from the SAT feeling that things hadn't gone well. Although he claimed that it hadn't affected him, the girl sitting next to him had a seizure right before the test started, and the paramedics had taken her away. Whatever the reason, Mike feared that he had answered several questions incorrectly, so we decided to go ahead and pre-cancel the test so that it would never be scored.

That meant the April SAT was going to be his only SAT score, since he was scheduled to take one of the SAT subject tests in June.

April came along, and as bad luck would have it, Mike's lacrosse team had a game scheduled for the Friday night before the SAT, ruining our ideal study-sleep-breakfast prep routine. We couldn't even do the normal "sick" day on Friday, since varsity players were not allowed in the game on days they were out sick from school.

That night, in a major incident of bad luck, Mike and another lacrosse player ran into each other on the field, and Mike was injured. He appeared to have a badly sprained ankle, but he refused to leave his team, since it was such an important game. The team doctor happened to be at the stadium, so he sent me to the emergency room of our local hospital with instructions on how to obtain a pre-formed cast.

I may have been the only person to ever go to our emergency room without the patient. I claimed that "the patient couldn't be moved," which was somewhat true since he actually refused to move due to his desire to watch the rest of the game. Major amounts of begging by me and cell phone intervention by the orthopedic surgeon finally yielded a cast, which I took back to the game so that the doctor could put it on the patient right there on the team bench.

That night, Mike took about fourteen ibuprofen pills (unknown to me) and got no sleep due to the incredible pain. He took the SAT anyway the next morning, and then went to the emergency room where an X-ray revealed that he had torn every single ligament on both sides of his ankle.

Mike received a 1480 on that test (that was the last year the SAT had a maximum score of 1600). Test-taking came easily to him, and he had been scoring in the high 1500s or even 1600 on his practice tests, so this was a disappointment.

We made a last minute change to his June SAT registration and switched him from the math SAT II to another try at the regular SAT, but he had to take it in yet another nearby town since there were no more SAT spots available in our town on that day.

June came along, and I was anticipating our normal routine for the pre-test week—check out the location of the high school in the neighboring town, take Friday off from school, eat a power breakfast Saturday morning.

But Monday turned out to be Meltdown Day.

Mike came in panic-stricken that night because he had just taken a practice SAT and scored another 1480. He announced that he had decided to delay retaking the SAT until the fall since he was never going to do better than a 1480 that unlucky spring. I knew that timing was impossible, since he still had to squeeze in two subject SATs in the fall, before applying in October to his first choice college. June was definitely his last chance to take the regular SAT.

I called our SAT tutor and whispered that Mike was suffering a crisis of confidence and we needed an emergency visit. We agreed that the tutor would visit on Thursday and administer a practice test, and that no matter how Mike did, the tutor would tell him he scored 1580. Sure enough, Mike came in beaming Thursday night and reported that everything was back on track and that he had just received a 1580 on the practice test.

Saturday, Mike returned from his SAT test and said that everything had gone beautifully. And indeed he did receive his target score of 1580, getting only one math question wrong on the whole test.

I finally told Mike about the fake 1580 practice score a couple of years later, when all standardized testing was safely behind him!

~Amy Newmark

19

A Life Saver

*Mother love is the fuel that enables
a normal human being
to do the impossible.*
~Marion C. Garretty

As I sucked on a strong peppermint, my stomach continued to perform the hokey pokey. I wasn't sure if that was the exact dance, but it certainly was "shakin' all about." There was something a little ridiculous about trying to fight a tsunami of nausea with the small life-preserver of a lozenge at 6:00 A.M. on a Saturday morning. However, my mom had assured me that it would somehow allow me to relax and to stimulate my neurons, allowing the correct responses to flow freely onto the answer sheet.

It was ironic that the test center had recommended eating a large, nutritious breakfast before enduring the infamous ACT. How a person whose entire future was resting on one number was possibly going to consider stopping at a local Bob Evans to down the "Sunshine Skillet" was beyond me. As I sat in the passenger seat, I reflected on the bland English muffin and low fat cheese stick that I had consumed earlier that morning. I felt that I had done an adequate job of eating a meal that would get me through the test, but it didn't seem to be settling so well in my stomach.

"Honey, you can't study for this type of test. You've been preparing for twelve years, learning all of this material," my mom carefully counseled.

Apparently, she felt the need to interrupt the staring match with my reflection in which I was engrossed.

"I guess, but what if I blank out? What if I don't score high enough to get into Miami?" I countered without pausing to take a breath.

"Oh, you'll be fine. What's the worst thing that could happen?"

Incredulous, I was trying to explain that all of my future success was riding on this moment, leaving me baffled as to why she was so calm. However, I made sure to contain my thoughts in my head and didn't have time to fully debate the subject as we had all too quickly arrived at my designated testing center.

Fighting my way through the hoodie-infested crowd, I finally determined in which room I would meet my fate. My fellow Hs, Is, and Js all fingered our two, super-sharp, number two pencils in anticipation of the maze of "bubbles" we were about to confront. However, the proctors, feigning concern, put our minds at ease as we spent thirty minutes becoming well acquainted with the answer document, darkening the circles to represent our name and other various personal information, so that one pencil was already out of commission before the test even commenced.

After much lollygagging, the test finally began and I felt a surge of accomplishment after finishing each portion. This feeling only lasted for the first few sections as I was then consumed with watching the other students who all seemed to be finishing before me. Was I going too slowly? Were they going to bomb it too and never get accepted to college?

Eventually, the last subject area was appropriately bubbled and I was relieved to be released to the parking lot, where I found my mom ready to rescue me from this Boston Marathon of academia.

"Well, how was it?" she asked in a chipper tone.

Apparently, the thirty year gap between when she was in my place and that day had allowed her to forget the four-hour torment. I couldn't even compose a coherent sentence, as all of my dendrites seemed to have been temporarily incapacitated.

The calendar was circled as soon as we returned home, to signify the date on which the rest of my life would be determined. When that day finally arrived, I was devastated to realize that the scores were only being sent that day and I wouldn't receive them for another week. While I was doing anything and everything to get my mind off the impending doom, my mom made a covert eight-dollar phone call to the omniscient ACT recording system. When she came up to my room and asked me if I wanted to know my score, she did not get her anticipated response.

"You called?" I fumed. "You spent eight dollars to find out my scores that would have come in the mail anyhow?"

However, being as thrifty as I am, I resolved that she might as well break it to me if the money had already been spent.

"No way. Seriously? You're positive?" I responded, as I was informed that I would definitely have my choice of colleges in the fall. Never in my wildest dreams did I think my score would begin with anything other than a two.

As my mom finished pretending to have something in her eye, I said "thank you." It was in this moment of sheer joy and overpowering sense of accomplishment that I recognized just how lucky I was to have my own personal cheerleader, no matter what the occasion. Even when my heart is beating at the tempo of a hummingbird, I can always count on a fresh bit of insight and encouragement—whether it is a peppermint, or a half-hidden tear of pride.

~Rachel Henry

20

Chicken Soup for the Soul

A Medical Dream

*In nothing do men more nearly approach the gods than
in giving health to men.*
~Marcus Tullius Cicero

There was a little girl who wanted to be a doctor. She wrote it in yearbooks and textbooks and anywhere she could. She seemed to have no other ambitions, and every action was on the path to this goal. Her grandma said to her, "I knew you were going to be a doctor as soon as you were born. I'm telling everyone. Just wait, one day you'll do it."

When she was thirteen, she got into a selective school that was known for its high rate of graduating students being offered places in medicine and law. It was the most prestigious school in the state, and many families believed that acceptance into the school guaranteed success later in life.

During the four years at the school, she met girls who were acclaimed artists, multilingual volunteers for the UN, representatives to government committees and accomplished scientific minds. The girl had none of these talents. She could debate well, but she wasn't a member of the Australian Debating Team like her friend was. She was good at writing, but she hadn't won a national writing competition and been published like her classmate had. The school liked her and thought she was involved and committed, but no one thought that she was particularly clever.

After a while, she stopped telling people that she wanted to get into medical school. The girls around her were much smarter, much more studious and far more likely to become doctors. She wasn't even very good at science.

When she was sixteen, the school organised a lecture to explain the complicated process of getting into medical school. They gave out pamphlets and advice and the girl carefully kept them in a folder labeled "University: medicine." After the session, the students crowded around to share doubts and concerns, but the girl went to library to study. She didn't have a photographic memory like her best friend, and never quite understood concepts as well as the teachers would have liked.

In July that year, she took a 6 A.M. train into the city for the Undergraduate Medical Admissions Test (UMAT). It was a three-hour exam feared by all the students, and the girl had been preparing for the past two years. It was a horribly cold morning, and her menstrual cramps were almost as bad as her nervousness. When the test was over, she phoned her mother, took the train home, and went to sleep.

During the many months she waited for the results, she applied to every medical school in the country. Some rejected her straight away. "Physics is a prerequisite." "We offer priority to students from rural backgrounds." "We prefer students from our own state." "Your predicted final marks were not enough to obtain an interview."

Some, however, were kind enough to wait for the UMAT results. She got 281 out of 300. The letters came dribbling in over the following weeks; she was offered interviews at five of the six universities she was eligible for. At school, there were girls who didn't get any interviews at all, and assumed that she was equally unfortunate. The girl still didn't tell anyone her results, and celebrated with only her parents and brother.

Soon, the high school final exam results came. Her marks were high, but not high enough for medicine. Some of her friends obtained such perfect marks they were offered scholarships straight away. Her parents asked the girl if she had considered any back-ups. She had not.

Still, her mother took her to an expensive store and bought nice clothes for the interviews. Her father bought plane tickets and took her around the country, waiting in corridors until the interviews were over. They were encouraging, but prepared for reality. It was very unlikely that the girl would get into medical school.

At the interviews, the panel asked her questions like: "What would you do about the issue of binge drinking in the younger populations? What are your best friends like? What do you think is the hardest part of medicine? When did you decide that you wanted to be a doctor?"

When the process was over, there was nothing to do but wait. And then one day, a letter came. We are sorry to inform you... The girl's parents made a promise to not show the letter to their daughter. They decided to wait for the next one. We believe most students prefer a place in a medical school located in their home state, and so we will not offer you...

After a few letters came bearing the same message, the girl knew her dream could only be achieved by acceptance into the medical school located minutes from her house—and one of the hardest to get into. Her parents became more worried, and her mother started to research alternative pathways to study medicine.

One day, the letter from that university came. The girl was waiting at the letterbox for the postman. Over the year, he had become accustomed to the mother waiting at the gate for him in desperation for acceptance letters.

The girl opened the package, knowing that her life was about to be defined in the next few seconds.

"We are pleased to inform you that you have been offered entry to the Bachelor of Medicine/Bachelor of Surgery course."

She called her grandmother—she was going to be a doctor.

~Pallavi Prathivadi

Chapter
4

Teens Talk

GETTING IN...
TO COLLEGE

Parental Pressure
and Support

Nobody can give you wiser advice than yourself.
~Marcus Tullius Cicero

Running Through the Woods

In youth we learn;
in age we understand.
~Marie Ebner-Eschenbach

I remember running through the woods. My blue silk dress was getting caught in the brush as we made our way from the dance hall to the parking lot. Through the trees, I could see my father's car racing up the school driveway.

I pulled off my shoes, which kept getting stuck in the damp spring ground, and Billy (the name I will use here) held my hand to steady me. Then we ran the remaining distance to his car.

I didn't start crying until we reached the main road and was certain my father hadn't followed us. Billy lit a cigarette and shook his head. Neither of us could believe the night had taken such a wrong turn, that my senior prom had spiraled into a disaster that was, we knew, only just beginning.

It was a right of passage in the 1980s, getting a string of hotel rooms after prom. It was understood that we had all lied about where we would stay that night, that we would dance and drink and party together, sleep four to a bed then get up, go home, and face the last summer before college.

But my story was not that of the typical graduating senior, and how this night landed me in college still amazes me over twenty years later.

I met Billy the summer before my junior year. He was beautiful and irreverent and the attraction was as instantaneous as my parents' concern. They had high hopes for me to attend an Ivy League school. I was the straight A high performer, the competitive figure skater who had just given up the sport to pursue my education. I had two years to fill out my already glorious resume, ace the SATs and fulfill my destiny. Billy did not fit into the equation.

None of this mattered. We were in love. That crazy, hormone induced teenage love that will not be denied. Not by parents. Not by the distance between our schools. Not even by the greater distance that resulted when he suddenly joined the Marine Corps at seventeen. I did what I had to do—got my grades, did my extracurriculars, started my college search. And in the spring of my senior year, I got engaged to my Marine boyfriend.

This meant one thing to my parents. Terror. And the terror grew as the acceptance letters began to roll in. Of the eleven schools I applied to, nine accepted me. And one of them was Brown University. The Ivy League. It was well understood what this meant to my family. My grandparents were immigrants who struggled to live The American Dream, to give to their children what they did not have with the understanding that those children would, in turn, give their own children even more. Neither of my parents had finished college, but my father still managed to land a job on Wall Street and work his way up the ranks. I remember the progression of affluence well. The small houses getting bigger. The Ford Pinto being traded in for the Cadillac. And my older sister going off to college. It was my turn to do my part and I was failing miserably.

There was no question that I was drawn to Brown. Nestled in the hills of Providence, Rhode Island, with its historic buildings, traditional college green and highly privileged student body, it felt important. But Billy was stationed down south and I had offers waiting for me there too. I was torn between my love for him and a family history that was ingrained in me from before I could remember.

The after prom plan was the last straw for my parents. I was on the dance floor with Billy, my bare shoulders pressed against the stiff fabric of his uniform, when the chaperone pulled me aside. My father was on the phone, screaming. His every fear was being channeled into anger about this one small thing, this thing that should not have mattered, and his words were more hurtful than they might otherwise have been. I, too, had been holding back my own anger and I unleashed it into the receiver, then left it hanging as I grabbed Billy and told him we needed to run.

We got to his house half an hour later to find his parents waiting with a police officer. My father had called ahead and told Billy's parents he was coming after me, and they were scared of what might happen. When my father arrived, there was little discussion. Thinking I had called the police, he was beside himself. He gave me two choices—come home with him now, or be forever disowned by the family. But it was not a choice I could make. Between his anger, my anger, Billy upstairs and my entire life unraveling before my eyes, I could not get in that car.

And so it came to be that I was disowned. I moved into an open dorm room at my school, where I was a day student, and they let me finish my last three weeks without charge for room and board. I am, to this day, forever grateful. Billy went back to his base in Mississippi, and I graduated without my parents in attendance. I spent the rest of the summer living with Billy's kind and generous parents, working at a sandwich shop and scrambling to apply to a state university. I was not able to see my three younger siblings, my mother, my older sister, or needless to say, my father.

What I did not know was that my mother had filled out the form to accept the offer at Brown. And near the end of the summer, she came to me with a formal, written proposal. They would pay for college if I agreed not to marry Billy until after graduation. Of course, I had become so detached, so irreverent myself, that I turned down the offer. The summer was almost gone and I still had no plan for college.

One week before the start of school, my mother came again,

this time without a formal document. This time, she said, they were willing to pay for Brown and see how things went. I was eighteen years old and I had a decision to make — one that went far beyond the choice of where to attend university.

In August of 1985, I packed up my car and drove north to Providence. I attended Brown for four years and graduated Magna Cum Laude. It took several months to reconcile with my family, and to realize that my life was moving on in a way that was incompatible with Billy's.

Brown changed my life, opening doors and giving me the tools I now use as a thinker, a learner and a writer. There is no question that it was the perfect place for me. And yet I thought about Billy for years, and still do, because he taught me about love. I found him recently through the Internet. He is happily married, and I am happy for him. We talked about the past and I was, after all these years, able to explain the choice I made.

Life is always about choices it seems, and the older I get, the more I understand this, and accept it as truth. Still, there are times when I can feel Billy's hand holding me up as I pulled my shoes from the mud in those woods.

~Wendy Walker

Follow Your Heart

The man who never alters his opinion is like standing water,
and breeds reptiles of the mind.
~William Blake

These were the headlines at the University of Colorado at Boulder in 2004, my senior year of high school.

University of Colorado Named Top Party School.
Sixth Rape Allegation Surfaces at CU.
Rape Scandal Rocks CU Football.

A New Yorker, I had never been to Colorado, but imagined it to be something like heaven. I imagined snow-covered mountains, sunny skies, ski resorts galore, and thousands of students waiting to be my friends. In my mind, it was the perfect (and only) college for me.

My parents, however, did not agree. They questioned my sanity—how did these headlines not bother or worry me? How could I be so set on a place like this? I had worked very hard all through high school, and graduated with an I.B. Diploma. Did I want to throw my studious ways aside and head to the number one party school in the nation? And on top of it all, why was I so insistent on traveling across the country to go to college?

I understood where my parents were coming from. No dad wants to think of his little girl across the country surrounded by a team of accused rapists. And no mom wants to imagine not being able to hop in the car and deliver homemade chicken soup to her sick child. Despite all of their best efforts to dissuade me, I was persistent. At the very least, I had to go visit this place that I envisioned to be so wonderful. I knew that once my mom saw all the beauty that was Boulder, she would support my decision.

Needless to say, my parents refused to accompany me. I attempted to bribe my dad with snow conditions and ski resorts. I begged my mom to come see the city that could potentially be my future home. Neither one budged. If they were going to play hardball, so was I.

I booked a plane ticket for a long weekend in Colorado, and planned to stay with a friend from high school. It was at that moment that my parents began to understand the depth of my determination. My hope to attend CU was not a passing phase that I would soon get over, but it was a feeling deep inside that would not subside. My parents agreed to pay for my plane ticket, but still would not join me on my trip.

From the moment I arrived in Colorado, all of my wildest dreams were confirmed. It was even more beautiful than I had imagined, and the people were even friendlier than I thought possible. CU was everything I had hoped it would be. I could not put my finger on just one reason why, but I felt at home at CU. I knew that it was where I belonged. As I followed behind fifteen other students, each accompanied by a parent, on the campus tour, I knew that I would attend CU in the fall. I had to.

When I returned home, I could feel my parents softening with each passing day. Even as I was accepted to other colleges, several with more prestigious reputations than CU, nothing changed my mind. And slowly, my parents began to understand. They understood that deep inside I knew that CU would fill me with a happiness I wouldn't find anywhere else. And in the end, all parents want their children to be happy.

On August 17, 2004, I arrived at the Stearns West Dormitory in Boulder. As I entered my tiny dorm room, I felt truly happy. I was in the place where I belonged.

Four years later, I am a proud graduate of the University of

Colorado at Boulder. And not once during those four years did I ever question my decision to attend CU. I followed my heart, and attended the school that I knew was best for me. And in the end, it was incredible, both socially and academically. On graduation day, I stood proudly with my class and looked out into the eyes of my parents. The pride and happiness in their eyes made all of our past battles disappear. They finally understood that I had followed my heart to the place where I knew that I would flourish and be truly happy.

~Kate Lynn Mishara

23

Validation

There is no telling how many miles you will have to run
while chasing a dream.
~Author Unknown

I was probably one of the few kids in America whose parents didn't want her to go to college. It's not that they didn't want me to go, exactly, now that I look back at it, but, just as everything else in high school, there was the major issue of money.

My family is very blue collar. My parents started (inadvertently) having kids very young, and I felt they were never able to achieve more than getting a factory job, just as their parents did before them, and trying to make ends meet as their family grew.

While growing up, it was fine to speak in theoretical terms about going to college. I would always say I wanted to go to an Ivy League school and then practice neurosurgery at the Mayo Clinic, and my dad would say there was absolutely nothing wrong with our state university. My aunt Mary, the only person in both extended families to go to school before me, had gone there and she was a big-shot lawyer taking in loads of money. So Dad suggested that's what I ought to shoot for.

The one thing I vividly remembered hating in high school was asking for money. When my junior year arrived, I had signed up for the whole course load of Advanced Placement classes. Even though the AP tests were only $22 at that time, my mom would question why I needed the money and, I believe, huff a little bit as she wrote out the check. I gave creative speeches about how much AP would save me at college, and that those $22 would be parlayed into thousands of dollars of tuition money.

By the time senior year rolled around, I sent out only two applications for college, one to the state university a little more than two hours away from my hometown, and one to a school in another state. I was quickly accepted into both, but this was the point at which I felt somewhat blindsided by my parents. My dad, at least, seemed to be against the idea of my going away for school. He wanted me to attend the extension in our county and save money by continuing to live at home.

The mere thought of staying home another two years was enough to turn my stomach. I was already attending some classes at "The Stench," because my high school didn't offer the accelerated classes I qualified for. Although it was a fine school, and many people did transfer from the extension to the main state school, I knew I wouldn't follow that path.

For whatever reason, I had been given more ambition than my parents before me, or my two younger brothers, both of whom opted for the factory scene rather than education. But I could see this ambition having an ending point, as if it were mistakenly siphoned into me and would be sucked out if I spent too much time in my small town. I could see in my mind's eye how discouraged I would get living at home for two more years under my parents' ironclad rule, either getting frustrated at the extension, or finding more value in the attention from boys—none of whom paid attention to me in high school—ending up pregnant and working barefoot at the nearby gas station. Not my idea of a future.

So every day after school, my dad and I had blow out fights about where I would go to college. His logic was very sound, especially considering where I stand now, three years after graduation with debt up to my eyeballs, but I just knew I would get nowhere staying in my hometown. He threatened to give me no financial help at all, and I said that was fine, I would be able to get enough loans.

Eventually I signed my family up for a tour of the state university.

My dad and I toured campus, and even though it was so cold my toes started making odd snapping sounds, my dad fell in love — or at the very least seemed very enthusiastic about every corner of the campus.

I could tell he was softened by this visit, but the fights about where I was going to get the money continued until the day I packed everything up into our minivan. It was then, at breakfast before we made our journey down, that my dad said he was proud of me. He hadn't thought I would actually leave, and he was impressed. As my parents dropped me off at my dorm room, my mom started crying hysterically, and even my dad teared up, kissing me on the forehead, which was the first time I could remember getting hugged and kissed by them in years.

At this point, my relationship with my parents changed. No longer were they the disciplinarians, but they became confidants, advisors and an excellent support system, and I became an adult. Sometimes I still expect to get yelled at for my decisions, but they've done phenomenally well to leave me to my own life, and to just be happy when I actually call home. No matter what happens now, I know standing my ground on where to go for school has been the best decision of my life, as I have gained both an education and a life experience I never would have been exposed to had I taken any other road.

~Michelle Desnoyer

My Personal Best

Success means doing the best we can with what we have.
Success is the doing, not the getting;
in the trying, not the triumph.
Success is a personal standard, reaching for the highest that is in us,
becoming all that we can be.
~Zig Ziglar

"You're going to make a C?" my mother questioned. It was that I'm-not-happy voice I knew too well. I shrank back as she continued. "Perhaps you have forgotten, but Cs are not acceptable in this household, and you won't be salutatorian with a C on your report card."

Oh, I had not forgotten. I knew what was expected of me. From first grade to high school, I had never made a C. In fact, fear of disappointing my mother was so strong that only a handful of Bs had ever crept into the mix of A and A+ grades that I brought home on my report card. But I had hit an impasse in high school—geometry. No matter how much I studied, I just didn't get it! I truly did not "see" how all the parts of those little triangles and trapezoids fit together. Friends in my advanced track classes tried to help me. I spent hours on the phone every night, going over problems with other honor students. And then the test would come and I'd make another C.

Until the year I took geometry, I was in the running to be salutatorian. It was a family tradition—sort of. My mother had been pre-determined as her class salutatorian. Then, because of a bout with pneumonia and several weeks of missed classes, her grades fell. It had always been quite clear that I was to step in and fulfill that missed dream for her.

I did try to please her — not just with my grades, but in my total high school persona. I was a class officer, inductee of National Honor Society, German Club Vice President, Choir officer, and I got the lead in the school musical. But it wasn't enough. It wasn't salutatorian.

After the conversation about the C in geometry, I buckled down and studied like I had never studied before. I went to my teacher before and after school for help. I worked extra problems, memorizing the steps. The last hope to raise my grade was the final exam. I would have to make an A in order to raise my overall average to a B. It was a long shot, but it was all I had left.

I'll never forget taking that final exam. My hands were so sweaty that I had to keep wiping my pencil on the hem of my shirt. I worked and reworked every problem. I stayed after class to check and recheck my work. When I finally turned in my paper, I was convinced that it was the best I could do.

After school, I rushed to my geometry teacher's room. Had she graded my test? She had. I made a B — a good, strong, solid B. While I should have been elated, I was heartsick. The B on the exam was not high enough to change my average. I would make a C in geometry on my report card and that was that.

I hurried home and shut myself in my room. I couldn't bear to face my mother. With the impending C on my report card, I would lose the salutatorian spot. I was devastated because I knew it would disappoint her so much.

I aimlessly looked around my room. On the walls hung my medals from All-State choir competitions, photos from National Honor Society events, and all sorts of honor certificates from various academic organizations. Was I really a failure just because I wouldn't be salutatorian? I called my school and asked to speak to the counselor. Explaining it all amidst tears, I asked what I had done to my scholarship chances with the making of the C and my impending drop from the salutatorian position. A little quick figuring produced my "standing." I would move from #2 grade ranking to #6 of 650 students, still in the top 1% of my class. I would still receive a scholarship. The top colleges in the country would still want me. I stopped crying.

The school counselor paused and then went on. "Let me ask you something," she said. "Did you study as hard as you could in geometry? Did you give it your best effort?"

"Yes," I replied quietly. "I gave it my all."

"And was that final exam you just took a representation of your best work in geometry?"

"Yes."

"Then you should be proud."

"But I made a C in geometry," I sputtered. "That's nothing to be proud of."

"Of course it is. It's your best. And it represents your character. You spent hours studying when you could have been out with friends. You tackled your worst nightmare and brought it to bay. You were fearless and dedicated. You were steadfast and tireless, fighting until the end when you signed your name on that final exam and turned it in. This is a victory, my dear. This is a personal best. Be proud of yourself."

I'm not an athlete, so the term "personal best" caught me a bit off guard at first. But I have learned that it means surpassing my last effort. It represents pushing myself to be further along than where I was the last time that I met this challenge. And that's what winning is all about, the striving to be better. It's reaching MY personal best, not my mother's.

And what are my dreams? Just what do I expect from myself? That one's easy now — my personal best — every time.

~Elaine Ernst Schneider

If You Build It

God's will is not an itinerary, but an attitude.
~Andrew Dhuse

In my family, we didn't make quaint gingerbread houses for Christmas, we made candy castles—McMansions made of industrial strength white frosting and all the Brach's hard candies, gumdrops, Hershey's Kisses and peppermints we could pile on without collapse. From the Walt Disney Cinderella castle, artistically replicated with ice cream cone turrets, to a full New York City block with a succession of vanity mirrors to depict the icy city streets and Nerds snowflakes, our candy construction endeavors were nothing less than extraordinary. You could say that my parents attacked this simple-made-extravagant holiday tradition much as they did their careers and education. They went big, and excellence was the only option.

My mom and dad met at a prestigious law school, and my father was an official admissions interviewer for his renowned Ivy League alma mater. Throughout my childhood, I listened to my dad talk about the amazing, if not super-human, students he interviewed. They all seemed to have published books, played in a few symphonies (many being first chair in the state before they reached puberty), took care of impoverished foreign family members, and were fluent in several languages. Oh, and it goes without saying they all had perfect scores on their SATs and took classes at local colleges to offset the boredom of the high school curriculum.

I was a good student as well, happily exhausted with my honors courses, sports and activities, though when my senior year rolled around, I was very nervous about getting into college. Not only because college was a very Big Deal in my family, but also because the school I wanted to attend was the ultra-competitive and hard-to-get-into University of Notre Dame.

Several teachers told me to kiss my application goodbye, and most everyone I talked to recommend that I adopt an Irish heritage. But despite their doubts, I had faith that Notre Dame was the perfect school for me (and believed I was qualified, regardless of my failure to play the violin outside anything but a school gym).

So that December, in honor of my college hopes, we decided to build a candy replica of none other than the Cathedral of Notre Dame.

Like any of our endeavors, we attacked the project with intensity. We got out the old encyclopedias and checked out library books for authentic architectural accuracy. We made sure we had the exact number of candy cane flying buttresses, and melted LifeSavers in the oven to best represent the stained glass rose windows. Like any big construction project, candy or otherwise, the cathedral took longer than expected to complete.

With every passing day of adding another gummy bear gargoyle or M&M doorknob, it was one day closer to when I was supposed to hear back from Notre Dame. I applied for Early Action acceptance, and I expected to find out if I was "in" right before Christmas. I was literally a bundle of nerves. Several of my friends had been accepted to schools with rolling admission policies, and the children of ND alumni were already glowing with pride. Meanwhile, my dad would come home and tell us how shocked he was that so-and-so amazing Ivy League applicant didn't even get pushed to the waiting list, let alone get accepted early. All the while I was preparing for finals, checking the mailbox incessantly for a thick envelope, and frosting on more nougat bricks to keep from biting my nails or going completely crazy.

Finally finished, the cathedral sat in the middle of our kitchen, taking up most of the table. It stood not only as an impressive Christmas decoration, but also as a sugar-infused symbol of my college dreams. We admired it for a few days, standing on pins and needles "waiting to hear back." Then, my mom realized we forgot something.

Looking at the candy-packed replica, with its Red Hot-accented towers, Now and Later-bricked side chapels and foil-wrapped bells, it was hard to imagine that we forgot a thing.

"The cross!" Mom said with worry. "We forgot the cross!"

Whoops. We did remember a lot of things, even the Teddy Grahams tourists, but truly, we did forget the cross.

With that revelation, my mom went upstairs to her jewelry box and removed a small amethyst cross, set in silver, from a necklace (as Twizzlers just wouldn't do for something that special.) She whipped up some frosting and placed it on top of the cathedral's center steeple.

The very next day I received a letter welcoming me to the University of Notre Dame Class of 2004.

~Alexandra Gierak

Under Pressure

Some mothers are kissing mothers and some are scolding mothers,
but it is love just the same, and most mothers kiss and scold together.
~Pearl S. Buck

My mother never read the annual college reports that came out in all the magazines. She didn't need to. When we came to America ten years before I'd be applying to college, she learned the names of the top ten universities and that was all she needed to know.

Destiny, according to her, lay at one of those tony schools. And the thousands of colleges that didn't happen to be in the top ten? She hadn't heard of them, didn't care to learn their names and, to her, at least, they did not exist.

The names decorating my college applications read like a prep school wish list. At the very top was Stanford. We lived fifteen minutes away from it and my father had once gotten a fellowship to teach there. It was always around and my mother assumed that, naturally, I would want to go. And, more importantly, that I would get in.

Swaddled in maroon sweatshirts from an early age, I wrote with pencils from the Stanford bookstore and rode my bike on the sprawling campus, learning my first tennis chops on the courts beneath its august palm trees. While my mother had a burning desire, I had a burning secret—I didn't want to go there.

The fights we had on the subject were long, painful and frequent. "I don't want to go," I'd yell.

"What do you mean?"

"I don't want to go there."

"You don't want to go to Stanford? How can you not want to go to Stanford?"

"I just don't."

"That's not a good reason."

"I don't!"

My reasons were many and I couldn't articulate just one. I thought Stanford was snobby and huge. The campus looked more like a town than a college, with its own lakes, woods, towers, fields and little villages. I wanted something smaller, more intimate. I'd come from a private high school where I knew everyone and everyone knew me. My favorite teachers and I laughed and joked in the halls. I'd been reading up on it and I wanted a liberal arts school.

None of the top ten that my mother had memorized, however, could be called "liberal arts." She looked at me like the Queen of England staring down a wayward chimney sweep. "Liberal arts?"

"Yeah."

"Why liberal arts?"

"I want something..."

"Yes?"

"More, well..." I'd learned the buzz word but not what it entailed. "It's too big!" I blurted finally.

"I think you'll manage."

"I hate you!"

"You're grounded!"

Etc., etc.

All personal preference aside, there was also the nagging, awful worry that I wasn't good enough to get into Stanford. That, even if I wanted them, they wouldn't want me back. I played varsity tennis, sure, but my only extracurricular was theater and my numbers didn't add up to 2400 and 4.0.

The fall of my senior year, my mother decided that I would apply early decision. Staring down at the application made me break out in hives. Early decision meant "I really want to go here, more than anything in the world!" Writing my application, I tried not to look like a total liar. I didn't want to go there, not for anything, and it seeped into every word I wrote. The day I sent my application off, my mother beamed with pride. I smiled, went upstairs and started my other applications.

Since my mother worked at home, it was hard to get the mail before her. I felt like the bully, trying to intercept the inevitable letter from the principal. I knew what was coming—I knew that my heart hadn't been in the application and the committee would see it.

One day in December, though, she was out running errands when the mail truck pulled up. The envelope from Stanford was thin, almost famished. I didn't want to open it—I wanted to take it to brunch and buy it chocolate chip pancakes. I smuggled it upstairs with my heart pounding and ripped the top. They regretted to inform me, it said, that I would not be joining the class of 2006.

"Shouldn't you be hearing from Stanford yet?" my mother would ask.

"Any day now, I hope." I tried my best to smile.

"Have you checked the mail?"

"No letter, not yet."

"Maybe that's good. They always send the fat envelopes after the skinny ones. It takes them longer to put together that acceptance package."

I couldn't take it anymore. One day after school, I put on my best weepy face and walked into her office. "I didn't get in," I told her.

"Are you sure?"

"That's what the letter says."

She didn't even ask to see it. At dinner that night, she didn't seem too sad. I thought the whole storm had blown over. I got into another school, a small, liberal arts program about twenty minutes from Stanford, called Santa Clara University. They gave me a near-full scholarship. I was so excited.

Then, a few months into school, my mom's mild reaction to Stanford made sense. She dropped the bomb. She didn't think Santa

Clara was good enough for me and she wanted me to start working on my transfer application. To Stanford. It was a nightmare. If my lack of enthusiasm came through on my first application, I knew that it glared obviously from my second. I sent it off. Needless to say, I didn't get in. Again.

As I followed my passion at Santa Clara, I worried that my mother would never be proud of me, because I didn't get in to Stanford. We'd spent my teen years warring over it. Her message had been clear — she just didn't think success was possible anywhere else.

Well, I misunderstood. She wanted me to have the best shot at happiness. She wanted to make absolutely sure that I would succeed in a life that she had worked so hard to give me. All this time, I thought it was about the prestige.

As I was finishing up the school I'd chosen, it finally hit me. It wasn't about Stanford; it was about a guarantee for my future. All I had to do was show her it was possible no matter where I went.

When I graduated from Santa Clara, four long years after the Great Battle of the Cardinals, my mother was ecstatic. Now she defends good ol' SCU to all her friends and brags about every single thing I do.

In following my heart, I helped her learn about an awesome school that was never on her list to begin with. Now it's at the top and she proudly thanks me for it. And success? Yeah, it's possible outside the top ten box.

~Mary Kolesnikova

Not College Material

Most of us, swimming against the tides of trouble
the world knows nothing about,
need only a bit of praise or encouragement—
and we will make the goal.
~Jerome Fleishman

"You're just not college material."

The words were echoed by school advisors all my school years. Up to this point in our family history no one had attended college or university. But, my dad felt differently. "You are going to university," he told me. He was determined that I would be the first one in our family to start a new generation that would have the opportunities that he did not have. So, in seventh grade when vocational guides were handed out outlining various tracks of study, I naively filled out the vocational guides that listed courses for the next six years that would prepare me for higher education.

"Son, you do not have what it takes to go to college," I was told by my junior high counselor as they reviewed my course selection. I went home and told dad what the teacher had said.

"Sit down," Dad said, "listen to me."

I sat down.

"Yes, going to university is going to be hard." Dad paused, struggling to find encouraging words. "Your mother and I can't help you with academics because it is beyond our education. So you will have to work harder than other kids from educated families, but you can do it."

Dad was right. I did have to work harder than other kids. In ninth grade algebra, my grades were not high enough to progress to tenth grade geometry. There was no option but to take summer school.

Throughout my high school years, there would be times I became very discouraged. However, my father was persistent. "Son, if you work hard you can go to university," Dad kept up his firm encouragement. "You will have choices that neither I nor anyone in your family ever had. You can choose a career that each morning you wake up you look forward to going to work."

Dad drove his point home several times by waking me up in the middle of the night to go to work with him. At the time, he drove a truckload of bread and delivered it to a town several hours north of where we lived.

"You want to do this for the rest of your life, than don't study and don't go to university," he would say as we unloaded the large racks of bread. That was how intent Dad was on me being the first to graduate from university.

Discouraging words from my teachers continued through high school. However, I kept plugging along. Then, in eleventh grade chemistry I became overwhelmed with the course load. It was obvious that I had to work harder than the other kids in my class. My lunch hours were spent with my chemistry teacher. I found out that he was an amazing man. He was the only teacher who believed in me like my father believed in me.

One day he sensed my discouragement. He stopped tutoring and just talked. "Son," he said. "I know you look at all the other kids and you get discouraged. However, you are different; you have something inside of you that they do not. You may have to work harder but you are going to succeed when many of them fail."

Forty years later, I still remember his words. Along with the words of my father, those words kept me from giving up. He was the only teacher who had that faith in me.

In twelfth grade I told my English teacher that I was preparing to go to university and needed a foreign language.

"For you English is a foreign language," she said looking at me in disbelief.

I graduated from high school and decided to go to the local community college instead of straight to university. It was true that my ACT scores in math and science were in the 90th percentile. However, my English was not good enough to get into college level English. So I took a remedial course. Due to an amazing biology teacher in tenth grade, my goal was to major in the life sciences.

In the end, my Dad and high school chemistry teacher were right. I was college material. The hard work paid off. I went from taking ninth grade algebra in summer school to getting a B+ in college calculus. I also received As in two university chemistry courses. Sure there were times during those college years that I would call my father and say "I quit." However, he would not let me give up. Finally, with my father and grandfather cheering in the crowd, I graduated from the University of Idaho with a major in bacteriology and medical technology. More importantly, I had the honor of being the first in my family to graduate from an institute of higher education. My own son will graduate from university this year. But my hard work did not stop there. I have since earned a Master's degree in counseling. Not bad for a person who "was not college material." Dad's lectures spoke louder. His midnight trips to work were not forgotten. The encouragement of my high school chemistry professor was not in vain. I was college material after all.

~Dennis Hixson

The Dreaded College Application Process

Success depends upon previous preparation,
and without such preparation
there is sure to be failure.
~Confucius

I've been arguing with my parents a lot lately. The reason? The dreaded college application process. I'm finishing eleventh grade and it turns out that I have more than a few "gaps" in the college resume that we juniors must submit at school. Gaps that my mom and dad are now insisting I "plug" over the summer. I gather that I need to work, demonstrate some kind of passion for "something" and perform community service. While I'm at it, a Nobel Prize nomination wouldn't hurt either.

Now I'll admit that I'm the kind of kid who just isn't a "joiner." I'd rather be home working on my own interests—most of which are, sadly, not going to help get me into college—than signing up for activities and clubs where I'll feel uncomfortable and will have no fun. I don't understand the need to create some persona for myself for the purpose of getting into college. I wonder how many college applications simply do not reflect the character of the applicant and therefore give no indication of what the student will do or how he or she will act on the university campus.

Yet my parents are panicking. Why did they allow me to give up piano lessons in the fourth grade? Why didn't they send me off to the Model UN competition? Why didn't they insist that I build houses with Habitat for Humanity?

You would find this last one particularly funny if you had met me. I am neither physically strong, nor well coordinated, and have absolutely no talent for construction. I would require so much assistance that I would definitely be a hindrance to one of these projects. And, for safety reasons, I would not want to step into a house that I had helped to build. Frankly, any community would be far better served by my parents sending a check equal to the amount of money it would cost to get me to the work site. The money could surely be spent more effectively, safety hazards would be prevented, and I wouldn't be forced to do something I'd hate. Good for the community, but bad for the college resume I guess. Can you imagine me writing that my community service activity had been to write a check?

I wish my parents would calm down, although I have to admit that the reality of the college application process has been brought home to me by the college counseling class that I have been taking at school. I understand now that colleges look at everything about someone to decide whether or not he or she is what they are searching for. Athletic prowess, artistic ability, the clubs you have been in recently, community service... these are all on the list. All of these on top of SAT scores and academic accomplishments. I would advise all you freshmen and sophomores out there to download a common application form and try filling it in. We did this in a counseling class and the number of unfilled lines on my paper was very depressing. Acing every history test just isn't enough, and I'm now more aware that I am lacking in a number of areas.

Another activity that we completed in our counseling class was a role play session. We each had to pretend to be the admissions director of a university by reviewing the profiles of several applicants and picking who we would admit to the university. I was stunned to see the differences in the selection of each class member and of our instructors. Our conclusions were so different. Think about this real-life example: one student application for a university centered on science boasted superb physics and chemistry grades, although nothing else about the application stood out. A kid strong in science, who wants to pursue an education and career in science. This makes sense. However, the reality for this student was that the college already had plenty of excellent science students and was after something more. It wanted to boost its tennis program. This meant that the advantage was with another applicant, a girl with good enough grades who could also contribute to the improvement of the tennis team. Strength in only one area of the application proved detrimental to the first candidate.

Learn the lesson now, freshmen! The college admission process is tough and competitive. When you consider the millions of teenagers across the country, even across the world, with whom you are competing for college spots, it seems almost incomprehensible that you will get in anywhere. Your goal must be to make admissions directors think, "Wow, here is a quality person who could contribute greatly to our school." You need to present a well-rounded resume, which shows you as the type of person who can make an impact on the school in more ways than one. It is a case of "what can you bring to this college that will increase our reputation and give even more high school students a reason to think about applying here?"

As I've said already, I don't particularly agree with this approach, as I think it results in many resumes which are fabrications, manufactured by kids, their parents and any external advisors, to paint a picture for college admissions departments. However, the process is what it is, so I offer you this advice: get started early and try and find opportunities for jobs, extra study and community service which most appeal to you. Leave it too late and you will be grabbing at anything that comes along as application filler. Much better to get a jump on the process and fill your time with activities you enjoy.

My parents and I have reached a compromise for now. I get to take a fabulous journalism class, for which I can't wait, but only after I've filled some of the larger gaps on my resume. I'll be teaching children English, although I don't see myself as a teacher, and I'll be painting a community center, although I'm sure I'm not much of a painter. Poor kids, poor building! But I hope to see you in college!

~Thomas Ranocchia

Chapter
5

Teens Talk
GETTING IN...
TO COLLEGE

Road Trips

And that's the wonderful thing about family travel:
it provides you with experiences that will remain locked forever
in the scar tissue of your mind.
~Dave Barry

Chicken Soup for the Soul

Mom's Tour de Force

A mother understands what a child does not say.
~Jewish Proverb

I've never been a fan of arranged marriages, not that I've found the right person on my own, but I certainly can't imagine my parents being able to find that person. However, it dawned on me recently that I did something quite similar—I let my mother make one of the most important decisions of my life, one that lead to a marriage of sorts... I let her pick my college. How we got there is interesting, and how it all turned out proves that despite all the stress, work, and sometimes strife involved, the college admissions process does work out in the end.

A high school overachiever and the first child leaving the nest, my college decision process was more dramatic than a night at the opera... and on a few occasions we wondered if the fat lady ever would sing. It all started in my sophomore year of high school when my (equally overachieving) parents decided we should get a leg up on the admissions process. I remember leafing through the large college guide I was given one cold winter weekend and highlighting those schools which interested me. It should come as no surprise then that most of them fell below the Mason-Dixon Line, and I ultimately ended up in North Carolina. But to get there my mother and I embarked on a journey that took us from the mountains of Tennessee to the banks of Lake Michigan and proved just how blessed I was.

You see, decisiveness is not my gift. And my mother indulged what I now realize was an absolutely erratic college visitation spree spurred on by my inability to make a decision.

It began slowly with visits tacked onto family vacations. I toured Tulane when my father had business meetings in New Orleans and William and Mary over a holiday trip to Williamsburg. But as I edged closer to senior year, with nary an idea of where I would end up, there was an increased urgency.

Soon my mom was leading our team of two. She created a handwritten spreadsheet to record information and my feedback on all of the twelve schools to which I applied. Our dining room table became College Central, as mom rewrote my college applications in her neat and steady print, kept us on deadline, and charted a series of road trips. My path to college consumed both of us. Mom was my partner, someone just as vested as me, someone who understood the trepidation, the work, and exasperation involved in getting into college.

Mom tracked down a former admissions counselor to answer our questions; she scheduled campus interviews, tours, and our accommodations around her work and my school. And we were off! We visited so many schools: big schools, small schools, urban and rural schools, from the blue hens to the spiders, and many schools in between. Sometimes my father came with us, sometimes my best friend, or grandmother. But often we were on our own. And that's the way I liked it best.

Despite my initial yearning for some place warm, the idea of attending Northwestern University, in Evanston, Illinois, lodged itself in my head like a pesky sinus infection. I toured the school and interviewed with a college representative, and then I was promptly rejected. Unfortunately, I had so obsessed over Northwestern that nowhere else seemed suitable. I baked and devoured an entire apple pie out of self-pity and then announced that I was no longer interested in any other schools. Looking at me across the dining room table, it's a miracle that mom didn't throttle me with our heavy college guidebook; instead (thankfully) she did what she does best; she turned the situation positive, planned an impromptu trip and we were off... again!

In Nashville, we got our first taste of country music; in Virginia, we saw the northernmost palm tree; and in Delaware, my parents offered me a new car if I chose the state university. But yet, I was paralyzed: nervous and frightened, stubborn and unable to make a decision.

The last school we visited was Wake Forest University in Winston-Salem, North Carolina. We almost didn't get there, as mid-way through the eight-hour drive, I announced in dramatic fashion that I still believed Northwestern was the only place for me. Mom pulled to the side of the road and said, "If you're not going to give this place a chance, I am going to turn around right now instead of wasting our time." She wasn't messing around. And she was right. I shut up, and we continued.

Arriving in Winston-Salem, we drove up a tree-lined hill that opened on a vast expanse of green. "It's beautiful," my mother said. But I scowled, reluctant to make a fast judgment, or even worse, be pushed to like it. After the campus tour, mom was obviously excited, "So what do you think?" she asked. I mumbled something about the sports arena being too far from campus, an amusing complaint from a girl who had no interest in sports. I was still stuck and my mom could see it.

The deposit would be due soon, and my parents had already spent untold amounts of time and money trying to help me. It was time to draw a line in the campus dirt. My mother made it clear that they would not be paying two deposits.

"Aimee," she said, "Wake has a great reputation; it's small, but not too small. Look around you—it's beautiful, the people are kind and it feels like a family. What's not to like?" I didn't answer. She continued, "I think I am going to go buy a sticker for our car, what do you say?" I agreed, not feeling compelled to argue about a sticker, able to accept it mentally by telling myself, "it's just a sticker after all." But we both knew it was more.

That night on the phone in our hotel room, I heard my mom

tell my dad, as if in code, "Well, we bought a sticker for the car, Dan." And I think they both breathed a sigh of relief. The sticker was the type of commitment that I could handle. My mother knew me and it seems she knew her psychology as well. The sticker turned into the deposit, and the deposit turned into enrollment. And at the end of my freshman year, my mother and I again looked over that vast green expanse of campus together.

This time things were different. This time it was my home. We were swinging on swings that had been installed as a student art project. They were engraved with words like "dream" and "trust" and "hope" and "love" and I was crying because I did indeed love this place. That I had fallen in love so quickly and completely, after so much hesitancy and doubt, made it all the sweeter and leaving it, even just for the summer, was one of the hardest things I had to do. My mother knew this. That was why we were on the swings. Just as I had to take baby steps to get to this place, I too had to take baby steps to leave it. So we swung for a while, and then Mom said, "Aimee... time to go." And though I didn't want to, I felt compelled to trust her. And as we walked up the hill to our car, where a streetlight illuminated the sticker that started it all, I knew why.

~Aimee Cirucci

"Good news mom. I was accepted to the college of your choice."

Two Tour Trips with Dad

Any man can be a father. It takes someone special to be a dad.
~Author Unknown

While on the phone with Kim, an old friend from summer camp, the topic of college visits came up. "I don't know what school I want to go to," she said, "but there are a couple of schools in Boston that I'd really like to visit."

"Me too," I said. "Hey, my dad and I were planning on going up there over February break. You should come with us!"

Perfect timing! It must have been serendipity, or else a lucky break. You see, I loved my dad, but as a high school junior, I couldn't imagine spending four straight days with only him. I was the oldest of four kids, two of whom were under age ten, so Dad and I were almost never alone. The closest we'd come to talking one-on-one were the ten-minute drives home from play rehearsals, with my five-year-old sister bouncing and commenting from the backseat.

And whenever we did talk, he tended to dole out advice that felt a lot like criticism. If I complained about the amount of schoolwork I'd been given, he'd say that I had to buckle down and study harder. If I slept in on weekends to recover from the studying, I was lazy. Even when he came to see the plays I performed in, he couldn't turn off the critique. It was always "You were great, but..." You were great, but you could have been louder. You were great, but you seemed like you were tripping over your words. You were great, but don't you think you were overacting a bit?

I knew he loved me, but sometimes I felt helpless in his eyes, always floundering, in desperate need of advice.

But, to his credit, Dad drove two chattering girls toward Boston for four hours. He did not complain.

The next morning, we were up at the crack of dawn so that we could squeeze two tours in. Somehow, amid arguments between Dad and Kim on how to navigate the subway system, I found myself on my first college tour. Kim seemed to be on a mission to out-talk the tour guide. She floated from family to family, chatting about whatever came into her mind, making observations and flaunting statistics she knew about the school. I just followed in a daze, overwhelmed by the blend of city aura and ancient grandeur of academia, trying to imagine myself as one of the students chilling on a ledge by a statue, so cool and casual and at home. My dad was, apparently, feeling the same way. I watched him look around in awe, shake his head and laugh, "It's a playground."

When my dad was a kid, he had to spend four years in the Navy before he could get them to pay for his schooling, which he completed at night while working during the day. He never had the teenage on-campus college experience, and as I realized that, it hit me just how privileged and lucky I was.

The trip progressed and we toured more schools. Kim did her outgoing thing, and Dad and I did our "hanging back and making the occasional snarky comment" thing. Kim argued with Dad about directions, and one night she confided to me that she was going to sneak out and meet her long-distance boyfriend the next day. "Don't tell your dad," she said.

I don't know if it was the excess of college store caffeine in my system, or the fact that I had not been alone for three straight days, but for whatever reason, her plan made me really angry. How dare she take advantage of my dad after all he had done for us on this trip? I was the only one who was allowed to lie to him!

It turned out Kim was not as stealthy as she imagined, and Dad figured out that she was trying to sneak off to meet a significant other. I thought he would freak out, but instead he very smoothly insisted on accompanying Kim to meet her boyfriend. I joined him on the awkward encounter that followed and, I must confess, laughed at Kim a little.

After returning exhaustedly home, I decided that my next tour would just be my dad and me.

Three months later, Dad and I bid the siblings goodbye and set off alone for the eight-hour drive to Ithaca and Syracuse, New York. I was a bit more optimistic about this second journey, but still wondered how we would coexist that long without exploding.

But somewhere along the endless stretch of road and Dad's mix CDs, we began talking. We talked about music (it turned out I really liked the CDs he made) and somehow, that turned into the subject of me. I found myself telling him about my life, pouring out tidbits about teachers, things I'd done with my friends, and eventually (against my better judgment) my insecurities. Ever Dad-like, he responded with advice. At one point he tried to tell me about the birds and the bees (that was awkward) but the biggest surprise of the car talk came from his observation about something I never thought he noticed.

"I've realized that when you talk about college, you aren't talking about acting," he said. "And you aren't acting in school plays as much as you used to. What's up with that?"

Well," I said, surprised, "I figured it's not worth it to study something I'm never going to make money from."

"That's stupid, Valerie!" he said angrily. "Never stop doing theater. You're really talented!"

I stared at him, waiting for the "but..." It didn't come. For some reason, over the course of the trip, the critique filter turned off for both of us. Maybe Dad chilled out because he wasn't under so much pressure to take care of four kids, or because he realized that in just two years, I would be gone. And maybe I stopped getting so defensive because I realized how much I would miss him.

Ithaca and Syracuse were cool, but the trip, for me, wasn't about school anymore. It was about the little things—the fact that Dad never made me drive even though it was a long, tiring trip; about how, once we found a vegetarian restaurant in Ithaca, Dad let us eat there two nights in a row even though he probably just wanted a burger and a beer; the amazing feeling that came from having someone focus on your feelings, care about your opinions. Sure it was only a weekend, but for that weekend, I had my Dad to myself.

One year later, on the eve of my acting school auditions, I practiced my monologues for the last time, performing them for my dad. I finished and told him, "That's it!" in a shaky, overcompensating voice.

He shook his head. "If they don't take you after that," he said, "I don't know what their problem is."

And for the moment, that was enough.

~Valerie Howlett

Finding the Right Fit

It is a wise father that knows his own child.
~William Shakespeare

My parents knew from the moment I brought home Cornell's glossy full-color brochure that I would hate it. Even with the university's J.Crew catalog-inspired photos of kids gathered around a fireplace, playing on a perfect blanket of white snow and engaged in other wholesome Ivy League activities, they knew that upstate New York was not the place for me. Even after I read a book by one of Cornell's leading women's studies professors, they knew that four years in upstate New York would be four years too many for a city girl accustomed to four-story bookstores, multiplex movie theaters, and a Starbucks on every corner.

Still, I was convinced that Cornell's rural surroundings and rigorous academics would mold me into the kind of intelligent, inquisitive woman I hoped to become.

Mom had said several times, "We want you to go to a good college, but I don't think you'll be happy at Cornell."

To which I pleaded, course catalog clutched to my chest, "Can't I just visit it and see for myself?"

"How many flights do you think they have from Seattle to Ithaca?" my mother answered. "Not too many."

"But students come from all over the world," I countered. "There has to be a way to get out there."

"Trust me, you won't like it."

Before she could launch into her speech about the virtues of her alma mater, how Simmons has an excellent communications program right in Boston and how this writer and that senator had done just fine at a women's college, Dad joined the discussion.

"This is silly," he announced. Usually a man of few words, my Dad only interrupted our mother-daughter debates when he had something really important to say. And we listened. "She'll never believe us until she sees it for herself. Let's humor her, and then we can move on to places she'll actually want to go, like NYU or Boston University."

"Who's going to accompany her on this fun little trip to the country?" asked my mother, always fixating on details.

"I will," he volunteered. And that was that.

• • •

That spring, instead of jetting off to a warm, sunny locale like Hawaii, where my parents always said they would go for a second honeymoon, or to a thriving historic city like Philadelphia, father and daughter boarded a cramped plane bound for Ithaca, New York. The town wasn't warm or sunny or particularly thriving, but if Dad was disappointed he never voiced a complaint. Ever.

"What should we do first? Do you want to drive around campus?" he asked.

I noticed immediately that the campus didn't look quite as welcoming and sunny as the photos in the brochure. Partway to the center of campus, our Honda Civic rental car was blocked by a group of students protesting in favor of the Kyoto treaty, an environmental policy which had hitherto eluded my consciousness. This was not the preppy oasis I pictured, where students discussed philosophy and literature over lattes, and reserved yelling for football games, but I refused to admit that half an hour into our trip.

A perpetual good sport, Dad said it reminded him of his college years. "Harvard, Yale, MIT, tear down the schools of the bourgeoisie!" he chanted, tapping the steering wheel in time. "Hey, there's something catchy about that chant."

The next day, we joined dozens of other eager parents and students on the traditional campus tour. Though it was already mid-April, our guide wore a wool pea coat, a funky scarf and the Birkenstocks that seemed to set the campus-wide standard in footwear. Rubbing her hands together for warmth, she lead us from one Gothic building to the next, commenting on the students' affinity for winter sports and the school's origins as an agricultural college.

As an aspiring journalist, I asked about the communications program in a last ditch attempt at redeeming the trip. She explained that it had begun as a school for local farmers to learn about reporting. "Even today, we're more interested in *The Farmer's Almanac* than *The Financial Times*," she quipped.

I was not impressed, and by the time she pointed out the bridge where "at least one student takes the plunge each semester during finals," I was ready to admit that this definitely wasn't the school for me.

Dad knew before my chattering teeth could form the words. "I think we've seen enough. Do you want to get some coffee instead?" he whispered conspiratorially mid-tour.

I hesitate to admit this next part, because I went on to become a campus guide myself, but Dad and I ditched the tour. We slunk to the back of the group and, as soon as our guide turned to cross the street, ran in the opposite direction.

Safely tucked inside what was probably the only Starbucks for twenty miles, we had a good laugh about our ill-fated trip.

"Can you believe that story about the bridge?" he said, giggling like a college girl at a party. "Is their suicide rate supposed to be a selling point?"

"I know!" I took another sip of my peppermint hot chocolate, preparing to swallow my pride and admit I'd been wrong. "And Dad, you and Mom were right about Cornell. What was I thinking? I would never go to a school that was this far from civilization."

The following week, Dad took me to visit Boston University. And just as he'd predicted, BU fit me perfectly.

~Susan E. Johnston

Tour de College Campus

Indecision becomes decision with time.
~Author Unknown

As our tour group hiked across the main quad, she lagged behind to pan the scene. Video camera smashed against her forehead, she zoomed in on the stately mustard-colored brick buildings. Next, she focused her lens on our tour guide, a confident junior who speed-walked backward and talked nonstop.

"This is the Science Building," he informed us. "Totally renovated last year. Any undergrad may conduct research under full professors. Stunning discoveries happening here on sea cucumbers. Do a semester abroad on any continent except Antarctica, and still graduate pre-med in four years. We have hundreds of activities on campus, but if you don't find the club you want, track down four other people and start it yourself!"

Video Mom recorded our walk down the empty hallway, then our entrance into the biology lab lined with algae-laced aquariums. It wasn't hard to spot her son. He was the one trying to blend into the wall tiles, staring straight down like he was planning to major in shoelaces.

"I may ask questions, but I don't video!" I whispered to my son.

Our countless dinner table conversations crystallized here on the campus visit. After months focused on college guidebooks, essays and SATs, transcripts and teacher recommendations—it was show time.

Moms and dads walked across campus, trying to imagine their sons or daughters living here — on their own, away from home. Will Ben ever hang up his wet towel? Or study with no one telling him to? Will Kaitlin get along with a roommate? We've seen more friend drama in high school than the entire theater department!

The students were full of questions, too. Will I get in? Do I even want to be accepted here? Is there anyone here who looks like me? What if I hate it? What if I flunk out? Who am I going to live with? How am I going to fit my stuff in a room the size of a closet? I wish I could move in today!

The information sessions answered some questions, but created more. "If your student is undecided on a major, that's great! Seventy-five percent of all students change their major at least once! Your student will likely switch careers at least seven times in his or her work life! Look around you — most of our students find their future mate here on campus! Reserve the chapel way ahead, it books up years in advance!"

I gulped. Sending my firstborn to college was hard enough without adding the stress of a future in-law.

For us, campus visits before knowing if your student was accepted had a different feel than the special days for admitted students many colleges offer in the spring. In the junior year, or senior fall, everything is possible. In the spring, the choices are real and defined. Attending our first admitted student day, we scanned the other high school students in the cafeteria eating institutional scrambled eggs. Imagine, that guy could be his roommate! Could the girl in front of us in line become a close friend?

As we rode hotel elevators and waited for breakout sessions in student centers, we started running into families on the same circuit.

"Weren't we in the same tour group last week in Iowa?" a mom asked me.

"I knew you looked familiar!" We chatted like old friends as our offspring slinked into the background.

Colleges design campus visits with as much care as the slick brochures that flood the mailboxes of high school students. On the covers, autumn leaves softly fall year-round on smiling students. They stroll across a sunny campus, un-stressed by papers, midterms, or roommate problems.

However, sometimes it rains. Or snows. On one campus visit, a persistent cold rain fell the entire day. At the coffee table, a concerned admissions representative noted that bad weather on a visit day definitely cuts the "yield" of potential students. "We have 299 days of sunshine here. Why not today?" he moaned.

A bored, cranky or hung over tour guide also can make a student — or parent — cross that campus right off the list. But if the tour guide mentions your student's favorite activities, the opposite reaction can occur.

"Here's where the guys all play Guitar Hero... we have all-night Mafia card parties in this lounge... our floor is so close and our RA is awesome... I've never taken a class before 10 A.M... our floor won the flag football championship. It's incredible — all of our games start between 10 P.M. and midnight."

Soon the buildings and admissions spiels ran together into one giant campus. In between official events, we tried to coax clues from our son. What did you think of this? How do you feel about that? But his mind was back home — figuring out his prom date or texting friends about playing Frisbee golf the next day.

We all were relieved when it was time to drive home after the last visit. Our next college trip would be to orientation, or freshman move-in day.

"Remember the mom when we were touring the dorm at that school in Texas?" My son laughed. "She wanted to know if the college would assign who got which bed."

"The classic moment was when that kid started snoring during the chemistry department session," my husband added.

"When we get home, it's time to do those pro and con lists," I reminded my son. "If only we had made a video!"

~Sue Lowell Gallion

Reassuring Words

Choices are the hinges of destiny.
~Pythagoras

L ike most of my friends, I started to really think about college the summer before my junior year. Unlike most of my friends, I knew what kind of college I was looking for. There was no doubt in my mind that I wanted to attend a small school with a strong Liberal Arts and Sciences program. At crowded family gatherings, I would constantly repeat my formula for the future to every aunt, uncle, or cousin who asked or was willing to listen.

As junior year got into full swing, a school organized college tour was slowly being planned. Many schools I was interested in were on the tour and I was excited to finally visit the places I had read so much about.

The trip itself was not the epitome of luxury. Eight people to a seven-person van and an all-inclusive roadside motel package allowed us to focus on the schools, not the lavishness of our rooms. But none of this mattered. Because I knew that on that trip I would find where I was going to go to college.

On the tour, we visited two to three schools every day, and every day I felt as though I had been smacked across the face. None of the schools I loved on paper, with their small class sizes and world-renowned English programs, were places where I wanted to spend the next four years of my life.

To put it mildly, I was crushed. After all, I already had my whole college future planned out, I just needed to pick a school, but then, in one weekend, it all came crashing down and I felt as though I was trapped in a cocoon of confusion. I spent the next week of school in a sort of daze, as though everything around me was in a thick layer of fog. All I could think, or worry, about was college.

One night that week, my dad was talking to my uncle on the phone while I was quietly contemplating my disaster of a future. "Max, Uncle Dave wants to talk to you," said my Dad. The conversation with my uncle started with talk of my baseball season, but soon drifted towards the looming topic of college. As I spoke, my uncle must have been able to hear the dissatisfaction in my voice. I stumbled over my words, trying to explain how none of the schools I had been looking at felt right for me. "No matter where you go, it's the right choice," he said, rather abruptly. As the conversation wandered back to baseball, my mind stuck to that one sentence and I felt as though a tremendous weight had been lifted off my shoulders.

As the college process got more and more strenuous as junior year ended and senior year arrived, I would always think of what my uncle said. "No matter where you go it's the right choice." When I got my first denial letter, made my final decision, and then second-guessed that decision, his voice came to my mind and I knew no matter where I went to college everything would work out just fine.

~Maxwell Schulz

Chapter
6

Teens Talk

GETTING IN...
TO COLLEGE

Placing Your Bets

You have brains in your head.
You have feet in your shoes.
You can steer yourself in any direction you choose.
You're on your own.
And you know what you know.
You are the guy who'll decide where to go.
~Dr. Seuss

34

Chicken Soup for the Soul

The Basement

*The conventional view serves to
protect us from the painful job of thinking.*
~J.K. Galbraith

"I just hope my daughter doesn't end up THERE. It's her basement school."

I watched my mother as another parent belittled her alma mater in front of her without a thought. I bit my nails as my mother bit her tongue. I could see the wheels of disbelief turning in her head. I felt terrible that I went to a school that would tell me that the state university she attended was not good enough for me or my peers.

My parents didn't buy into the polo shirt-boat print shorts combination culture abounding around me during high school. I had transferred from a public middle school into a K-12 private arena in which pearl necklaces and summer vacation houses were flashily displayed with nonchalance. My parents constantly reminded me that, unlike some of my new peers, I would not be spending four hundred dollars on a pair of shoes. They vetoed frivolous expenditures and preached that my siblings and I were owed nothing by the world or our socioeconomic bracket.

When it came time to apply to college, the differences between my parents' mentality and the attitudes perpetuated by my prep school once again became apparent.

We had an entire course dedicated to college admissions

counseling our senior year. Our counselor worked around the clock to make contacts with Admissions Officers across the country and get our school's graduates admitted to the best schools in the nation. My high school published a list of the colleges that graduating seniors would be attending in the area newspaper. At the end of April, my high school ordered a massive sheet cake and divided it into squares, printing the name of the university each senior would attend on each square. Going to college in the first place was a given; going to a prestigious college was expected.

We were to construct metaphorical houses for our prospective college lists: safety schools in the basement, likely admittances on the first floor, less certain prospects on the second floor, reach schools in the attic, and the most selective school as a satellite dish on the roof. My high school college counselor never really mentioned the option of attending a state school. The idea was seen as somehow beneath members of my graduating class. Our sizable tuition bill was an investment for the Ivy Leagues, not for the in-state school down the road.

But my mother went to that in-state school down the road. And she was very quick to remind me that it was an institution undeserving of my peers' upturned noses. The fact that my mother is one of the most intelligent adults I know convinced me that there was no shame or embarrassment in being a state school graduate.

While my peers and their parents discussed where they were applying, their legacies, and their application woes, my parents kept their mouths shut. They refused to believe that college applications should dominate my senior year. They would not give college admissions the weighted importance in my life that other parents did. Even though I was "freaking out" about my future, I had the rare set of parents who were not doing the same alongside me. I felt pressure from myself and my high school, but not my home.

When constructing my application "house"—safety school in the basement, reach school on the roof—my mother made sure I put at least one state school in the virtual abode. I didn't end up enrolling at a state school, but if I had, I can only hope I would have graduated from there with as much intelligence and wisdom as my mother did. After all, I like the basement in my house a whole lot more than the roof.

~Emma Lee Goode

I Just Knew

Whenever you find yourself on the side of the majority,
it is time to pause and reflect.
~Mark Twain

Most people grow out of their "I want to be famous" stage. Somehow, I didn't. From the moment my grandmother took me to see *Cats* when I was four years old, I decided I wanted to be on Broadway and there was no changing my mind.

Twelve years later, I was still pretty sure that's what I wanted to do. I was visiting New York University with my stepmother because one of her friends taught an acting class at Tisch and said I could sit in on it. I thought it was the coolest thing ever, and I walked out of the class and onto the streets of Greenwich Village thinking "If I could go to school for this, I would be the happiest person alive." I watched the urbane NYU students walk past me, their clothes vibrant and funky, and decided I would be a performance major if it killed me.

But things changed as I started actually applying to college. My grandparents, who always wanted the best for me, found a college counselor who lived a town over. She was skinny and blond and looked at me knowingly when I sat on a leather sofa opposite her. I felt lost in a sea of applications, median SAT scores, possible majors, and resumes. I hoped she could help me keep my head above water.

Unfortunately, she didn't seem to get me. She'd never had a student who wanted to go to school for performance, so she consulted some books. I'm sure if I had said I wanted to be pre-med, she would have known what to do in an instant. Instead, she was trying to improvise.

"How about Catholic University? This list here says it's good for drama."

I tried to keep an open mind. "Do they have musical theater?"

She looked at me blankly and then opened my file. She clearly had no idea.

When she looked at my qualifications, she decided I shouldn't settle for NYU. Because I mentioned I also wanted to be academically challenged, she made a list of schools I had thought were out of my reach. She rattled them off: Yale, Harvard, Princeton, Brown, Northwestern, Vassar. Sure, I'd considered some of them. But did I really belong at Princeton? I hadn't thought so.

I'd spent my high school years staying in the upper echelon of a student body that was large and diverse. Fights broke out often at school and parts of the building were in disrepair. It was easy to flounder in a school where classes were sometimes large and teachers were often disorganized. I lived in a privileged area, but my high school definitely didn't reflect that.

So in retrospect, my college counselor's idea to pit me against students coming from the most elite private schools, who had had years of tutoring, was unfair. I had the grades and the SAT scores to get into the schools, but something told me I wasn't going to shine in a batch of applicants whose parents hadn't gone to art school, like mine had, or who had been on winning sports teams (my school had none).

Still, the allure of the words "Harvard graduate" seeped into my long-term goals. I started having interviews and visiting the schools, convincing myself they were right for me. I remember my tour at Yale with my mom on a rainy, dreary day. I walked through the beautiful buildings, glancing down the empty corridors. The few students I saw walked by in sweatshirts and jeans, heads down and books in hand. Where were the fun, artistic types that I wanted to hang out with? As much as I convinced myself they did, no one really looked like me, or the person I so desperately wanted to become.

I had interviews with alumni and told them how badly I wanted to go to their schools, knowing in my heart I really didn't. I wrote an essay for Vassar about why I wanted to go to the school and had my stepmother read it for me. Her criticism was succinct and stung at the time: "It sounds like you don't want to go here."

I had an interview with a Princeton alumnus in a Starbucks in my town. I remember trying to look at him as the sun coming through the window made me squint. I could only see the outline of his head from where I sat, fidgety and uncomfortable. Knowing I liked singing, he asked me whether I thought musical talent was more about "nature and natural talent" or "lessons and nurturing that talent." I labored through an answer and wished he would stop "picking my brain" and just ask what kinds of extracurricular activities I was into.

I still auditioned for NYU, but not Tisch. I did a summer program before my junior year with the Steinhardt School Vocal Performance program and knew that the faculty liked me there. If I had the grades for Brown, I surely had the grades for NYU. Plus, I had something else, something a lot of applicants didn't have—a passion.

As I started to hear from schools, I was largely unsurprised. Waitlisted. Waitlisted. Waitlisted. Rejected. Rejected. Rejected. I spent my birthday, March 31st, with my best friend, checking our Yale and Brown accounts. Luckily for our friendship, we had the same outcome. Rejected and waitlisted, respectively.

But NYU accepted me. They sent me an invitation to come to a luncheon for a few select accepted students. They asked me to join their scholars program. They gave me a small merit scholarship. Finally, it was nice to be wanted.

Best of all, it was nice to breathe a sigh of relief when I realized I had been given a sign. I didn't want to go to Harvard to study business. I didn't want to go to Princeton and be an engineer. I wanted to sing and I wanted to be in New York City, where the students were cutting-edge and exciting.

Today, I'm a junior at NYU and I couldn't love it more. I found a way to double major, so I get to be academically challenged as well as explore singing and performing. I'm now one of a teeming mass of NYU students who congregate around Washington Square Park and set the trends for the rest of college campuses across America. And if I see a tour pass by, I think of myself walking the streets of Greenwich Village as a prospective student. I try to smile at them and look as happy as I am, because I want them to see me and think "Hey, that looks like someone I'd want to be friends with." I want them to have that same gut feeling that I had. Because although it took me a while to come to terms with it, I just knew—at four years old, at sixteen years old, and now. I just know I'm where I belong. And I say thank you to Princeton for rejecting me and confirming that.

~Madeline Clapps

The Only Person in the World

Labels are for filing.
Labels are for clothing.
Labels are not for people.
~Martina Navratilova

I think I might be the only person in the world who was happy to get a rejection letter from one of the most prestigious universities in the country.

I, Alexandra Swanson, was just regretfully informed that I was not accepted at this time to Tufts University in a letter hastily delivered to me by my anxious mother when it arrived at 9 A.M. on a Saturday morning. I was asleep before I got the letter, and I went right back to sleep after I read it, a content smile on my face.

You might be reading this and wondering why I even applied in the first place. I did want to apply, for those of you thinking that it was merely my parents pressuring me to do so. I toured the university; I liked what I saw; I applied.

The school was absolutely fantastic, of course: a lush, green campus in the middle of Medford (a town, incidentally, in which I actually lived temporarily). The foreign language and English programs were excellent. And, of course, there was the reputation which could not be denied by anyone.

Now, I was always the "smart one" of the family: the daughter who wanted to be the first female president, the cousin with the best grades, the niece who awed everyone with her ability to read at the young age of two. It seemed only natural that I would attend an Ivy League school and go on to be wonderfully successful.

Well, time went on, and procrastination became my deadliest enemy. No longer were my grades perfect, and Harvard became an unattainable goal.

But Tufts? I felt I had a shot there.

Actually, half the reason I applied was to fulfill that role as the "smart one." I felt that I had to prove something to myself, because in a way, I had let myself down by slacking and not receiving all As (at least, that was how I felt about it).

I had, of course, found my strengths, which did not lie in the field of math and science (and I'm sure any university to which I applied could tell you that). I had an absolute and undeniable passion for writing.

In school, my role changed from the "smart one" to the "writer," and the essay was my favorite part of the application. Tufts also required its applicants to answer a few different questions in 500 words or less. I was particularly proud of one I wrote when asked to describe myself:

Those of you who know me would know that I carry around a gigantic bag all the time full of anything one might possibly need (and quite a few things that no one but me would ever need). So the answer to my question was written about each of the things found inside my bag and the part of my personality attributed to each.

So Tufts was my favorite application—I know: how many people pick a favorite college application?—but as it turned out, it wasn't my favorite school.

Ever since deciding to go college hunting on a whim with my best friend, I had discovered and fallen in love with Northeastern University.

Yes, it was a little weaker in its Foreign Language Department than I would have liked, but the concepts of being right in Boston and having the co-op experience were too good to pass up. Not to mention that my grades were good enough to easily make the Honors Program, and the Honors students had pretty amazing dorms.

Even though Northeastern wasn't even on my original list of colleges to look at, I was completely hooked. I toured it a total of three times, each time becoming more and more convinced that this was where I not only wanted to be but where I was meant to be. Something just felt right about it: a feeling that I really can't put into words, though the writer in me is striving to try.

Northeastern's letter was the first acceptance I got as well as the first reply from any school at all.

When I got that e-mail informing me of my acceptance to the university as well as the Honors Program, plus a Dean's Scholarship, I was so ecstatic that I literally screamed.

Before I received any other letter, I sat my parents down and said quite calmly, "I'm going to Northeastern."

Both of them were startled but gave me the typical reactions, my mother saying, "But what about Tufts? If you get in there, you should go: you'll get a much better education, and employers will be more likely to hire you."

My dad's reaction: "I don't think this should be just your decision. We should sit down and talk about it together."

Most other people I talked to agreed with my mother, and I was completely ignoring my father's input, not wanting him to be responsible for the decision about where I get my education.

I was becoming resigned to the fact that if I got into Tufts, Northeastern would be a distant dream, especially since I could get better financial aid for Tufts.

I tried to reassure myself, repeatedly reminding myself of the fact that Tufts was by no means a bad school, and I would learn a lot there, but I was still praying for the slim chance that I would be able to attend Northeastern.

So when I received that rejection letter, I was happy. Maybe I was the only person in the world who was happy about a rejection from Tufts, but I was.

I have now completed my first wonderful year at the school of my dreams. Seven amazing professors, two awesome roommates and twelve months later, I am only upset about one thing:

Why didn't Tufts like my writing?

~Alexandra Swanson

Clueless

When you cannot make up your mind
which of two evenly balanced courses of action you should take—
choose the bolder.
~William Joseph Slim

"Check the box that has your top choices for your future career," the guidance counselor instructed our class, "and put your pencils down when you're finished."

I stared as my classmates located their boxes and filled them in. How did they know what they wanted to do? Had I missed something?

I had no idea what I wanted to do with my life!

As if sensing my dilemma, the counselor said, "For those who aren't sure, pick your two favorite hobbies and choose careers along the same lines."

Good grief. I contemplated all the things I loved to do in my free time and narrowed it down to two... but they were different as night and day.

I love writing, novels especially, so it seemed natural when one of my options was to major in English with an emphasis in Creative Writing. I didn't want to go into Journalism—I preferred reading nonfiction but writing fiction.

My other choice was to go into Culinary Arts. That job seemed more practical to me. I would be active as opposed to stuck behind a desk. I would learn to cook well enough that I could help my family with the cooking. The problem was... the cost for the culinary school closest to home was approximately $30,000 a year. Even though it was worth it—the tuition price included a full set of knives, uniforms, and the classes—I didn't have that kind of money.

Both options were very tempting.

I scowled in frustration and leaned back in my chair, analyzing my future.

"If you're having trouble selecting a college," the counselor said, "I would advise researching them on the Internet."

That sounded like a good plan. At home, I looked up both of the majors. Apparently, not many schools had Creative Writing options, which made it easier to narrow down colleges. And of course culinary schools weren't on every street, either.

The next morning before school I stopped at my counselor's office. "I'm having a bit of trouble deciding what to do," I admitted.

"Well, for the majors you've told me, I would go on campus tours first," she instructed. "Also talk to the representatives who come to recruit the seniors, and see what you can learn from them."

A week later, a promoter came from Johnson and Wales—my primary choice for culinary school—and gave a speech about the college. "If you're not sure whether you want to become a chef," he said, "we have a three-day camp that will make or break your decision. It's $195 and I promise it's worth it!"

Things fell into place after all the advice I'd received in the past week. I was very lucky to have supportive parents who were determined to see me happy with whatever I chose to do. They signed me up for the culinary camp, and when spring break rolled around, we hit the campus tours.

We had three English schools on our list and Johnson and Wales as the culinary school we wanted to see. Two schools were located in Denver, Colorado, one in Greeley, Colorado, and the fourth in Fort Collins, Colorado.

The first school we visited was one of the Denver schools. I loved it! The dorms were amazing, and some of the classes I would get to take as a Creative Writing student sounded amazing (Shakespeare, Romanian Literature, Dark Romanticism...).

My parents, however, hated it. The school was built in the middle of the city, and there were six bars less than a mile from campus. We left discouraged but still hopeful that one of the other campuses would have something that satisfied everyone.

Of the remaining two Creative Writing colleges, I eliminated one instantly. The third and final university—Colorado State University—was incredible. The campus was gorgeous, and the classes sounded so fun! We actually got to sit down and talk to one of the English professors while we were there. I liked him right away. He had long white hair like Ebenezer Scrooge and wore a billowy white shirt under an old-fashioned black vest. He had pants tucked into knee-length black boots. He taught classes on Chaucer, and he fit the profile of a man who loved the classics.

That was enough to convince me that if I went into Creative Writing, I would definitely go to CSU.

My parents and I were also blown away when we visited Johnson and Wales University. That campus was stunning, too—and much smaller than CSU. Smaller than my high school, in fact. The schooling techniques were fantastic... students got Fridays off from class and could do an internship anywhere in the world during their sophomore year. It looked like so much fun!

The problem still remained the price, however. Johnson and Wales' nearly $30,000 a year was almost double the approximately $17,000 that CSU required. I threw myself into applying for scholarships as I waited for the culinary camp to roll around. Until then, I got a job working as a food prep buffet attendant at a local restaurant, which taught me so much about cooking. I also began writing for the Christian Writer's Guild, a program that had students submit one extensive writing lesson every two weeks.

In the end, I chose the culinary route. It was expensive, but my family was continuously supportive. My parents helped to pay for school and my grandparents gave me the idea to cook on a cruise ship. Suddenly I was facing a fantastic future that exceeded my wildest dreams! Looking back, I can see throughout all of this that the most important thing to help me decide what I wanted to do with my life was getting involved. The campus tours, the culinary camp, and the Writer's Guild all influenced my thoughts about the future, and in the end, they helped me decide what to do with my life.

~Amy Anderson

"The guidance counselor took a leave
of absence ... to find himself."

Poor Little Smart Girl

A wise man makes his own decisions,
an ignorant man follows public opinion.
~Chinese Proverb

"So you're applying to Harvard? Maybe Yale? Possibly Princeton?"

My guidance counselor barely took her eyes off her computer screen as she asked these questions. The boredom in her voice was obvious and her hand hovered above her mouse as if she was waiting to tick an appropriate box on the screen. I could practically smell the indifference wafting around the room.

"No, actually, I'm not."

She didn't miss a beat.

"Columbia? Perhaps Penn?"

"No."

"Cornell?"

I studied her profile and realized that if I didn't put an end to it soon, she'd just rattle her way through whatever list was designated the best of the best in that year's college guides.

"No. I'm applying early decision to Providence College."

That got her attention. She turned so violently that her short bob swished around her head and she had to brush a few stray locks down from her glasses.

"Excuse me?"

"Providence College. I'm applying early. I'm hoping to be invited to the Liberal Arts Honors Program."

She raised a slim eyebrow, wordlessly inviting me to go on.

For my part, I didn't think there was a lot left to say. I was an honors student at a world-renowned international school. I was secretary of the National Honor Society, on the board of the Social Services Club, a member of the Mandarin Honor Society, Captain of the swim team and in my spare time I was a lifeguard within the expatriate community. Combined with the fact that I did all of this while living abroad and managed to get much higher marks on my SAT and ACT than the average student, and I was well aware that on paper I was an ideal candidate for most colleges.

My guidance counselor shuffled some papers on her desk. I could tell she was stalling for time, but since I was just counting down to the bell, I had all the time in the world. After she gathered her wits, she launched into a spiel that I had come to know well. A spiel that I had privately dubbed "You Can Do Better."

"You Can Do Better" generally started with an educational authority flattering me, telling me that I was a smart young woman and that I could do whatever I wanted to do. Then it moved along into cajoling me, making arguments that usually ended with "You see what I mean, right?" When I didn't—as I always made a point to do—it moved along into threatening me, telling me that I would regret not attending the very best school that I could get into.

What everyone who pushed this talk onto me forgot to realize was that, as they were so fond of saying, I was a very smart young lady. I knew exactly which was the very best school I could get into, and it was the very best school for me, not the very best school in an annual guide or arbitrary alumni survey. I was also well aware that I didn't want to go to most of the "major" colleges or universities, I wanted to go to one that was small enough to feel like a home, urban enough to provide an array of activities and dedicated enough to remain committed to undergraduate teaching. After all, if I was going to spend four years somewhere, I wanted someone to know my name. I did not want to be another face in the crowd or, worse yet, in a giant lecture theater.

Grasping at straws, my counselor reminded me that my high school had a long tradition of academic excellence. Alumni were astronauts and internationally known musicians. Students were routinely offered scholarships and internships. I stopped listening midway through because I'd heard it all before. Instead, I watched the leaves of her plants dance in the breeze of the air conditioner. I watched a bead of sweat trickle down the window glass. I counted along with the ticking of the wall clock.

"Do you understand?" my counselor finally implored, holding her palms open above her desk as if by that very act she was opening wide the gates of Heaven.

"You know, I'm a smart girl," I finally said, and she nodded along. "And I know that a lot of students would love to be in my position right now."

She continued nodding, her head bobbing up and down so passionately that I wondered if she'd hurt her neck.

"But this," I spread my hands out across her desk, "this I don't understand. I know where I want to go, and I know why I want to go there. I have my reasons and they're good reasons."

Her nodding faded, then stopped.

"So I guess really I do understand. I just wish everyone else could too."

I gathered up my backpack and made as grand an exit as I could manage. For days, I arrived home each evening with a knot in my stomach, sure that my parents would have received a letter telling them that not only was I throwing away my future, but that I was being impertinent while I was doing it. That letter never came, but one day that winter a thick envelope from Providence College did. Inside was a letter admitting me to the college. Following that was an invitation to enter the Liberal Arts Honors Program. Following that was notification of an annual academic scholarship.

I never took these things in to my guidance counselor as some other students did. I tucked them into a folder and slid them into my desk drawer. I understood. My parents understood. My first choice college understood.

~Beth Morrissey

The Seeds
of an Idea

If a man aspires to the highest place,
it is no dishonor to him to halt at the second,
or even at the third.
~ Marcus Tullius Cicero

The college admission process can be a terrifying thing. At least for me it was. Nothing short of an axe-wielding mass murderer can be scarier than filling out all those long pages about yourself and your academic record for strangers into whose hands you are placing your future. Combine that with the fact that I am a homeschooled senior, which took the process to a whole new level of challenging. Nevertheless I made it through the long, dark tunnel of applications and nervous anticipation and emerged unscathed.

It would be a lie to say that I didn't start thinking and worrying about college until junior year or so. The truth is that ever since I was a little girl the idea of college had been planted into my head to grow and thrive. When senior year came around it blossomed. My mother was a careful gardener and she made sure those ideas and dreams were seeded carefully and with love.

I started researching different colleges as early as my freshman year, back when I was still in a public school. I'd go online and sort through the vast wealth of information about community colleges, liberal arts colleges and four-year universities. The first choice was the easiest. What type of school did I want to go to? I knew I didn't want to go to community college. I wanted more than an associate's degree. But did I want a liberal arts education or did I want to go to a more prestigious four-year university? I decided I preferred the latter.

So I began the difficult task of picking which colleges seemed right for me. I used a variety of tools, tests and search engines, and by senior year I had my choices narrowed down to five schools. My top choice was based entirely on personal preferences and my own ambitions: Northwestern University in Evanston, Illinois. It wasn't too far from home and it was famous for its excellent school of journalism. It was just what I wanted; the only problem was that it was top-notch and accepted only the best of the best.

After narrowing down my search, it was time to begin the actual application process. But before that there was one more thing I had to accomplish: standardized testing. I wasn't particularly thrilled.

Early in senior year, I woke up one morning feeling very, very nervous. It was time to take the ACT test.

"Don't worry. You'll do great," my mother reassured me. I wasn't really convinced.

Still I hopped into my car and drove to Rockford College, the site of my testing and ironically one of the five colleges I was applying to. As I parked my car and stepped out into the crisp autumn air I was amazed to see so many other high school students just like myself, nervously looking around and wondering what to do, pencils and calculators in hand.

I entered the big brick building with the rest of them and eventually made it to the classroom I would spend the next four hours searching the files of my brain for all the correct answers for the most important test I'd ever take in my life. When I received my answer booklet, the nervousness began to magically drain from my body. I was taking the test and it wasn't so bad. It was just one more step on the lengthy road to college, but I had taken it and I was that much closer to my goals.

Weeks later I received my results. Envelope in hand I rushed toward my mom. I was almost bobbing up and down with excitement.

I ripped open the envelope and retrieved the papers within. My eyes fell upon the thirty printed on the page and I was stunned and relieved. I had received a good result. My mother's smile widened and her eyes lit up when she saw what I had seen. Yes, everything was going to be just fine. I had received a good result and anything could happen, anything at all.

That sense of relief and calm lasted until I got the letter from Northwestern University. Knowing that the envelope I held in my hands determined my future, I was reluctant to look inside. Finally, I took a deep breath, opened the letter and read my future.

It was a rejection note.

I did not cry as my hopes and aspirations fell down around me and shattered like fine china, but I was crushed. The smile died on my lips and I felt cold inside. Even knowing that I was not the only person to ever get rejected from their first choice school didn't make me feel any better. At first I felt totally lost and so I looked to my mother, that gardener of ideas, for guidance.

"So you got rejected from one school," she said. "Don't forget about the four others you were accepted to." She smiled. "It isn't the end of the world."

And it wasn't. She was right. I had been accepted into those four other schools. My second choice school was still a really fine institution. I put the letter aside and decided upon Loyola University in Chicago. I would attend my second choice school as if it were my first. I was still in charge of my future and I was still going to college. Summoning up a smile I filled out the housing contract for Loyola.

I am just finishing up senior year now. Soon I will be going to Loyola to register for fall classes. And you know what? I still have that envelope, that letter of rejection. I keep it because it helps me persevere. As a homeschooled student, I had an added difficulty when it came to getting accepted to college, but I still did it, no matter the fact that my first choice was denied to me. We all face rejection in our lives but that's not what matters. What matters is what we do with the experience, whether we choose to dwell on the bad things in our lives or whether we learn and grow just like those tiny seeds that were first planted in my mind so long ago.

~Tawnee Calhoun

No Silver Platter

Jumping at several small opportunities may get us there more quickly than waiting for one big one to come along.
~Hugh Allen

Like most teenagers, I felt I would be ready spread my wings and be on my own as soon as I graduated high school. My life would be so much different than my mom's. She was already married and had me to take care of when she got her high school diploma.

I was sure attending college was the first step in an amazing, fulfilling and exciting life. I was just as sure this first step included getting as far away as possible from my family and the small Wyoming town where I had grown up.

For a while, college was a dream that I didn't share. My mom was single with five kids and worked as a supermarket cashier. She had enough to worry about. So being the independent spirit I was, I took it upon myself to start researching colleges.

Oh! The places I could go! The pamphlets started coming in, enticing me with expansive campuses and intelligent faces in far away places. One college even spoke of the chance to spend my sophomore year in Italy! Representatives from colleges far and near showed up at my high school to persuade us to apply to their schools. The possibilities were endless. I was so excited to be the first in my immediate family to get a college degree.

When I worked the closing shift at my part-time job at a fast food restaurant, I wouldn't waste time when I was mopping the lobby, knowing that I had to get home to finish my homework. I was sure that my grades, while not perfect, would be good enough to gain access to whatever college I deemed worthy of my presence.

My first lesson about college was harsh. Academically, I was prepared. Financially, I was not.

When my mom looked over some of my dream schools, she thought for sure my head was in the clouds. Just because I wanted something so badly didn't mean it was going to be possible. Good grades were important, but it wasn't the only consideration. The tuitions were just way too high. My family had always been on a tight budget and not able to save for much of anything.

I thought about saving a lot of money over the summer. I thought about working full time while going to school. Then I thought about books, about rent, and about a social life. Math was never my strong suit, but the numbers just weren't adding up to the tuition and the good life at any of my dream schools. There had to be another way.

I dove into the scholarship battle, swimming through the paperwork and essays the best I could. For someone who liked to watch from the sidelines, it was strange to suddenly be in competition for my future. I found I wasn't the only one who wasn't getting their dream school handed to them on a silver platter.

Allowing myself to dream more realistically, I applied to good universities that were public, rather than private, and therefore much less expensive. I was accepted by all of them. But even with some help that was being offered by the schools, I was still falling short. I knew I wouldn't thrive in school if I was constantly worried about making money to pay the rent, or buy books. How was I going to gain the "Freshman 15" if I didn't have enough money for food?

I knew I didn't want to wait "one more year" as some suggested, in order to save up more money. I had seen too many people say they were going to do that very same thing, and each year passed with them saying "next year." I didn't want to take the chance. Instead, a different chance was given to me.

One afternoon, I was called to the guidance office. My counselor announced that I was eligible for a Full Ride Scholarship. There are no sweeter words to a high school senior on a tight budget! Of course, there was a catch. It was only for two years, because it was for a community college. My fantasy of large lecture halls suddenly shrunk to classrooms of standard size. And the college was in the next town, about fifteen miles away. My dreams of traveling to an exciting new city and meeting new people were replaced with thoughts of driving down a familiar highway and taking classes with some of the same people I'd known since kindergarten.

The counselor focused on the benefits, understanding my collegiate expectations. I could still take part in the whole "dorm life experience," as this college offered on-campus housing. Later, I would be able to transfer to a university as a junior. It was a great way to start a college career, he said. And I might have more individual attention than I would if I went straight to one of the larger colleges. I took a packet of the literature I had always passed up before and told him I'd think it over.

My mom's eyes brightened as I told her the news. She was excited for me. Looking through the classes, she pointed out ones that sounded interesting, envisioning a fun and intellectually stimulating schedule. I began to realize that sometimes the dream and the goal can be different things, and knowing that may be one of the first steps in growing up. What I really wanted was an education in order to grow as a person. Who's to say that couldn't start fifteen miles from where I first learned the ABCs?

Once I accepted the scholarship, other things fell into place. I had won a few local scholarships, easing even more of the burden, as well as reducing the time I would have to work while going to school. After learning more about my family, my counselor thought I might be eligible for a Pell Grant, a loan that wouldn't need to be repaid. He said my mom and I could find out about it at the financial aid office at the college.

My mom was proud of me, her eldest daughter, getting to do something she had never had the opportunity to do. We were relieved that the financial aid meant I wouldn't have to spend most of my potential study time working.

Learning about financial aid didn't just help me, though. Mom got a Pell Grant for herself, and began her own college journey, with me.

Looking back now, I'm glad that I stuck around home. I excelled in my studies at the community college and it was a great preparation for university. I even ended up meeting people from all over the world—a few of my roommates were from Paris and Tokyo!

The biggest honor, though, was getting to experience English 101 with my mom. We were cooperative yet competitive classmates, often bouncing ideas off each other after dinner. My arrival into the world may have delayed her college experience, but by staying close to her, I like to think both of us grabbed onto our dreams.

~Tina Haapala

Chapter
7

Teens Talk

GETTING IN...
TO COLLEGE

Essays, Interviews,
Auditions and Self-Doubt

*Too many people overvalue what they are not
and undervalue what they are.*
~Malcolm S. Forbes

Ten Things
I Like about Myself

It took me a long time not to judge myself through someone else's eyes.
~Sally Field

My personality
My writing
My hair
My teeth
My smile
My sense of humor
My taste in music
My recipes
My style of fashion
My signature

~Morgan Anthony Richardson

Filling Out the ACT Application

Nobody can make you feel inferior without your consent.
~Eleanor Roosevelt

I knew that filling out the application to take the ACT was going to take a while. I knew I'd have to have a Number 2 pencil that was actually sharp and a check from my mom to pay for the test. I knew that the test was important and that I had to take it if I wanted to get into college.

What I didn't know was how rotten just filling out the application was going to make me feel.

Filling in all those little ovals for my name, address, date of birth, test center codes, college codes, etcetera, etcetera, etcetera was bad enough, but my heart really sank when I opened the booklet and saw the ACT Interest Inventory, a list of seventy-two questions that asked if I would "dislike" doing a certain activity, feel "indifferent" toward it, or "like" doing the activity.

How am I supposed to know if I'd like planning a monthly budget? The only budget I plan is how much money I can spend on CDs each weekend. And would I like, be indifferent, to or dislike attending the lecture of a well-known scientist? That would depend on who the scientist was, what he or she was lecturing about, and how much sleep I'd had the night before. But my favorite one had to be "engrave lettering or designs on a trophy or plaque." Having never seen anything engraved in my entire life, I'm thinking that might be kind of fun to watch but I don't think I'd actually want to do it. Does that mean I'm indifferent to engraving?

I'm guessing that these "interest" questions are supposed to help me decide what kind of career I might want to pursue, assuming I get a high enough score on my ACT to get into college. I suppose they're also supposed to make me think about what I want to do with my life. That's something I've been hearing a lot of lately but I sure didn't expect the people who wrote the ACT application to join the chorus.

I slogged through all seventy-two questions, thinking that I had to be near the end. Wrong! Next came the Student Profile Section, 177 questions about basic stuff, like what I wanted to major in (as if I knew) and how much money I'd need (lots). Then came the part that really got to me. High School Extracurricular Activities. I had to answer Yes, I did participate in this activity (Y) or No, I did not participate in this activity (N). Activities included stuff like debate, music, student government. Speech. Athletics. Science. Community Service. It was downright depressing to see that I'd hardly participated in anything at all during high school. I could just imagine the person looking at my Student Profile. "Look at this kid! He didn't do anything for four freaking years! He'll be lucky if he gets a job indifferently engraving trophies some day!"

After finishing the entire application, I stared down at all the little black ovals dotting my form. The Ns in the High School Extracurricular Activities far outweighed the Ys. For several minutes, I just felt terrible. Personally, I don't think "profiling" someone with a set of statements like "Wrote an independent paper on a scientific topic which received the highest possible grade given in my school" is going to get a whole lot of takers. I know there are probably millions of other high school kids like me who went through high school studying, doing homework, hanging out with friends, and just making it from one day to the next.

Then it dawned on me: This isn't a picture of me. This doesn't really say anything about who I am or what I like. It's just a generalized survey, not a life story. That made me feel a lot better. That, and the fact that I was finally finished with the application. Getting up, I went to find my mom to get the check that would cover the application fee. I've heard taking the test is hard. I'm thinking it can't be that much worse than filling out the application. And I'm pretty sure that none of the questions will have answers that are either "like," "dislike," or "indifferent." True or false is a whole lot easier.

~Joe Musolf

"Good grades, tests, forms to fill in, applying for scholarships and loans... College is a lot of work BEFORE you even get in!"

The Essay I Didn't Write

Hope is grief's best music.
~Author Unknown

I was an average student by all accounts. My mother thought a little better of me, but my teachers thought a little worse, so really, "average" averaged out.

Junior year was supposed to be the most important year. I was supposed to work ridiculously hard in all of my classes, be diligent about finding schools I wanted to apply to, and be well ahead of the game in studying for the ACT, the SAT, and preparing the common application. Especially the Essay.

Anyone who has applied to college in the last ten years knows why I'm capitalizing Essay. It is the X factor, the swing state of college applications. It can make a sub-par student interesting and extraordinary, it can knock the squeaky toed all-rounder out of top place because they don't have as much potential and personality. It's the greatest equalizer for a high school student.

Like I said, I was average—mostly because I was friends with the National Merit Scholars (all twelve from my school came primarily from my social group) and I saw them studying themselves to death and being exhausted and stressed out and none the happier. I also had a small problem with people telling me what should be important instead of letting me choose it for myself.

So I resisted. I didn't put in the extra effort, I didn't search for schools in my spare time. I chose to go on the optional class trip to

Spain for two weeks on spring vacation instead of visiting schools and buying sweatshirts, and I was pretty smug about it.

But then the school year ended, and I was in a bit of a panic. I was completely unprepared for senior year, for applications, for the Essay, for the ACT and the SAT.

My mother, having seen this very predicament in her firstborn, was prepared. That summer she pulled out a dry erase board and handed me a pile of books to look through. As I began picking my list, she would write it on the board along with their application procedure, whether they took the SAT or the ACT, what essays I had to write, where it was, pros and cons. It was a pretty impressive board.

We began visiting schools at the end of the summer. The list ranged from Mount Holyoke (beautiful), Georgetown (my dream!), Amherst, Williams (nixed after we visited, so bleak), Sarah Lawrence (I literally cried after my interview when they grilled me on whether women's rights were adequately represented in my recreational writing), Middlebury (loved the writing program), Gettysburg College, Wheaton (they had their own M&Ms, I was totally impressed) with so much in between. It was a whirlwind tour filled with car ride wardrobe changes into the all-important interview outfit and random little hotel rooms, and of course the ever present books detailing everything we had to know about each school.

The summer ended, I had my condensed list of applications, and half the names on the board had been erased. It was a manageable list of things, except for that essay.

Senior year started with another assembly. This one explained to us how we would have a special guidance program taking up our free period for this semester to help us through the process. I was horrified that my increasingly precious essay writing time was being taken up by guidance, but there was little I could do.

The first two weeks were a blur. Tests were scheduled, review books purchased, stress levels ratcheted up—the most important year, the final chance, had passed, and now I was coping with the aftermath, trying to scramble everything together and find something to write about that would define my life and my personality.

It was the third week of school, early on a Tuesday morning, when everything changed. After that morning, all the stress took on a suddenly different perspective, and new worry and fear clamored over the noise of which college I would go to, what essay to write. That morning, the idea of what was most important in my life radically changed.

It was September 11th, 2001.

Strangely enough, I wasn't one of the thousands of kids that year who decided to write about 9/11. I considered it—there were a hundred different ways to approach it, to tie it in to my life, to the way everything had changed, to the perspective that it gave me.

I didn't want to. I didn't want to write about terrorism, about fear, about my father being scheduled on a flight from D.C. to Boston that day. I refused to write about when my mother showed up at school in the middle of the day to check on me because the phones were jammed; I thought, when I saw her in the hallway, that my father must have died.

I didn't write about the quiet in the halls as we first heard about it, and the noise thereafter, as if we were all afraid of that silence. I didn't write any of it.

I ended up writing about a teacher who completely changed my life. She told me I was an amazing writer, and because it came from a woman who knew so much about so very many things, I believed her. She died not long after 9/11.

In a year marked by so much loss, I chose to write about her because I would carry her encouragement in my heart for the rest of my life. I didn't write about any of the loss, the fear, the collapse of the trusted social exterior. I wrote about the hope.

~AC Gaughen

44

Chicken Soup for the Soul

Typing Out Your Life

Truth is rarely writ in ink; it lives in nature.
~Martin H. Fischer

There is nothing more terrifying than the idea of putting your entire, amazing, charming existence on paper. In a page or two. On a certain topic. To determine the rest of that entire, amazing, charming existence. Ah, such is the joy of the college essay.

Even though I always prided myself on my writing, I sat and stared at my word processor. I slumped into the chair at the college counselor's office. I glowered at my mother across the dinner table. The question on the tip of my tongue was always the same: "You mean I have to get the whole thing, my whole life, out in about two pages?"

Where to begin? I'd emigrated from Moscow at the age of seven. That definitely had to go in there somewhere. I loved punk music and was a fixture at the San Francisco clubs, my French was pas mal, I was a renegade with a skillet and a pile of eggs. All of these things were me, too, but the question remained—which would make the cut?

The closer it got to the application deadlines, the more I tried to figure out Application Me. Real Me was tossing and turning at night while Application Me would tap dance on the admission officer's desk, putting on the best possible show to get me into the school. Would she be a funnier, more witty version of me? A more profound, chin stroking deep thinker? I had to create an Application Me that reflected the Real Me and then let her do all the work.

I gazed in the mirror with a sculptor's eye. In crafting my application, which parts of my large personality, sharp mind, loud laugh, big pores would I cut out and which part would I leave on to make me more attractive to the college admissions committee? Hmm.

When I actually wrote the essay, I shared all I possibly could about myself in hopes of leaving them wanting more, as in, Big Fat Envelope more. The One ended up being about my interest in psychology. It focused on the fact that my childhood memories of Russia were completely different from what I saw when I went back for the first time my junior year.

An emotional topic, it let my writing sparkle, it showed my interest in the human mind and, helloooooooo, my worldliness for traveling all the way across the freaking planet. I thought I had a home run. I read it over a few times, jiggling my foot in a dizzy rhythm against my computer desk, printed it out and sent it off.

Now that I'm done with it, I can honestly say that writing a college essay is the worst part of the process. So many decisions to make, such high stakes. You in a nutshell and make it snappy, funny and eloquent, thanks. Having done it not once but twice now—I just got into graduate school—I've got a few things I want to pass along. A whispered hint to my fellow essay-writing hopefuls.

First, take your hands off the keyboard, jump up from your seat and scream: "I hate these things!" Louder. "They are horrible, awful, insane, criminal, out of their gourds!" That's good. I like that. Essays are a pain.

Next, spit out the essay you want to write. Just sit down, shush up that critic in your head. You know the one. She's always sitting on my shoulder, even right now. "Don't write that," she says, her brows knit together. "That's stupid. They're not going to like that. You think that's funny? Ugh, who ever let you into college in the first place?"

Kick her off your shoulder and write the essay you want to write. The one that's going to get you into college, the one that sparkles with your amazing wit and personality. Now put it away for three days.

When you come back to it, you will want to take a dirt nap. The stuff you thought was so funny three days ago will fall flat. You'll find yourself rambling on without purpose and you'll discover sixteen spelling errors that a second grader would've caught.

This is good. Now, find your point. What's the number one thing you want your admissions guy or gal to know? Mine, and I think everyone can agree with me here, was: "I really want to get into your college, please, please, please, please, pretty pleeeeeeeeeaaaaaaaaaaaaasssssseeeee."

Figure out why you belong at that school, gosh darn it, write toward that point and keep all the fun things you salvaged from your first stab at the essay. Weave them together and you'll get a brand new version, full of personality and purpose.

When you think you're done, have five people read it. People who are smart and won't just say: "I loved it, it was, like, so brilliant, you are ah-mazing!" Then, change the font and read it again. You'll catch stuff you've never seen before.

Last but not least, try to relax. My essay expounded on my life-long commitment to psychology. Two days after I got to college, I switched my major to English and Theater. The essay you write has to be you in that moment, but you don't have to apologize if that person changes when you hit campus. It happens to all of us.

The only promise you do have to keep, though, is this: that you will write the best you, the best essay, the best intentions you have. Print it out, stamp it, slip it in the mail. Then, kick back and let Application You take over and do the grunt work. You've earned it.

~Mary Kolesnikova

Let It Shine

It is well for people who think,
to change their minds occasionally in order to keep them clean.
~Luther Burbank

"Thank you." I tried to smile through stiff, trembling lips, but as soon as I stepped into the hallway, tears filled my eyes.

Music was my life, and ever since I'd started playing bassoon in eighth grade, I'd dreamed of college auditions. My dreams were all the same—me, playing brilliantly; professors from famous music schools becoming so excited they'd accept me on the spot. "We can offer you a full ride. Please don't go to Julliard—we want you here!"

I'd been hot stuff in high school, but now those college auditions had started. And so far, real life couldn't be further from my daydreams. Here, in these marble halls swarming with talented kids and hundreds of thousands of dollars' worth of instruments, I felt like a complete fake.

Nobody here cared that I had the first seat in honors orchestra, two years running. They seemed to look right through me and know I didn't practice six hours a day—that my bassoon teacher was just an assistant high school orchestra director instead of a symphony musician.

This audition had been the worst yet. I was so nervous I'd made one mistake after another. The two auditioners didn't smile or try to help me relax. After my etude, one just said, "That sounded bad."

By the end, when they asked if I could name the "Big 5" orchestras—something I could normally rattle off in my sleep—I only came up with three. All I wanted was to leave.

I fled, bumping into kids talking about "last summer at Interlochen," and "my audition at New England Conservatory." What was I doing here? Why had I ever thought I was anything special?

We had been planning to go out for a special dinner, and Mom must have been starving. But when I found her in the coffee shop, I just muttered, "Let's get out of here." It was already getting dark, and we soon found ourselves fighting rush hour traffic in a strange city. Mom's white-knuckled hands clutched the steering wheel as she scanned overhead signs for our route out of town.

Usually, I helped navigate, but all I could do was huddle against the door and try to breathe around the lump in my throat. What was the use? I'd applied five places, including two "safety schools." At one, I'd only gotten a conditional acceptance because I couldn't pass their weird theory test. I hadn't formally auditioned at the other one yet, but I'd gone for a tour back in the fall and played for the bassoon teacher. He'd pretty much ripped me up, too. I couldn't imagine how my other auditions were going to go—if I went through with them.

It was hard going back to school on Monday. My friends weren't serious musicians, and they all figured I was on the road to fame and fortune. I couldn't possibly explain what I was going through, so I just didn't say much. Why, oh why, did I ever want to be a music major? Wasn't it enough, just coming up with the grades and the SAT scores—without having to take all these auditions, too?

But the truth is I already knew why. I'd never played an instrument at all till I was twelve, but as soon as I picked up a bassoon, I felt like I'd finally come to life. If I didn't follow through with this, what would I have? What would I be?

The winter went by in a blur of homework, more auditions, senioritis, and icy slush. Kids were coming to school and saying they'd been accepted. One of my best friends got into Harvard.

Things for me had gotten better—and worse. I'd been accepted at two music schools. But I also got put on the waitlist for one of my two brand-name conservatories. Now, I realize that was a compliment to my playing in itself—but then, all I could think was that I wasn't good enough for them. That I wasn't good enough to be a performer at all. I still hadn't heard from the other conservatory, but I hardly wanted to—it was where the teacher had said my etude "sounded bad."

Spring came, and I was sitting in Region Orchestra rehearsal. The other students had come from school districts all across our half of the state. Most of them, it seemed, planned on music careers, too. It was the usual business of trying to come in at the right time, passing notes and funny pictures, and trying not to get caught up in the "where are you going to school" conversations.

The guest conductor was talking. I was in my spot, jammed in with too many other bassoons, right in front of the horns and the trombones, way at the back of the stage. Suddenly, there was my orchestra director, waving his cell phone at me from down in the auditorium seats. "Call from your mother," he mouthed.

Great. I felt the conductor's glare on my back as I squeezed out between the rest of the orchestra, feeling like Little Miss Rudeness.

"Hello." I didn't try to keep the grouchiness out of my voice when I answered the phone.

Mom just launched into a tune. "Let it shine," she sang.

"Yes?"

"Don't you recognize the song?" she asked. "It's from the Orange County movie soundtrack, where the girl gets her acceptance and starts jumping up and down."

"What??"

"Guess who got in?"

At first, I didn't even understand what she was saying, but finally, realization and happiness flooded over me like a hot shower. The big conservatory I'd run away from in tears—they wanted me!

The orchestra was taking its break now, too, and I turned and screamed, "Guess what?!" I spent the whole rest of the day telling everyone my good news. People were giving me high-fives and asking all about my auditions and what my plans were.

That had to be one of the best moments of my life. But then a weird thing happened. After the excitement died down, I realized I wasn't so sure where I really wanted to go to school. The conservatory was impressive—and it was attached to one of the most elite universities in the country. But, even with my scholarship package, it still had a price tag to match. And attending any classes at the university meant a bus trip to the other campus—if I could ever squeeze it in.

I started to realize that although one of my "safety" schools wasn't the easy target I'd first thought, they'd accepted me—and I really liked the place. The music school was part of a big, academically strong university, where I'd not only be able—but expected—to take liberal arts classes. And my financial package covered a big chunk of the cost of going there.

I agonized up till the last day, but in the end, I knew what I hadn't been able to see going in: sometimes the "best" school isn't really the right school. Sometimes, the right school is what's best for you. I was grateful for the confidence boost, but I didn't need to go to a big-name school to know what I was cut out to do in life. What was more valuable was what I'd learned about myself and what mattered to me in the long run.

~Marcella Dario Fuentes

The Right, On Time Essay

There's nothing to writing.
All you do is sit down at a typewriter and open a vein.
~Walter Wellesley "Red" Smith

"You can write the essays later," I said to my son, "Let's just keep going here." Josh, a restless high school senior, and I, his helpful fifty year old mother, were both being held hostage at the kitchen table, as we forged our way through the pile of his college applications. Every few minutes the digital ring tones of a Led Zeppelin song rang from his cell phone, and he'd have to inform the friend, "I'll catch you later, dude." Sitting with me to help answer the questions was holding him up from his abundant social obligations. I was just thrilled (besides weary and bleary eyed) that we were making progress on the college applications.

It had been obvious from the start that Josh was not as concerned as I about deadlines. The kid was hardly ever home anymore. When he was home, this is how our talks usually went:

Mom: Have you e-mailed any of the coaches on the list yet like the guidance counselor suggested?

Son: No

Mom: Have you gone to websites of the colleges on your list yet?

Son: No

Mom: Did you get the applications yet from the guidance counselor?

Son: Yes. I have them.

Mom: Oh, good. Where are they?

Son: At school. In my locker.

After the applications were home and filled out, a few weeks went by without the required essays. I grew anxious.

I decided to step in and help. Some of my attempts thus far to "help" Josh had not been well received. "I wish you hadn't done that, Mom." Josh inhaled sharply when he discovered that I had e-mailed the college football coaches on his list to assure they knew about the awards and honors Josh received. I had even attached a short video clip of him making a touchdown. "My guidance counselor and I are putting together a letter and DVD to mail to all the coaches." Oh. I gulped, sheepishly. "Well... geez, I'm your mom... I'm like your agent."

Josh didn't seem to find my charming banter during the guided tours of the colleges helpful either. "Mom, you can just drop me off at the college," he suggested as we were driving to visit the last college on our list, "Then you can like go to the mall and go shopping or something and then come pick me up."

When the deadlines for the applications were making me frantic I looked over the parts asking for essays. They asked, "Describe your career goals," and "What skills and experience do you currently possess."

Easy, right? I mean, what parent couldn't list the skills and strengths of his or her child? And what mother doesn't love to share what she knows would be the best career path for her son or daughter to take? I typed up some ideas.

The next day, I blocked Josh's exit from the house with a maneuver worthy of our school's star lineman and handed him my work. "Here," I pleaded, "Look these over."

After a few weeks went by and still no essay materialized, I went a step further. I composed three slapdash essays. Yes, I had some twinges of guilt about writing them, but, I reasoned, they were only rough drafts. Josh could pick one and tweak it.

"This is just an example of what, maybe, you could write for your essay." I explained as I dropped my masterpieces on his bed where he had been reading. Before turning to leave him in peace I added, "They're just, you know, some ideas, you could use, if you want. You know, just to give you... some ideas."

"Thanks, Mom," he said with as much enthusiasm as if I handed him a stick of gum or something.

And that was the last I ever saw of my wonderful essays.

A few days later, Josh handed me some papers, "Can you proofread this for me Mom? It's my college essay."

"Sure," I replied, watching my athletic son turn and walk away.

Curious as to which of my essays he picked, I read it immediately.

"I can still remember everything about that day—the field, the grass, the weather, even where I was lined up in the pre-game stretches..." he began. This essay wasn't one of mine at all, but a fully original one that Josh had written, all by himself. In it he shared what he had learned about himself by overcoming a terrible football injury.

As I read his words I saw how it was so him, his voice, his thoughts, his experience. And I recognized with a kind of wonder that it was... good. (Only a football player, though, would take two pages describing a game, play by play, in a college essay. I had to smile.)

"This is really good, Josh," I said.

"Thanks." A shy smile spread across his face, causing, as it always did, his left eye to close slightly.

"But I don't think the admissions people need to read a play by play of the game," I offered gently. (Josh did cut some of the game from the essay.)

I read his essay over again later, and a few times again after that. I cried a bit, partly because of revisiting the pain he had gone through with his injury, but also for this insight into my son. His heart and his life spilled out of every sentence.

His essay was way superior to anything I could have written for him, because it was him.

And I realized this was what his senior year and getting ready for college was about: me letting go, and my son taking the reins, and both of us knowing he could.

~Donna Paulson

Chicken Soup
for the Soul

Life Lessons
from a Female Dog

Fill your paper with the breathings of your heart.
~William Wordsworth

When my daughter was applying to colleges last year, I gave her some unsolicited advice—don't waste too much angst on your essay. It's the body of your work in high school that counts. Nonetheless, my daughter did want to give these admissions gatekeepers a taste of her personality, and she did spend quite a bit of time on her college essay. After she clicked the mouse and sent the common application zooming the cyber air waves, she let me read her essay.

Yikes! The title of her essay was "Life Lessons from a Bitch"! I froze in my tracks. "What the blankety-blank were you thinking?" I blasted at her! Then, I blamed myself for not being a "helicopter mom" and insisting on reading her essay before she cursorily submitted it.

Upon reading her words, my stance softened. Her essay tenderly described what she had learned from raising her puppy, as well as lessons learned from caring for and breeding Sweetie, and finally the lessons learned from the death of her dog. I misted up. It was a good essay in my opinion, the opinion of a doting mother. Of course, I apologized to my teen and blamed my initial over-reaction on my own silly anxiety regarding college admissions.

My daughter was rejected from some colleges. And, she was

accepted by others. The college she chose to attend was a recipient of that essay with the questionable title. Did the bold title help her? Hurt her? Who knows?

My point in rehashing this anecdote is that although mothers and fathers think they know best, they just might not. My advice to a fellow parent who's now wearing the moccasins I was in a year ago is: "Down, Boy!" Roll over, play dead, whatever it takes to force you, the over-involved parent, to back off.

Let your kid apply with minimum intrusion from you. Stifle the censoring Jiminy Cricket and get off your kid's shoulder! It will turn out okay. And, unlike the popular '50s TV show *Father Knows Best*, sometimes, it's the kids who actually do know best and can teach us a lesson or two.

~Erika Hoffman

Really Scary Interviews

There are very few monsters who warrant the fear we have of them.
~André Gide

G etting into Oxford University is tough. At the College I was applying for the odds of getting a place were sixty to one for the English course. Round One was an application form and two essays; Round Two was a grueling three-day interview process. To get to Round Two, I somehow had to convince a tweed-jacketed professor, his mind honed and perspectives inconceivably distant from my own, that I was worthy to study under him.

To have a chance, I knew I had to say a lot in those two essays. I struggled for weeks trying to decide what to write about, how to infuse a mere 4,000 words with the magical spark that would shoot off the page and ingrain my name in the tutor's mind. I asked teachers and friends for ideas but their advice seemed deeply unhelpful. "Write from the heart," one person said. "Choose something you're interested in," said another. What I wanted was for someone to tell me the formula, the topic, even the line of argument that would win me that place. Normally a free thinker who hated to use other's ideas, my creativity was rendered rigid in the face of that blank page and what it represented.

Late one night, exhausted with nervous tension, reality hit me as I stirred my coffee. I sat there staring into the still brown surface and I realized I was trying to predict the unpredictable, to reach into the minds of these learned scholars and work out how they think and what they like. If I could do that I wouldn't need a university place—I'd already be set for life.

So I cleared my desk, turned off my phone and began to write. I didn't stop to look at lots of textbooks, but I stopped to think—a lot. I wrote about what I like, squeezing out my own opinions in my own voice. One paper on Conrad, one on Shakespeare's *Tempest*. I asked a teacher to check them through and, sensitive to my delicate state, she was completely positive. I checked the mailing instructions, posted the essays off and tried to forget about the whole thing.

I got through to the Second Round, and was invited up to Oxford to spend three days living in college and trying to convince the course tutors I could handle anything they could throw at me. I settled into my fourteenth century college room with about thirty-five other hopefuls, all of us trying to navigate the awkward border between camaraderie and competition. On day two I had my first interview, where I watched in disbelief as the jovial-looking tutor tore my precious Conrad essay to pieces without batting an eyelid. "You didn't think of this... consider that... read this... write that...."

I made a handful of hopeless contributions through gritted teeth and welling eyes. Although I managed to hold it together in the interview room, the tears were flowing before the door closed behind me.

"I've got no chance," I wailed down the phone to my mum. "I might as well come home." With the gentle, well chosen words that only my mum could have found just then, she convinced me to stop second guessing, hang in there, and go through with the rest of the interviews. Her last piece of advice was the only flawed one. "Go shopping," she said, "give yourself some calming retail therapy." Gravitating to the book shop, all my positive thinking crumbled when, in the literature section, I caught sight of the piercing eyes of that heartless interviewer staring from the cover of a Conrad biography. He was a Conrad expert, it turned out. What did I do? Let's just say that the phone bill was horrifying.

In my final interview with the Shakespeare professor, my *Tempest* essay wasn't even mentioned. By this point, I was sure I'd already been rejected and this was the final nail in the coffin. Clearly they were just going through the motions with me; they probably hadn't even read the second essay. I left Oxford in mourning; having both fallen in love with the place and become convinced I would never get the chance to study there.

The letter of acceptance came a few weeks later, and my first year of studies whirled by in a rosy haze of disbelief at my luck. I passed the first year exams, and on the last night of term the English department met for a celebratory dinner. I ended up sitting next to the tutor who had so heartlessly destroyed my Conrad essay. When, emboldened by the relaxed atmosphere, I told him how I had felt at the interview he just laughed. "I remember your essay," he said. "You argued an interesting case. It was completely wrong, but it was interesting. It's the interesting part that got you the place."

The Shakespeare professor chimed in. "We don't expect much knowledge in school leavers," he chuckled, "It's curiosity we're looking for in those essays. We want to see that you can think for yourselves."

"So why were you so abrasive?" I asked with obvious irritation. "You reduced half of us to tears!"

The Conrad expert nodded. "Of course," he said. "I needed to see if you would hold your ground, answer back, if you could sustain a conversation with me. You're all here because you saved the tears for after the interview. University can be the longest, most important conversation you'll ever have. You need brains—everyone knows that—but you need courage too. We don't have space for people who don't dare have something of their own to say." I left the restaurant in a thoughtful mood, only to have my reverie interrupted by the Shakespeare professor poking me in the ribs. "I enjoyed your *Tempest* essay, by the way," he muttered with a bashful grin, "but we were having such a good chat about Hamlet, I clean forgot to mention it!"

~Andrea Gosling

Audition

Always act like you're wearing an invisible crown.
~Author Unknown

My three-year-old daughter Carolyn picked an apple from the bowl on her Nana's table, took a bite, and murmured, "I feel strange." She fell to the floor, the apple rolling dramatically from her hand.

My mom was horrified, and jumped up from her chair. I continued to drink my coffee. I had witnessed this hundreds of times. Carolyn was Snow White, and had reenacted the famous poisoned apple scene. This was her debut, the first time she played a role for an audience. It wouldn't be the last.

Drama has always been a part of our household—not always in a good way. She had her share of door-slams and eye-rolls on the way to winning awards at speech competitions and landing leads in school plays. So it was no surprise when Carolyn decided to go to college to study drama.

In the summer before twelfth grade, while we were on vacation, we toured New York University. The campus visit was very upbeat. The dean of the theater department was encouraging, but he stressed that getting accepted was no small feat. NYU was a highly competitive school, and required great SAT scores, excellent grades, stellar recommendations, extracurricular activities, and... an audition.

After the presentation, we were led to a reception room. As I gathered brochures and information sheets and the requisite coffee and chocolate chip cookies that are part of every tour, I noticed Carolyn looking out the thirteenth floor window. Before us was New York City—Washington Square Park, the Empire State Building, the flood of cars and people and life. She loved the rhythm, the heartbeat, the opportunities, the future. "Why would anyone go anywhere else if they could go here?" she said.

That day we bought an SAT prep book to take on the rest of our vacation.

So Carolyn prepared. Like other students, she studied for the SATs and labored over the admission applications and essays. But she also had to worry about the audition. Working with her drama club director, Carolyn prepared the two required monologues. Her chances of acceptance to her dream school were hanging not only on the accumulation of four years of work, but also on an audition. She had one shot to prove she had talent.

Although NYU was her first choice, she investigated other schools. Her second choice had a great program, and would be a fine place to live and study. She sent in her applications and scheduled her second choice audition in Boston before NYU's, just so she could get a feel for the process.

We drove the five hours to Boston. Even though this was not her first choice, it was a very competitive school and Carolyn knew the stakes were high. She was nervous when I left her at the audition, but when we met just a few hours later, she was beaming.

"I think I really nailed it!"

As we walked through the chilly dusk of Boston, she gave me the details. "The professor who ran the audition was really nice. I did my monologues. Then she asked me to do them different ways—like a cartoon bird, and running around the room in circles. It was crazy, but it was actually fun. Then we talked for awhile. She smiled a lot." Carolyn paused. "I feel really good about it."

The NYU audition was a week later. Again, she was nervous, but gave me a happy smile when I wished her good luck.

After this audition, however, there were no smiles, just Carolyn acting stoic, holding herself together. "Let's go home," she said, not wanting to stop for dinner before the long ride home.

When she was safely in the car, she burst into tears. "I did everything wrong. I'll never get in."

And for days, that was all she would say about it.

Finally, weeks later, she let me know what happened.

"There were several professors conducting the auditions. They all looked really friendly except for one, and that's the one I got. He asked me to start my monologue. He took notes and wasn't even watching at the emotional parts to see my facial expressions. Then he stopped me in the middle and asked me to do my second piece. He didn't let me finish that piece either. He asked me to do it a different way. 'Do it without moving.' 'Don't say that line angrily.' And I tried to follow his direction, but I couldn't give him exactly what he wanted. He asked me some questions, and I felt like I answered every one wrong. Then he said thank you and that was it. The whole thing took about fifteen minutes. That was my chance and I ruined it."

Still she waited for the early decision envelope, confirmation of the bad news so she could move on. Every day when she came in from school she asked, "Any mail?"

Finally the much anticipated letter arrived. The envelope was thick—a good sign according to conventional wisdom. Carolyn came home with some friends, and I immediately handed her the envelope.

She ripped it open and glanced at the letter. She jumped up, then fell to the floor, the letter dramatically drifting from her hand. Her friends looked horrified. I had never witnessed this scene, but I knew my daughter. She was in.

The rest of the day was a flurry of phone calls, a celebratory dinner, and lots of cheering. Right before bed, Carolyn and I sat at the computer and ordered an NYU sweatshirt. For the millionth time that day, we talked about the audition. Whatever Carolyn did must have been right. Despite his stony reaction, the not-so-friendly professor liked what he saw. The acceptance letter posted on the refrigerator proved it. "I'll never doubt myself again," Carolyn said.

"Yes, you will," I told her. "Everybody does. But when you do, remember this moment."

~Lauren Andreano

Teens Talk

GETTING IN...
TO COLLEGE

Getting the Letter

*Climb the mountains and get their good tidings. Nature's peace will
flow into you as sunshine flows into trees. The winds will blow their
own freshness into you, and the storms their energy, while cares will
drop off like autumn leaves.*
~John Muir

The Acceptance Letter

Necessity has no law.
~Benjamin Franklin

There's a scene burned into our brains from movies and television. A fresh-faced teen, perhaps long-haired, but in a good and studious kind of way, runs to the family mailbox to receive the parcel that bears either his acceptance or denial (or waiting list, though this third dramatic option is seldom used in Hollywood for reasons of pace) into the college of his dreams. The destiny to finally leave where he grew up, the little house on whose grassy front yard he now stands, is in the piece of paper in his hands.

The scene is an obvious choice for filmmakers, for its suspense, poignancy and ability to push the narrative. Plus, it's what happens in real life. To high school seniors applying to college, the mail is a very big deal. Monitoring its contents on a daily basis is not uncommon. Any envelope with university stationery can stop your breath.

In the movies I've seen, if the parent, while sifting through the bills and fliers, encounters the envelope first, he or she waits and gives it to the son or daughter, to whom it is rightly addressed, to open. The parent then sits patiently and reads the letter simply by reading the child's face.

Having been exposed to this cinematic scene so many times, I was of course awaiting "my scene" the year I applied to college. I was applying to Washington & Lee University, a small liberal arts institution in Virginia. I was applying early decision, which supposedly meant three things:

1. It's where I wanted to go most.

2. If accepted, I was fully committed to going there, and nowhere else.

3. It reflected a specific desire to attend that boosted my chances of getting in by about 15%.

I would find out in late December, not in the spring as one would for regular decision, so if I got in, I could spend the last five months of my senior year slouching off, within reason. There were suburban legends about A- students getting Ds the spring semester of their senior year and colleges reneging their admission, but it had never happened to anyone I knew.

Weighing all the formulas for getting in; SATs, grades, sports, awards and honors, community service hours (in this last category I was lacking), my father said he was 85 to 90% certain I'd get in.

A businessman by nature and trade, I remember him quoting this figure to me over breakfast. Sitting in the dusty morning sunlight of our kitchen, his glasses on a string around his neck, he had about him eggs, bacon, heavily-buttered toast, coffee, and a pack of Lucky Strikes. The college rankings issue of *U.S. News & World Report*, the big fat dictionary-like guide to colleges, was open to the Ws.

"85 to 90% certain," my father said again. "I'd be very shocked if you didn't get in."

Both my older brothers had attended fancy schools, and now that I, the youngest, was due up, my father had the swagger of a baseball batter who's going to hit three-for-three. Not that getting into a good college wasn't important to me, it was, but to my father it justified every endeavor of childhood, from wrestling tournaments to guitar lessons, in a strange, though harmlessly obsessed way.

Some days after that breakfast, I came home from school at the usual time after wrestling practice, and found the mail as it typically was, in a somewhat neat pile on the corner of the table. Sure enough, there was something from Washington & Lee. It was a normal, letter-sized envelope. Both sides were covered with translucent grease spots and the under-skin of the flap was bumpy and coated with a congealed white substance.

My mom was unloading the dishwasher. My father had just appeared from the living room at the sound of my arrival.

"What the heck happened here?" I said, holding up the battered envelope.

At first, the envelope wouldn't really rip. I tore harder and the lid just kind of separated slowly, like a mouth full of peanut butter. Right then, in the corner of my eye, I noticed the Elmer's Glue bottle on the windowsill above the sink.

"I think it's glued," I said.

"Sorry sweetie," my mom said, and set down a stack of plates and came nearer to put her hands on my shoulders. "Your father had to open it. When he saw it was a small envelope his face turned purple. He looked like he was about to have a heart attack and so he just had to open it."

That was the other great theory our family entertained about college mail. A big envelope meant you were in, as it would be stuffed with accompanying forms and brochures about dorms and meal-plans and such. A small envelope meant a single sheet of paper whose basic message was, "Sorry, but..."

For whatever reason, the good folks at Washington & Lee admissions sent me their congratulations with a simple two paragraph letter. According to my mom, this had almost killed my father.

"You should have seen the color of his face," she went on. "It was like all the blood in his body just rushed to his head when he thought you didn't get in. Your father had me boil a kettle of water and we sat there holding the envelope over the steam to get it to separate."

So as a victim of petty mail fraud, I didn't get to experience my acceptance letter in the traditional cinematic way. By the same token, my father, a proud and supportive man who deserved to feel a sense of triumph at the last of his sons making good, had a rather anti-climactic moment as well. Whenever I feel the need for a fond memory, I just think of the old man sitting at the table with the glue and the scissors like a kid in art class, trying to do the best job he can.

~Max Adler

"She got her college acceptance
letter."

51

Acceptance

Everyone has inside of him a piece of good news.
The good news is that you don't know how great you can be!
How much you can love!
What you can accomplish!
And what your potential is!
~Anne Frank

Flip... flip... flip... nothing yet.

Getting the mail had become an art form for my seven-teen-year-old hands. I would arrange the mail. First the junk mail, next the colored envelopes, and then the glorious white crisp envelopes. Those glorious envelopes held my future within their grasp. They would read "Congratulations" or "Thank You."

Yes, it was college application season. The time when students were in a frenzy. Many, like me, were nervous wrecks. I felt like the school day would never end. Every second felt like an eternity. The pressure was piling up so high, I could hardly concentrate on my school work. When was the letter coming from Tennessee? Did I get my financial aid? If not, could I afford it? No, I didn't make it in? Yes, I did! These questions circled my mind all through the school day while I crunched on my pencil with my back teeth.

"Does that pencil taste good?" Tracy laughed as she pretended to eat her eraser.

"Actually I don't taste it anymore!" I smiled back at her.

"You're still worried about your college stuff, huh?"

"It's all I can think about. I've become obsessed. I don't even go anywhere. I just wait!"

"You need to just relax. It'll happen. You should come out with us this weekend!"

"I don't know, maybe... but I have a hot date."

"Who is he? I want details!"

"He's tan, holds a flag, and he is about my height," I said through a smile.

"Who? Wow, that's pretty short!" she said, leaning in so I could give her a name.

"My mailbox" I whispered in her ear, half laughing.

"You really need to get out more! Seriously, come out with us this weekend."

She looked at me with mixed emotion as she turned back to her class work. She didn't understand. She had already been accepted to four top universities. It seemed she effortlessly got As. Her SAT scores were through the roof and she didn't even have to study! Unlike me, she was struggling to pick a college from the many she was accepted to. I had some universities I had been accepted to, but the only one that mattered was the University of Tennessee. I don't know if it was the orange T, the amazing women's basketball team, or maybe because it sat exactly 2,142.15 miles away from my home. I was just obsessed with getting accepted. It took me about eleven days to finish my application. One day to fill it out, and ten days to make sure it was perfect. What was taking so long? Did I put the wrong address? Was a 4.1 grade point average not enough? It was my SAT scores. They must have been too low.

I was already setting myself up for disappointment. All the other acceptance letters had arrived. They all began "Congratulations..." Two letters telling me "Thank you..." also had arrived. Yes, I had seen the big "Thank you...but you have not been accepted" letters. They usually came in small, plain, morbid envelopes. They were short, not so sweet, and to the point. Those dreadful letters filled with back handed compliments and feelings of insufficiency. I hoped to never read another "Thank You" in my lifetime. The word now made my stomach cringe with anger.

Ring... Ring... Ring.... Yes, school was out! Only 20 minutes and I would be at my mailbox. Maybe the letter was already there waiting for my fingertips to rip it open. There was a traffic jam that day, so I arrived at my mailbox in exactly 33 minutes. I raced up to the copper handle and pulled the mailbox open.

Empty. Nothing!

How was this possible? Not even a scrap of junk mail or a past-due bill? I scrunched my eyes with disappointment. I slowly felt the hot tears staining my face. How long would it take? I slipped to the curb, pounding my fist on the warm cement. Why are they not responding? I'm not good enough for them. Questions on top of ideas flooded my brain. I was so confused, upset, and disillusioned. I slowly picked myself up from the ground, wiped my tears away, and began to walk toward my front door empty-handed. I knew my mom would be sitting at the table waiting to hear the news from me. She would be waiting for a thumbs-up. Sadly, she wouldn't get it today. As I began to turn my key I heard whispering and the phone click. My mom met me at the door with a huge smile on her face. I looked in her eyes filled with mystery and excitement. She waved the brightly colored folder up and down as she smiled.

"You made it!" she screamed.

"I made what?" I looked at her puzzled as she jumped up and down.

"You are accepted to UT!" she screamed, scooping me up in a hug.

"Are you serious? Thank God!" I let out a sigh of relief and joined my mom in celebration. We celebrated at the door until our limbs were exhausted.

"Congratulations... Congratulations..." I read the paper over seventy times. It was in a beautifully decorated folder and came with a certificate of acceptance. This was the real deal. I was really accepted! I felt my body release all the built-up anxiety. I suddenly felt exhausted. My mom stared at me as I gathered my things. She smiled sweetly.

"Are you happy?" she asked, through her smile.

"I am. Now I feel like I am smart."

"Baby Girl, you don't need that paper to tell you are smart. You have always been my genius."

I hugged my mother as tears escaped our eyes. I realized all this time I wasn't obsessed with finding a college. I was obsessed with finding the feeling of "acceptance." After all, if these universities wanted me, I had to be a little smart. As I hugged my mom that late afternoon, I finally felt the "acceptance" I had yearned for.

~Alexsys M. Echevarria

Fate's Compass Points South

A wise man changes his mind, a fool never.
~Spanish Proverb

The sun shone warmly as we loaded luggage into the coach bus for our senior-year orchestra competition in Virginia Beach. I'd worked hard in high school, and my worries were coming to an end, save one looming anxiety—college acceptance letters.

The air was ripe with the fruition of a long college application process. Notification letters would soon start trickling into mailboxes. Everyone knew the deal—a thin letter was bad news. A thick envelope or a packet meant acceptance.

That morning, Mom had dropped me—and my luggage—off at school.

"Do you want me to drive to the high school to say bye before you leave this afternoon?" Mom asked.

"Nah, I'll be alright."

"Okay," she said, disappointed.

"Unless," I added, "a college letter comes today!"

She smiled.

"But if it's a little one," I added nervously, "open it first. I don't want bad news before our final orchestra competition."

I looked for my mom while loading my suitcase, but I hadn't seen her. The orchestra director instructed us to board the bus, and I complied. But a nagging feeling lingered, and I watched the parking lot. As the after school rush ended, I saw Mom's blue station wagon.

I stood up.

"Where are you going?" the director asked.

"My mom said she'd come if I got a college letter," I managed to say. "Please? Can I go?"

He smiled. "Sure."

I'd applied to a handful of colleges, and I'd only visited them once — briefly. I'd take a closer look once I got accepted. Still, I'd grown up in Connecticut and had my heart set on a New England college. Somewhere with rolling hills and old academic buildings that emanated tradition. Growing up in a busy suburb of New York City, I was used to the competitive atmosphere of the North. I couldn't see myself anywhere else. Of course, I hadn't been to many other areas of the country, and I realize in retrospect that I had no basis for comparison.

I'd set my heart on a small, private college — smaller than my high school. Looking back, I don't remember much about why I liked it. I remember large dorm rooms and a cozy little coffee shop that served four-dollar muffins. In my infinite high school wisdom, I'd considered factors like dorm rooms and intramural sports, but not academics or available majors. Still, I set my heart on this one college and wished for acceptance. I made myself a bracelet with the school colors and wore it secretly for good luck.

Mom knew I was setting myself up for disappointment.

"I know your guidance counselor approved of the schools you've chosen," she said, "but I have one more idea. My old high school friend mentioned a college — in Lancaster, Pennsylvania. Franklin & Marshall College."

I scowled. "Pennsylvania?"

"It's a small college, like the ones we've been visiting. It's known for teaching critical thinking. You'd really enjoy the types of classes they offer."

"But Pennsylvania?!" I protested. Clearly, Mom had more insight than I, but in my adolescent obstinance, I failed to consider more relevant attributes than location.

"You remember all those vacations we took to Amish country," she reminded me. "The people are nice, the farmland is beautiful."

Again, I scowled. Farmland was nice, but it wasn't the bucolic, rolling New England hills.

"And there's the snow," Mom mused.

That was true. I loathed the snow we got in Connecticut.

"Surely it'll be worse farther North," Mom said as if reading my mind.

"Okay," I conceded. "I'll apply. But no promises."

I left the charter bus and ran to Mom's car. "Congratulations!" she said, handing me a large envelope from Franklin & Marshall. It contained an acceptance letter and scholarship notification.

I couldn't help but smile. Still, during the long drive to Virginia Beach, I wished I'd heard from my first choice college.

When I returned from the trip, Mom and I visited my grandmother in the nursing home. Suffering under the first stages of senile dementia, she remembered our names some days; other days, she didn't.

"Mama!" Grandma said, indicating my mom. "And Bubey!" she said, giving me a big, wet kiss. She didn't know our names today, but at least she recognized us.

"How are you?" I asked.

"Nananana!" she sang.

"Mom?" my mother asked. "Do you remember who we are?"

Grandma thought a moment. Then she laughed, embarrassed that she could not.

"Well," Mom continued patiently, "Your granddaughter Valerie has some good news to tell you."

Grandma turned to me. "Bubey?" she asked.

I told her that I'd been accepted to Franklin & Marshall. She smiled, and her lips moved, though she did not speak.

"Pennsylvania," Mom repeated. "Do you remember Pennsylvania? You were born there."

"Nanana!" Grandma sang again. The rest of the visit went much the same, with mom and me talking while Grandma sang along happily.

But as we turned to leave, Grandma spoke, serious and celebratory, in a moment of lucidity.

"It's wonderful that Valerie's going to Franklin & Marshall. I'll know she'll do great things there," she said.

"But I haven't heard from my top choice yet," I said, surprised and discouraged. But grandma only answered with more singing. Her lucidity had passed.

A week later, I'd heard from all the schools except my first choice. I was too nervous to check the mail, so I sent my little sister instead. I watched from my top-floor bedroom window as she opened the mailbox and frowned, holding a small envelope. I fought tears.

I was rejected. I tore off my bracelet and decided the universe was unfair. I'd wanted to go to that school more than I'd ever wanted anything in my life. If I wanted something so bad, how could the universe possibly not allow it?

I drove to visit Franklin & Marshall College with grandma's prophetic conversation replaying in my mind. I mingled with other recently-accepted students. I got along well with a girl from New Jersey — it later turned out we'd be housed in the same hallway, and a year later, we'd choose each other as roommates. When Mom and I stopped at the grocery store to get snacks for the hotel, the clerk looked busy, so I bagged our groceries. Before we left, he turned to us. "Thank you for bagging," he said.

Our jaws dropped. We'd lived in our hurried Connecticut city so long that we weren't used to anyone slowing down enough to say "thanks." I knew then that I would attend F&M.

When I visited my grandmother again, I described the college visit, but she answered only in babbles. Her doctor said she couldn't understand us. Still, looking at the twinkle in her eye, I suspected she knew more than anyone. Maybe her smile reflected the four wonderful years she knew I'd experience at F&M, or my personal growth, or my future husband from F&M...

An open mind is the best kind to have. Though we like to think we know best, sometimes there are unseen forces which, incomprehensible at the time, are only acting in our best interest. In my case, fate's compass had pointed south, and I'm glad I followed.

~Val Muller

Receiving the Letter

If you don't like the news,
go out and make some of your own.
~Wes Nisker

G rowing up in a small town in Westchester County, New York, I had felt pressure to be accepted to a prestigious college or university since the first day of my freshman year in high school. I worked hard to make honor roll, high honor roll, and principal's list. I took every honors and advanced placement course that I could fit into my schedule. Joining clubs (and ultimately becoming president of them), making varsity teams, participating in community service projects, taking on part time jobs, as well as studying with an SAT tutor were all thought to be essential to gaining entrance to my "dream college." But I also knew that in order to win over the admissions council, I would have to have something that would make me stand out, that would make the college feel like they needed me there.

So diving became a huge part of my life. I had been on my high school's varsity diving team since eighth grade, and on various club teams since I was about nine years old. I was captain my senior year, and had done exceptionally well on both my club and high school team. I didn't wait for diving coaches to approach me when choosing which schools I wanted to apply to. No, I did it the old fashioned way. I spent hours poring over Barron's college books, and after making a carefully constructed list of my favorite colleges, I drove up and down the entire East Coast with my parents, visiting each and every one of them. They ranged in size, Division I to Division III, and soon I had used up all of my allotted overnight college visits, resulting in a handful of coaches promising me admission and scholarships to their schools. By the time September of my senior year rolled around, I had fallen in love with one small, prestigious college in upstate New York. After having been assured that there was a spot on the team with my name on it, I applied to the school, Early Decision of course, and waited the seemingly endless two months to hear back.

I remember the day I received my letter. I had spent the twenty-four hours leading up to it analyzing every detail of my high school career, thinking of the countless hours I had put into being the Editor in Chief of my high school yearbook, secretary of the math honors society, captain of the diving team, treasurer of peer mediation, all my volunteer work, and every final exam grade I had worked my butt off for. I was positive that I deserved to get in. I was beyond anxious. Was I going to collect the big brown package, or the thin white envelope? The pressure was almost too much.

When I opened my mailbox, my heart sunk to the ground. It was a meek little envelope, and when I tore it open to see if I had even snagged a spot on the waiting list, I found I was fully rejected. It was a crushing blow. I sat around for a day sulking, thinking I did something wrong, or that I hadn't worked hard enough, and of everybody I thought that I was letting down.

I thought of my two best friends who had both gotten into the same liberal arts college in Pennsylvania, Early Decision, the day before. How was I supposed to tell them I was denied? But they were more than understanding and supportive, and made me realize that maybe the school was too small for me anyway. I had lived in a small environment my entire life. Maybe I had other options that I wasn't even considering.

A week went by, and I continued my application process. I had to put things into perspective: I was a great student, I did everything I could, I applied to a dozen excellent schools, and one was bound to take me. How was I to know for sure that my original top choice was just right for me? I didn't attend the college; I just did a simple over-night, and one night couldn't predict my entire college experience.

As it turns out, I was accepted into a highly regarded state univer-sity which holds an equal, if not greater, reputation than my "dream school." And the best part was, I wasn't even accepted because of athletics. I applied to the school solely based upon academics. Soon I visited the University, and found that I loved it even more than the small college I had my hopes set on. Luckily, I had found the motivation to continue my application process, squeeze out a few last minute schools, and got into one of the best that I had applied to. Now I can't wait to attend college this coming fall.

~Jacqueline Palma

A Matter of Life and Death

To give vent now and then to his feelings,
whether of pleasure or discontent,
is a great ease to a man's heart.
~Francesco Guicciardini

I found out that my grandfather died the morning I received the news that I'd gotten into my first-choice college. It happened on a balmy December morning in Nairobi. Just minutes after I received my long-awaited early acceptance e-mail from William & Mary, my mother told me in a whispered voice that her father, who had been ailing for the past week, had finally passed away, and that she'd be leaving immediately to spend the funeral week with her mother and many sisters.

It was strange—I knew that one event was supposed to fill me with happiness, and the other with grief, but I felt neither. In some strange way the feelings seemed to cancel themselves out, leaving me with the will to feel something... but without the ability to do so.

One thing was certain. I'd wanted to get in to William & Mary, and badly. My sister was already a sophomore there, and when I'd visited her I'd fallen instantly in love with its reassuringly steady brick walls and all of its civilized and sculpted greenery. I imagined it to be everything that my rather solitary high school experience wasn't, and felt all too ready to leave behind the feeling I had in Nairobi of always being an outsider — the walled-in white girl who didn't fit in — and the incestuous society of the all-too-small fifty member senior class at my international school.

So I did feel an initial burst of relief when I first heard the news of my acceptance, but that was immediately tempered by the fact that I was supposed to feel something about my grandfather's death. While I wore a William & Mary T-shirt to school that day — an early and somewhat presumptuous Christmas gift from my sister — I felt that it was almost wrong to publicize my good luck, that the people congratulating me were doing me a disservice. I should be sad.

The thing was, I'd never really known my grandfather except as a shadow of himself. He'd had some sort of nervous breakdown years before I was old enough to know about such things, and had been reduced to a crinkled-up man, older than his years, who was, in my memories, always bound to his La-Z-Boy armchair.

When I tried to summon up loving memories of him, all I could think about was how no one had ever really listened to him. He would start grumbling about how savvy my Aunt Beatty's cat was, embarking on long and uninteresting vignettes about her various exploits, and he would be utterly ignored by everyone, not even acknowledged with a polite bow of the head. Whenever we were over, I would pretend to listen, if only because it seemed absolutely necessary that someone should do so. And that was it. The fondest thought I could summon about a man whom I'd known all of my life. Was that terrible? Did it make me a bad person? Certainly I hadn't spent much time with him, but he was flesh and blood, one of my closest relatives.

The truth was, my feelings about my mother's parents were complicated ones. I didn't think she'd gotten the love she needed growing up, and it killed me to stand by and watch as year after year she continued to try to win the approval of her blasé parents, only to watch her get shot down time and again. They never understood her, could never understand how willingly she had let my adventurous father take her away from her small town youth, away even from the country, and while they accepted her love in good grace, they never thought to show her affection in return.

Her childhood had been more of the same—I remembered well the story she told about how she was found sitting in the middle of the road when she was a mere two years old. She laughed when she told it, but to me it was the kind of thing that wasn't even funny in retrospect.

Reflecting on that day, some six years later, I realize that I wasn't emotionless after all. In fact, it was probably the first day that I really experienced what it is to be an adult; that, though we might want an easy answer, a right and wrong, it doesn't often exist. You can be happy, sad, angry, and guilty, all of these things at the same time. And sometimes, when you're not sure how to express yourself, that barrage of conflicting feelings can leave you with the hollow and misleading sensation of emotionlessness.

~Angela R. Polidoro

Meant To Be

Patience is the ability to count down before you blast off.
~Author Unknown

I'd been crying for hours.

Ever since I got my thin envelope from Harvard, my first choice college, I'd felt like my world had fallen out from under me. I threw myself on my bed and sobbed until I finally ran out of tears. Worse than the most agonizing breakup or the most violent fight with my best friend, my Harvard rejection tore my world apart. I felt like my future had been taken away from me—before I'd even had the chance to have a taste of what it could be.

I'd set my heart on going to college only a few years earlier. A conversation with my guidance counselor at school had opened my eyes to the world of possibilities that college had to offer me. I could go across the country—or around the world. I could learn whatever I wanted. I could build a future for myself that before I could have only dreamed about.

You see, my high school—a large, underfunded, public school in Southern California—wasn't exactly a feeder school. Only about half of the freshmen who entered each year would make it all the way to graduation day and, of those, only a handful went to a four year university. Before this conversation, I figured I'd maybe go to a community college for a few years, then get a job in town, never venturing more than a few miles from home. My world felt small and inescapable.

But college felt like the way to create a different destiny for myself. It was my way to break away from what I'd previously thought I could be and try for something so much more. I set my sights on the best, Harvard, and spent the next three years turning myself into the ideal Harvard candidate. Excellent grades, great test scores, and a perfect mix of extracurricular accomplishments. All I needed was an acceptance letter and a scholarship.

A few years of hard work later, here I was, crying on my bed, my world shattered by a little envelope containing only one piece of paper.

My mom came into my room and sat on the edge of my bed. "Why are you crying so hard? It's only one school."

"You don't understand!" I wailed. Harvard embodied everything I'd always dreamt of, and now it was officially out of my reach.

"You applied to six other schools, I'm sure you'll get into one of them. You're so smart and you've done so well. Any of them will be lucky to have you."

"But, they're not Harvard."

"Why do you want to go to Harvard so badly anyway?" she asked.

I was quiet for a moment. It was like I was really thinking about it for the first time. "Because, it's the best, I guess."

"But, maybe it's not the best for you. I know you'll get into the one that's right for you." My mom is a big believer in fate and, at that moment, so was I. Maybe I'd gotten carried away in all the hype around Harvard.

Six days later, on March 31st, I'd been rejected by three schools (including my infamous Harvard rejection) and accepted to three more, but without enough financial aid for any of them to be a viable option.

I had one school left: The Johns Hopkins University. Deep down, I knew that this had to be it. This had to be the school I was supposed to go to. My mom had to be right. I tried not to stress and to focus all my energy on visualizing that fat envelope with its acceptance letter and big financial aid package. I tried to believe in the power of positive thinking.

April 5th came and I still hadn't heard from Hopkins. Where was my letter? All my friends were starting to make plans for the next year and I was still waiting by the mailbox, praying that I wouldn't be left behind.

April 6th: still nothing. My mom told me to relax, it would come. She too believed that this last school would be the answer to our prayers. It had to be.

On April 7th, I woke up early, too stressed to sleep in, even though it was the middle of Spring Break. This had to be the day. I paced the house, waiting for the sound of the mailman driving down my cul-de-sac.

Finally, at 2 P.M., I heard him. I walked slowly to the mailbox, almost afraid of what I might find. Doubts clouded my mind, what if this weren't my fate? What if I couldn't go to college?

I reached in and pulled out the stack of mail. Magazines and bills, all piled on top of a big, white envelope. My heart stopped. It was from Hopkins.

I almost passed out. It was a big envelope. I was in. But, of course, for me that was only half of the equation. I'd gotten into three schools already, but none gave me enough financial aid to actually attend.

I ripped open the envelope and looked inside.

Full scholarship.

I screamed and cried all at once. My mom was right. Some things are meant to be.

~Jennifer Lee Johnson

"I won a full ride scholarship ... and *he's* a walk-on."

The Most Important Subject

The value of identity of course is that so often with it comes purpose.
~Richard Grant

My eyes start to blur as I stare at the screen,
They're so sick and tired of this trying routine.
Click-Send-Click-Send, applications are done!
Finally feeling like the battle is won.

But it's not — It's only just begun.

Now I'm waiting and hoping and praying.
I'm constantly biting my nails.
I'm wondering what I'll be saying,
In April when I get the mail.

Will I be an Ivy League girl?
Using words like "facetious" or "clout?"
I'll watch my career unfurl,
As a chemist or lawyer, no doubt.

But wait — I may have a different plan,
That puts me at a state school,

Drinking beer from a can.
I'll scream, "GO!" at the game,
I'll pray our team breaks the tie,
With my arm wrapped around
My fraternity guy.

"Hold on," I think now, of a place I could go
That doesn't have frats or fans that scream "Go!"
And everyone isn't pretentiously smart.
What if I just want to do liberal arts?
I could stroll on the quad with my hair uncombed,
Textbooks in hand, walking alone.
Birkenstocks on my feet, flowers in my hair,
Trying to make everyone in the world more aware.
"Peace for all!" I could scream, "Go green! Save the whales!"
At the front of the protest I'd stand, without fail.

Or maybe, I think, I don't have to decide,
I could just be myself and go with the tide.
I could wait to see where I end up, at which place,
And not try in advance to be someone to save face.
I'll make friends where I go,
I'll have fun and I'll grow.
Maybe learn bigger words,
Paint my face and scream "Go!"
Maybe go head-to-head with my political foe.

But all I can hope, as I wait for the letters,
Is that, wherever I go, my four years make me better.
I want to learn everything, I want a degree.
But mostly, I just want to learn about me.

~Madeline Clapps

Chapter
9

Teens Talk
GETTING IN...
TO COLLEGE

The Waiting List

The world is all gates,
all opportunities,
strings of tension waiting to be struck.
~Ralph Waldo Emerson

57

Lilacs and the Waiting List

Keep on asking, and you will be given what you ask for.
Keep on looking, and you will find. Keep on knocking, and the door will be
opened.
~Matthew 7:7-8

I could feel my face wilt into a disappointed grimace. The letter from Holy Cross, the one school I really wanted to attend, had come in a dreaded small envelope. By April of my senior year, I could clearly recognized what the envelope size conveyed about its contents—large manila envelopes, full and ripe with promise, were the heralds of glorious acceptances, while the thin, white business envelopes were forerunners to the dismissing lines, "We regret to inform you..."

I sighed as I began to slowly ease open the flap, trying to delay the inevitable as long as possible. True, my college counselor had told me that Holy Cross was a "reach" school, and based on my high school grades I would sit in the bottom 25% of my class all four years if I managed to get in. "But Holy Cross is my school," I had argued. "That is where I want to be." He had smiled skeptically and turned to schools that were more in my "range."

Holy Cross had been the only school I really wanted to attend since the moment I set foot onto the tree-lined main drive for the first time. I can't explain the sense of belonging and rightness I felt as

I wandered the old corridors and manicured grounds on my tour. I had visited lots of schools, been wowed by meal plans, dorm set ups, curriculum options, and diverse extra-curricular activities. But any interest I had in them disappeared as I toured Kimball, the main dining hall, and Dinand, the grand library. This was where I was meant to go to school—I could feel it, and I eagerly mailed my application with butterflies in my stomach and a quick kiss on the envelope.

Yet the months of waiting, checking the mail everyday, had lead to this disheartening moment, standing in my kitchen with my coat still on, slipping the thin, uncaring paper out of the cold white envelope. I scanned the page, looking for some sign of either acceptance or rejection. Blah, blah, blah, "we had a great applicant pool this year," yada yada yada, "we can't offer spaces to everyone," something-something-something, "placing you on our waitlist,"—huh?

"What does it say, honey?" my dad askd, his voice full of anxiety for me.

"I didn't get in, but I'm on the waitlist." I said, rereading the letter. Being relegated to the waiting list seemed a strangely anticlimactic end to my passionate desire to be accepted.

"Well, at least it isn't rejection," he said brightly.

"Yea, but still," I said, a small tear sneaking out of the corner of my eye. "I don't want to be on the waiting list; I want to be accepted. Holy Cross was the one school I cared about. It doesn't matter where I go now, because it is all ruined. No one gets in off the waiting list, it is a consolation prize. It's a way of saying 'thanks for trying; we liked you enough not to flat out reject you,' but everyone knows it's the same thing." My lip quivered; I was on the edge of dissolving into childish crying.

"So then let's go out there and tell them so."

"What?"

"I'm serious. Let's drive out there so you can tell them how you feel. What have you got to lose?"

"That sounds lame, dad," I pouted. "Stuff like that doesn't work."

"OK, do what you want. But, if I were you, I would make the effort to show them how much I want it."

Frustrated and annoyed, I went upstairs and busied myself in my room, my father's advice swirling around in my head. It was a silly idea. They wouldn't care if I showed up, begging to be let in. It would be a waste of everyone's time, not to mention very embarrassing for me.

However, I mulled the situation over for a few days, finally coming to the conclusion he was right. I had nothing to lose. I might as well try, or else I would never know. On Wednesday morning I asked him if he would drive me out there Friday. He smiled and said, "Of course."

The butterflies in my stomach felt as if they were threatening to leap out of my mouth as we pulled up in front of the vast and daunting admissions building. We walked in and took a left down an echoing and empty hallway. My dad stopped part way down the hall and said with a smile, "Good luck, sweetheart."

At the end of the hallway, I turned right and presented myself to the admissions secretary. I asked if the officer who conducted my interview would have a minute or two to chat. Fifteen minutes later, I was ushered into the same bright meeting room where I had my first interview and found myself seated across from Mr. Luis Soto, my admissions officer. He smiled as he held my fate in his hands.

"What can I do for you, Nacie?" he asked pleasantly.

"Well, sir, I am here to tell you that I love this school and would love an opportunity to be here. I was put on the waiting list, and just wanted to come out here to tell you how much going here would mean to me — it is my only dream for college, sir — and that I would use my time here to the best advantage. I am seriously dedicated to doing my best here, and wanted to let you know that if you gave me a chance and reconsidered my application that you wouldn't regret it." I took a deep breath; the words had tumbled imploringly from my mouth before I could stop them or check their desperate tone.

Mr. Soto was a young man with a calming presence and a sweet manner. He looked me over for a minute before he smiled broadly.

"OK, well that is the kind of thing we love to hear. Congratulations, you're in."

My voice caught in my throat and I choked, "I'm sorry?"

"We want people in the class who want to be here, who will make the best of this education. I'm glad you came to talk to me. I'm happy to offer you a position in the Class of 2007."

"Thank you," I said, my voice small with disbelief. "Thank you. Thank you!"

I was still saying thank you as I shook his hand and walked, dazed and elated, out of his office and back down the hall. I couldn't believe it. I started to cry from happiness and sheer mental overload. My father was sitting on a bench, his hands clasp anxiously on his knees. When he saw my tears he assumed the worst, and began to console me with an "Oh, honey..." before I was able to tell him the good news. Then his face lit up and he wrapped on arm around me as we walked out of the building.

As we left the campus that day, new Holy Cross T-shirt and hat in hand, we walked down a set of stairs that had lilacs growing on either side. My dad stopped, took a deep breath, and said, "I hope you will always remember the day you got into Holy Cross you were here with your father and everything smelled like lilacs." I smiled at him as we pulled out the phone to call my mom.

The four years at Holy Cross were even more wonderful than I thought they could be, and I never lost that feeling of belonging. I had an opportunity to learn about everything from archaeology to organic chemistry to Freudian psychology to English poetry and graduated magna cum laude with an honors degree in history. So much for the prediction I would be in the bottom 25% of my class. It's true that I haven't, and will never, forget the day I got into Holy Cross. The whole experience taught me two of the best lessons I learned during my college years: don't listen to other's predictions for you, and if you truly want something, never, ever give up.

~Nacie Carson

58

From Waiting List to Wonderful

We must be willing to get rid of the life we've planned,
so as to have the life that is waiting for us.
~Joseph Campbell

One week in March, all of the letters arrived.

Of the ten schools I applied to, one rejected me, four accepted me, and five of them put me on the infamous waiting list, otherwise known as college purgatory.

Surprisingly, I had a much easier time being rejected by my top school than being considered a "maybe" by half of the schools on my list. How was I good, but not good enough? That terrible week, I berated myself with questions and possibilities.

What would have made me that much better? An award-winning essay? An SAT score above 1500? A 4.0 GPA instead of 3.95? Five perfect SAT II scores instead of two? AP scores of all 5? I was such a dedicated student ever since I learned to read and write, with great grades and test scores. Great, but not perfect.

What would have made me that much more well-rounded? Six days of ballet a week instead of five? Playing a varsity sport as well as dancing? Two volunteer activities a year instead of one? Ten extracurricular activities instead of five? I had always been involved at my school and at my dance academy, and I was a volunteer EMT for two years. I barely had time for homework and college applications as it was.

What would have made me unique? Playing the tuba? Speaking Urdu? Being an Olympic gold medalist? Interning for the Governor? I spoke fluent Spanish, had studied abroad, and had a competitive internship in New York City. Apparently, that didn't help me stand out.

Eventually, I came to terms with the fact that despite being perfectly qualified for the Ivy League, I had just not made the cut. There was nothing I could have done, since the system doesn't work in favor of the applicants, but rather to benefit the needs of the school.

I also learned to look beyond the name and history of the school to decide if it was right for me. I chose a competitive school in Washington, D.C., and it was the best experience of my life. I don't think any other school could have given me the same advantages, and I can't imagine having gone anywhere else.

During my four years of college, I met my best friends. I became an expert on Latin America. I explored the city, and took advantage of lots of the great events, conferences, and celebrity appearances around campus. I explored subjects I never would have otherwise considered, such as Urban Sociology and Creative Writing. I co-founded a ballet company, which has now become an important student institution at my school. I studied abroad, and traveled the world. I graduated with a double major, in the top two percent of my class.

Now, a year after my college graduation, I think back on that terrible week in March and smile. I wish I had known I wasn't in purgatory, but in fact right outside the Heavenly Gates of college paradise.

~Rachel Glickhouse

59

Getting In...
from the Waitlist

Everything you want is out there waiting for you to ask.
Everything you want also wants you.
But you have to take action to get it.
~Jules Renard

I approached the only free computer in the library during seventh period—one of two that sat on a mahogany, chest-level table with no chair. I would only be a minute. It takes several minutes to read an entire college decision letter. It takes less than a minute to recognize an acceptance or a rejection.

As the Boston University website loaded, I felt several pairs of eyes sneaking annoyingly curious glances at my computer screen. Or, at least I think I did. When you're waiting for a college decision letter, you think your computer screen, your mailbox, and your telephone are the center of the universe.

An odd detachment washed over me as I skimmed the letter. I logged off and shuffled, in a daze, back to my study table. I stopped to ask my friend Meredith if she had heard from Stanford yet.

"Yeah... I, well, I was recruited for tennis, but... well... I was rejected." The tears that had splashed down her face left barely visible paths on her cheeks—like dried up rivers.

I sat down. I had been waitlisted, and didn't know what to think.

That night I logged into my e-mail account and found that Villanova had posted my admissions decision. The page loaded quickly.

Rejection letters never say the word "rejection." I wanted to scream and cry to whomever had come up with such a flowery way of saying that Villanova didn't want me. That day, I had accepted a place on a waitlist and been rejected by my final school. I knew I would not have a stress-free end to my senior year—simply because I didn't want to go anywhere that had accepted me, and BU, the only school I would consider attending, had sent me to admissions limbo. The rest of the night was eerily unremarkable considering the events that had taken place. *Wheel of Fortune* came on at six. I read a few scenes from *Death of a Salesman*. I cried through all of it.

The next day at school, I saw my college counselor, Mrs. Cady. There is no way to describe her other than "peppy." Mrs. Cady was my eternal cheerleader. In an oppressive, strict environment where I truly believed I had not thrived, Mrs. Cady, with her colorful sweater sets and bouncy blond ponytails, was one of the few faculty members at school who saw me for who I was.

I spent the time walking from my classroom to her office trying to mold my face into that of a happy person. I reached her office. On the door was a poster of Wake Forest—a purple-y evening shot of the campus, with its winding paths and charming streetlamps. I looked at that poster—the poster that had become so familiar to me through countless visits—and knew I would cry.

Mrs. Cady nodded and handed me Kleenex after Kleenex as I tried to express my feelings—embarrassment, fear, confusion—an overwhelming sense of being out of control.

"I've messed up so much," I gulped through sobs. "I shouldn't have listened so much to people. Why didn't I pick safeties I actually wanted to go to? Why would I ever think I would have a chance at these schools? I'm nowhere near good enough." As I was talking, her utterly empathetic, sensitive blue eyes made me think the worst—I had let her down after she had believed in my ability to succeed.

I looked at the clock. I had missed two classes, and what felt like ten years worth of tears had emptied out.

"Molly, you're so intelligent. You're beautiful, funny, and just about the friendliest girl I've ever met. You have so much energy. Why not channel all of that energy into getting off the waitlist?" Mrs. Cady reached out and grabbed my hand. "You'll have to put down a deposit somewhere else, just in case. But I know you. And if I were director of BU Admissions, you'd be my first choice off the waitlist. Now let's get busy!"

Being removed from a waitlist is a long shot at any school—they can be thousands of students long—but Mrs. Cady made me believe that it wasn't a long shot. I owed myself a chance to be at a school that would make me happy.

We began seeing each other daily, her helping me craft e-mails to the admissions office, me begging to hear about her conversations with admissions directors about me. Soon, I forgot that I was on the waitlist at all. All things BU consumed me. And not once did Mrs. Cady consider the possibility that I would not attend my dream school.

My mammoth, excruciatingly crafted letter to the admissions director was so vivid I forgot there were words, not pictures, on the page. I wrote about seeing my op-ed pieces printed in newspaper ink in the student paper, *The Daily Free Press*. I forced him to envision me gliding silently down the Charles River as a member of the BU Sailing Team. I told him I am the type of student that never puts her hand down. I let him see beyond my transcript. When the admissions director read my initial application, he saw my C+ in Algebra 2. In my letter, he saw me. He saw what I would bring to BU. And oddly enough, the more I wrote about what I would bring to BU, the clearer it became that all those college rejection letters were no reflection of my self-worth. In fact, I was one of the most interesting people I knew!

After dropping the letter in the mailbox, I tried to enjoy the end of my senior year. We watched movies in class and teachers encouraged us to bring in chocolate chip cookies and Dunkin Donuts. Dr. Marker, my French teacher, was leading a rousing game of French charades one day when a student delivered a note to the room. I was to come to the college counseling office, immediately.

I walked briskly, not pausing to wander the expansive hallways and stare at graduate composites from the 1800s. Mrs. Cady was standing outside her office when I arrived.

I'm not sure how she told me, or even if she told me at all. I was in. I sobbed a choking sob, first out of pure relief, and then pure joy.

"I knew you'd do it," Mrs. Cady whispered. I felt her cheek against my own. I was sure my tears were making her face wet, but when I pulled away, I realized she was crying, too. The other college counselors emerged from their offices, clapping, some wiping tears away, others laughing and shaking their heads at the amazing difference a college counselor can make in the life of a student.

There were no streamers, no balloons falling from the sky, no music. But there might as well have been. That moment was the beginning of the greatest party of all time. Come on—what other celebration lasts four whole years?

~Molly Fedick

From Rejection to Waitlist to Acceptance

Today is your day!
Your mountain is waiting.
So... get on your way.
~Dr. Seuss

Growing up in a small Wisconsin town, I always knew I was destined for Bigger things. Of course, one never quite knows what that means. I knew what it DIDN'T mean—it meant not going to University of Wisconsin and not majoring in engineering like every other person in my family. It was like a cult growing up. The Johnson cult of engineers. They indoctrinated you, and it started young. Me, on the other hand, I had an attitude problem and hated anything related to science. Engineering was not my forte.

"Fine," my engineering dad said. "Then what WILL you study in college?" At this point I had only convinced him the engineering thing wouldn't work, but he still thought I would buckle under the pressure and go to UW Madison. Ever the logical thinker, he made me research careers.

I'm creative, I'm good with people, I'm persuasive. I won a jack-of-all trades award in fifth grade. I'm tenacious, engaging, good with words. Marketing? Too much math. Advertising. Perfect. Dad said,

"Okay, if you aren't going to be an engineer at the best engineering school, what is the best school for advertising?"

So I looked. And looked. I filled out surveys, I spent hours on the Internet, I grilled strangers. I researched every single four year coed university that had advertising as a major. Every. Single. One. There had to have been over one hundred.

Slowly but surely, Syracuse University emerged as The School. More specifically, its famed S.I. Newhouse School of Public Communications. Even more specifically, it cost about a trillion dollars. My dad, in his unwavering support, said he would consider helping me with the costs if I obtained some scholarships and got accepted to Newhouse. The Arts & Sciences school wouldn't cut it—why pay an extra $30K a year when I could get a liberal arts education at UW Madison?

My visit to Syracuse was in the summer, and warnings of Easter blizzards were willingly brushed aside. I brought home an Otto the Orange T-shirt and proceeded to wear it to school every day. I became that girl. Anyone who would listen (and people who wouldn't) got an earful about how I would soon be getting out of our small town and into the best communications school that ever existed in the history of the world. My peers, who probably couldn't find Syracuse on a map (I'm not even sure I could at the time) soon knew that SU had 12,000 undergrads, that Bob Costas was an alum, that it's colors used to be rose pink and pea green, that it was three hours from New York City. I plastered a postcard of the campus into my locker and called my dad's secretary every day, asking her to hike up our driveway and check the mail for my acceptance letter.

University of Wisconsin-Milwaukee. Accepted.
Virginia Commonwealth University. Accepted.
University of Wisconsin-Madison. Accepted.
University of Colorado at Boulder. Accepted.

Syracuse University. Nothing yet.

By this time it is March of my senior year. I go with my best friends, four boys, on a spring break trip to Panama City, Florida and I enlist our friend Fuller to keep checking the mail for me. He begrudgingly agrees. We party in Florida and I call Fuller every day to get the mail.

"Liza, it's here."

"Well come on Fuller, open it."

"I don't want to... I'm scared."

"I'm going to kill you... open it."

"Liza.... You got into the Arts and Sciences school."

I cried and cried and cried and cried and cried. I was absolutely devastated and felt hopeless. I had been such a fool. The boys said all the wrong things.

"They don't know THE Liza Johnson."

"Maybe you don't want to go there anyway."

I just kept crying. There was no chance my dad was going to pay to send me to an Arts & Sciences school that cost $38,000 per year.

My Aunt Peg, an extremely strong woman, decided it was her turn to try and console me. "Liza, you are going to write them a letter and you are going to tell them that they have made a mistake. They made a mistake and you are going to let them know."

You don't disagree with Aunt Peg.

When I got home, I contacted the school. There is no waiting list, they said, and there is nothing I could do but enroll in the school of Arts & Sciences, get a 3.8 GPA or above for 30 credits (A WHOLE YEAR?!) and apply to internally transfer to Newhouse. But, they said, it is "unlikely."

So I wrote those jerks a letter. I told them they had made a mistake, and they would regret it when I ruled the world. I told them everything I wanted them to know and it was straight from the heart because I had nothing more to lose. And in the meantime, I had absolutely NO idea where I was going to go to school.

Two weeks later, I got a letter informing me I had been placed on the Newhouse waiting list in response to my letter of appeal... the list that I had previously been told did not exist. I did not know that

I had written a formal letter of appeal, or even that I could. I decided to give it my all, and replied with some more writing samples from the award-winning school paper. Newhouse said they would get back to me in May.

Two weeks before high school graduation in mid-May, I still had no idea where I was going to college. I was actually wearing my Otto the Orange shirt, when I heard my dad say, "No Lisa Johnson lives here. The dean of admissions for Newhouse? You must want to talk to Liza Johnson. One second."

I picked up the phone. They had a place for me in the Newhouse School of Public Communications. Once again, I cried and cried. I had done it. I went for what I wanted and didn't stop until I got it.

I went on to receive $20,000 in scholarships. At Syracuse, I met hundreds of people who came with the intention of internally transferring to Newhouse after a year, only one of whom actually did (nice job Alexis). When they heard my story, they would say "I didn't know you could appeal." I didn't either, but it didn't stop me. Now I have an advertising degree and work in Chicago at a marketing firm. So don't be afraid to go for what you deserve.

~Liza Johnson

61

The Campaign

Oh I'm gonna try with a little help from my friends.
~The Beatles

Deciding where to apply for college is, for most people, a very difficult process. With so many schools and so many different possibilities, it seems impossible to pinpoint a "dream school." But if anyone asked Kyle, my best friend's older brother, where he wanted to go to college, his answer was always, "I will go to Notre Dame." This was the answer that I heard when I first met Kyle, a nine-year-old whose entire wardrobe consisted of Notre Dame apparel. Later, I learned that such a definitive answer should not have been a surprise. After all, Kyle's first sentence as a baby was "touchdown Notre Dame!"

Kyle's dad was the ringleader of such brainwashing, wanting to set high goals for his children. But Kyle's mom was concerned that Kyle was setting himself up for failure by emotionally tying himself to one school so early. When high school came, Kyle worked extremely hard. By his senior year, Kyle had established some excellent credentials — salutatorian, varsity tennis, varsity basketball, president of the National Honor Society. He earned a reputation that made his college application shine, but with a school like Notre Dame, thousands of "shining" students apply each year and not all are accepted.

In the fall of Kyle's senior year, Carrie, a Notre Dame admissions ambassador, visited his high school. He arrived at her presentation a half hour early, and he hung on every word that she said. After she finished talking, he approached her individually and asked what he needed to do to get into Notre Dame. She suggested that he should not apply early because his SAT scores were too low, but rather that he submit his application with the regular pool. Kyle followed Carrie's instructions explicitly and sent in his application.

The only other school that Kyle applied to was Holy Cross, a school near Notre Dame that just recently converted into a four-year college. Many, including myself, wondered why such a successful student would not have applied to other prestigious schools, but Kyle remained resolute in his decision. He did not want to take a spot at a school that he did not truly want, because he did not want take away the dreams of an applicant who truly wanted to go to that school the way he wanted to go to Notre Dame. With the applications finished, the waiting began.

During those first days of April, Kyle expectantly waited for the mail. And then it came, his future determined by one letter. But as soon as Kyle saw the envelope, he knew that it would not contain good news. Kyle's small envelope contained a letter telling him that he was placed on the waiting list.

I do not think I could find a word strong enough to describe Kyle's disappointment. The day he found out, he cried and played basketball in his driveway through the night. And that next week, Kyle, the person who never stopped talking even when you asked him to, did not say a word. It was during that week that the kindness of his fellow students truly manifested itself. For every other student in Kyle's senior class who was on the waiting list at Notre Dame took his or her name off the list so that Kyle would have a better chance of being accepted. Kyle's dad let the week pass and then he asked Kyle, "So what do you want to do now? Do you really want to just quit?" Kyle and his dad were not ready to give up yet.

Kyle's dad called Carrie, the admissions ambassador who Kyle had met that fall and asked her, "What now?" Thankful for the calm and polite demeanor of Kyle's dad, she gave this advice: "All that I can tell you is that in the event that Notre Dame decides to take anyone off the waiting list, you have to prove that Kyle is the one who wants it the most."

From there, the letter writing campaign began. Kyle received over 200 letters of support from teachers, friends, family, and even the bishop. Kyle forwarded Notre Dame three to four letters a day, along with countless e-mails. Soon, Carrie called Kyle and told him that he could stop sending the letters; he replied that he would stop when she sent him his acceptance letter. The letters were just the beginning. Soon after, Kyle sent Carrie a box of photos that demonstrated just how intrinsic Notre Dame was to his family life. The pictures ranged from Notre Dame football games, to Christmas with Notre Dame-related presents. Finally, Kyle called and asked for an interview, but there were no interviews for waitlisted students. However, Carrie did promise that if Kyle flew out to Notre Dame in late April, she would give him thirty seconds to state his case.

So state his case he did, but the waiting only continued because Notre Dame was still unsure whether they would take any students from the waiting list. It was not until late May that Kyle got the phone call. While Kyle was at a tennis match, Carrie called his house and opened the phone conversation with Kyle' sister, Megan, by saying "I hate to have to tell you this over the phone..." With an opening like this, Megan's heart sunk. But in the next breath Carrie said, "Please let Kyle know that we took him off the waiting list?" "What does that mean?" Megan asked, still unsure if this was good news. Carrie replied, "We moved him onto the list of accepted students!" When Kyle got home that night and heard the news, it was evident that all of his hard work had finally paid off.

This year, Kyle graduated from Notre Dame, and after graduation took Carrie out to dinner. They reminisced about the day that Kyle was accepted and Kyle learned that he was the last person accepted to Notre Dame that year. I frequently think back to the day that Kyle was accepted. That day serves as a great reminder that hope and perseverance and hard work can truly make miraculous things happen.

~Lauren Gibbons

No Second Guessing

All my life, whenever it comes time to make a decision,
I make it and forget about it.
~Harry S. Truman

"I have no doubt you will get in, Kathleen. You're the strongest candidate from Memphis this year."

Honestly, I couldn't believe Mr. Simmons had said it. Without wanting to appear too eager, I smiled. "That's wonderful to hear. Because if there is one place I want to go to college, it's Dartmouth." I meant that, with one hundred percent conviction. Since visiting my older brother at Dartmouth two years earlier, I had had my heart set on going there.

Deep down, I never really believed what Mr. Simmons said—it didn't matter that he was president of my hometown alumni association, that he had interviewed every local candidate and had seen all of our applications. I wanted to believe him. But I had seen enough of life to know that it's never over until it's over. As I drove home, I decided not to put too much stock in those words.

Nonetheless, they haunted me for the next few months. Sometimes, as I retrieved books between classes, I'd catch sight of the Dartmouth wrapping paper that lined my high school locker. I'd catch myself thinking, "I'm going to go there. I am. He said so." I'd imagine myself walking across the Green or sitting in an English class, like the one I had attended with my older brother. I daydreamed about how I'd decorate my dorm room, and I guessed what my roommate would be like. As I pulled my Dartmouth sweatshirt over my head, I'd see myself wearing it across campus. I knew the thoughts were dangerous, and I'd try to push them away.

And then, one afternoon, as I walked into the kitchen after school, I heard my mother call out from the family room, "You have mail on the island."

I looked down and spotted the Dartmouth return addresses. It was thin, way too thin.

Hands shaking, I ripped open the letter. No sooner had I read the first clause then I started yelling expletives, which were in no way allowed in my very Southern household. But my mother gave me some leeway that day. She knew what that letter had meant to me, and she had surely anticipated what such a thin envelope signified. In just a few seconds, so much of my hard work, so many of my dreams, so many of my plans seemed to count for nothing.

Mom appeared in the kitchen doorway. She stood there silently, probably wondering what would happen next.

I was crying at this point. "I've been waitlisted." With the letter in hand, I rushed to my room. I picked up my phone and dialed my brother's dorm. No answer. Next I called the office of the student newspaper. I guessed he was there doing whatever sports editors do each day. But he was gone, and I found myself suffering through an awkward conversation with another student.

"Could you please tell Chris that his sister called?"

The stranger said. "Sure. Did you get your letter today?"

Who was this guy? And why was he asking about something as personal as my letter?

"Just have my brother call me at home? Thanks." I hung up.

Within twenty minutes, the phone rang. I picked it up.

"Chris?" I asked.

"Yeah, it's me."

"I'm waitlisted."

"No way!" He was as speechless as I had been. Tears were running down my cheeks.

"Kathleen, you should have applied early decision."

"Chris, that doesn't matter now. I've got to go."

You should have applied early decision. That's very easily thought and said in hindsight. But in the fall, as I had completed each application, I wanted to see what would shake out at each school—if I would receive scholarships, be admitted to honors programs, be admitted at all. For whatever reason, back then I was ripe for challenge but not for committing to one place, despite all of the enthusiasm I had for Dartmouth.

After I received my letter, I thought a lot about why I was waitlisted. I knew most of the other candidates from my hometown, and I knew a lot about them: their personalities, their extracurricular involvement, their grades, their special talents, even some of their SAT scores. I knew that on paper, and even in person, I came out ahead of many of them. When I talked with Mr. Simmons, he seemed just as confused as I was, which led me to one conclusion.

I was being considered in light of my brother's activities at Dartmouth. And admissions officers had reasons not to love him.

My brother had been very active at the *The Dartmouth Review*, Dartmouth's only independent newspaper and a highly conservative one at that. During my brother's years at Dartmouth, the *Review* had run articles that were highly critical of the college president. The ensuing controversies had put Dartmouth in the national spotlight. Regrettably, it seemed that I might be being punished for that—that someone, somewhere might have feared what a second Whitman would bring to campus.

Although I admired my brother, I certainly was not him. I didn't care for my brother's politics and his occasional conservative rants. In fact, I was the one who would one day intern on Capitol Hill for Senator Al Gore. But the admissions officers didn't know that. Was admitting a lesser candidate simply easier than taking a chance on another Whitman?

On the day that the waitlist was instituted, I received a call.

"Congratulations, Kathleen! Welcome to Dartmouth!"

It was too little, too late. Lots of thinking, coupled with admission to honors programs at other highly regarded and less expensive universities, had diminished Dartmouth in my eyes. I would never know why Dartmouth denied me admission the first time around. But in a few weeks' time, I had realized that the world and my future extended far beyond Hanover, New Hampshire.

On the night that I decided to attend the University of Virginia instead of Dartmouth, I stood in our darkened kitchen drinking a glass of water. As I drank, I stared out a large picture window towards the moon. My dad walked in and quietly stood beside me. Finally, he broke the silence. "Are you sure that you're doing the right thing?"

I've never interpreted that moment as my father doubting my decision. Instead, I think he was asking because he was afraid I one day might question what I had done.

I lowered my glass. And as I looked out into the night—dark, uncertain, but bathed in a warm glow—I practically whispered, "I'm sure."

But you never can be sure. And to this day, I occasionally wonder how life would be different had I gone to Dartmouth. Admittedly, I didn't love my undergraduate years, but that was a tough time in my life. It might have been tough anywhere. I'll never know if life would have been happier at Dartmouth and somehow better in the years that followed. But why second guess? As lives go, mine's been a darn good one.

~Kathleen Whitman Plucker

Chapter
10

Teens Talk
GETTING IN...
TO COLLEGE

Now It's Our Turn
to Decide

*I think that somehow,
we learn who we really are and then live with that decision.*
~Eleanor Roosevelt

A Sign from Above

A peacefulness follows any decision, even the wrong one.
~Rita Mae Brown

I'm a born worrier. If I see a penny on the street, I always pick it up. Not for good luck, but just in case I might actually need it someday. A little paranoid? Maybe. But then, you just never know.

When it came time for me to decide where to go to college, I was stuck between two schools. I fretted, I agonized, I debated. And after carefully weighing out the pros and cons of each one, I still couldn't see a clear choice.

One afternoon, with deadlines fast approaching and feeling like it was time to do SOMETHING, I picked up both of the acceptance letters and went into the backyard. I sat down on an old swing under the trees, and with one letter in my left hand and the other in my right, slowly swayed forward and backward. I kept staring down at those letters, without really seeing them, in a totally perplexed daze.

Finally, out of nowhere, something popped into my head.

"I wish I had a sign."

Now let me just say, I was not then, and am not now, the sort of person who is heavily into "signs." And that day was the first day I can remember ever thinking of any kind of sign other than the "Do Not Disturb" or "Reduced for Clearance" or "Sharp Curve Ahead" sort.

And there is something else—it wasn't even a true thought.

Certainly, it was not a prayer. It was not even a real wish. It was more of just a passing feeling or sensation. Like, say, for instance, "root beer would be good" or "my big toe itches." Just one tiny tick among the millions of fragments that pass through my brain everyday—most of which I'm barely conscious of, if at all.

And I wouldn't remember this particular bit except for what happened next.

Immediately after the "I wish I had a sign" blip, something fell onto the letter in my left hand and went SPLAT smack dab in the middle of it. The "something" was the sort of "stuff" that only comes from birds. And whatever bird happened to be flying overhead at that particular moment had perfect timing—and aim.

I looked up at the sky, grinned broadly, and laughed.

"Subtle," I said, out loud, even though no one else was present.

That's right. That was it. That was my sign. By way of airmail. It's not exactly a burning bush, but you take what you can get. Besides, the spontaneous combustion of shrubbery would have only sent me into a panic anyway.

After that, the decision was a cinch. I, of course, went with the school with the unbesmirched letter, and it turned out to be just fine. Also, I am forever grateful that the bird's miraculously guided "stuff" hit that piece of paper instead of my personal self.

More than that, though, the whole episode reminded me that I tend to take stuff a little too seriously. That I should lighten up. That the "stuff" that unexpectedly falls into my life—or onto a piece of paper, if I'm lucky—is sometimes just the thing I need to get unstuck or, at the very least, have a good laugh. An indication that a change in direction or, just as importantly, perspective is needed. That the "stuff" really could be more than what it appears to be sometimes. It could be a sign from above. You just never know.

~Michelle M. Lott

Money Matters

Money often costs too much.
~Ralph Waldo Emerson

Growing up, I always liked being part of a big family. I lived in a house with my seven siblings, three of whom are older than me, my parents, and whatever pet we had at the time (a snake, a guinea pig, a vicious dog). I had an endless supply of playmates and people to talk to, and there was never a dull moment in our house. I never minded the hand-me-down clothes and was only occasionally bothered by the complete lack of privacy.

But by the time my senior year of high school rolled around, it occurred to me that having seven siblings wasn't going to work in my favor. Sure, my large, crazy family gave me lots of material for college essays. But putting eight children through four years of college education wasn't going to be easy on my two parents' salaries, especially since my mom was a Spanish teacher and my dad had recently been laid off.

I listened as my girlfriend at the time rattled off the eleven schools she was applying to, all of them with tuitions upward of $30,000 a year. I nodded as my guidance counselor pushed me to apply, apply, apply, not realizing that even the $50 application fees were a drain on the family income. I had always been a procrastinator, but now I saw that the only way I was going to go to college was if I got my act together and applied for scholarships—lots of them.

My parents had been telling me throughout high school that

they could only afford to pay tuition for a regional branch of the University of Connecticut. So far, three of my siblings had taken advantage of that offer, at least partially, and one had actually finished her four years at the main branch two hours away. I looked at my list of schools I'd made at the behest of my guidance counselor and girlfriend, who kept talking to me about how "promising" I was, how I could and should go elsewhere. I was in Advanced Placement classes and had good SATs. I had taken a trip to Africa to build a school for poor children. I was a Hispanic immigrant, in classes where everyone was white and privileged. According to my guidance counselor, I was a shoo-in at so many really good schools. I was only hurting myself by giving up.

But I took that list and cut it down anyway... to two schools: University of Connecticut and University of Michigan. That's it. I cut out anything that would have been a "reach" because I figured that since I was unsure I'd even get in, I could be very sure I wouldn't get enough financial aid to make going there feasible. I thought that being accepted and knowing I couldn't go because of money would hurt more than never applying in the first place.

My dad took me aside, as we waited to hear from UConn about a scholarship, to talk to me about paying for college. I'd always quietly known that my parents thought that I had a very promising future ahead of me, maybe more so than some of my siblings. I had made the transition from living in Argentina and coming to America seamlessly when I was a kid, had always impressed my parents with my grades and my motivation since then.

Which is why my dad, unbeknownst to my siblings, told me I had more options than I thought.

"We'll do what we have to," my dad said to me in Spanish, "Even if it means taking out loans or going into debt." I appreciated what he said and the burden he offered to take on, since he was currently between jobs. But it didn't change my mind about anything. As far as I was concerned, my options were, and had always been, slim.

You could say I got lucky or that things just happened to work out. But when I heard from UConn and Michigan, all the news was good. Michigan accepted me, but the scholarship was nowhere near what I needed. Plus, I didn't think I could convince my dad that the education I got there would be worth the years of debt and the financial drain.

But the news from UConn was even better. Full scholarship, plus $5,000 a year and a paid internship for Citibank every summer. I would be getting paid to go to college. I wouldn't have to pay for books or housing. My family wouldn't have to pay for anything.

My dad beamed with pride when we went to the luncheon to accept my scholarship at the end of my senior year. I was one of only fifteen students who received it out of the entire freshman class, and he knew it. My mom and my sister cried when they called my name and I knew for certain that my education wasn't going to cost me anything. They were so happy to see that I had seized the opportunity they couldn't have given me otherwise — but would desperately have tried to.

And although I wish I could have shown the people who really believed in me what I was capable of doing and where I could have gotten in, sometimes things just aren't as easy as people make them out to be. Now, maybe my younger sister will be able to get four years somewhere other than the branch of UConn that's down the street. Maybe she'll get to live in a dorm and study something that really excites her. And I'll know it's partially because I made a few sacrifices and a few choices, and that makes it worth it.

~Juan Casanova as told to Madeline Clapps

A Dream on a Postcard

The difficulty of life
is in the choice.
~George Moore

I n April of my senior year in high school, I used an orange, white, and black index card to determine my future. The card felt flimsy in my hand on the night I filled it out. I treated the small rectangular paper unkindly, tossing it from hand to hand, flexing it back and forth until it sprang from my fingers and onto the floor.

I watched it.

"I can't believe this," I muttered into the cell phone pressed snugly against my ear.

"What?" my friend Nico responded quickly, his voice a little sharp. We'd been silent for the minutes I'd spent twisting the index card between my fidgeting fingers. It was the type of pause that best friends can withstand comfortably even over the phone.

I wondered if he'd forgotten he was talking to me, absorbed in the TV show he was most likely watching as we spoke.

"I can't believe this little thing is all it takes," I said. "I check a box, put it in the mailbox and then I'm going to Princeton."

I was surprised at myself. In my terror of making a decision I'd refused to utter the phrase "I'm going to Princeton." Never mind the fact that the day before my acceptance to Princeton I'd run around the house screaming excitedly that I was going to Columbia, the first school I'd been accepted to.

The next day, when I saw the wide white envelope with the Princeton University seal sticking out of the mailbox I felt dread sink like a honey-covered anvil down my throat and into my gut. It'd been a week since I'd gotten into both schools and with the arrival of more acceptances came the horror of decision-making.

"So then you are going there?" Nico said, seizing on my word choice immediately. He is uncommonly quick about certain things.

I sighed, dragging the index card closer with my fingertips. When it was on the carpet right in front of me, I shifted to lie on my stomach with my face right above the paper, propped up by my elbows on either side of the index card.

"I don't know," I muttered into the phone.

Nico didn't answer. We'd talked the college decision thing over so many times that all the words had reached their expiration dates and he knew that sometimes not talking is the only way to make sure you're not pressuring someone. Still, he stayed on the phone because the sound of a friend breathing is a pretty tremendous form of sup-port. So I lay on my carpet, feeling its fibers imprinting themselves on my legs, examining a Princeton University Admissions Response card and listening to Nico watching TV.

The carpet I was lying on had left its imprints on my thighs countless times. I'd spent hours sitting on the floor instead of at my desk, my notes spread around me like oversized flower petals, puz-zling out calculus problem sets. Nico was usually on the phone for those, guiding me toward a right answer.

Other times it was one of my girlfriends on the phone or sitting on the floor with me—Jen L. with her patient nods, Lori with her sarcastic jokes, Jen C. with her excited hand gestures or Angela with her secretive smiles—and we were talking enthusiastically about the guys who'd sort of flirted with us that day.

Much of my North Rockland High School experience not spent in the building itself, or sprinting around on the track behind it, was spent on this carpet doing homework, studying and talking to my friends.

And now, Princeton was sitting on my carpet with me and

offering itself up in all its ivy and ivory glory. It should have been so easy to say yes. But it wasn't. It was choosing between top schools and good schools and realizing just how much money was involved in this, my first real adult decision.

The people around me were acting like I'd already said yes to Princeton. Who, after all, says no? My dad had fallen in love years ago with the idea of his daughter going to Princeton, a school he never even dreamed of back in Haiti, and why on earth would I stand in the way of that? The people at school—my teachers and my friends (with a few notable exceptions)—all seemed to assume upon hearing of my acceptance that the decision had been made the instant I saw the big envelope in the mailbox.

There were little things to consider: Did I really want to go to college in yet another suburb? There were somewhat bigger things to think about: Could I really even handle the work at a top school like that? Princeton felt like an academic dive into the deep end of a pool wherein relief was going to be found way, way over my head.

And then there was the big one: the money issue.

What about my younger sister, Vicky? How were my parents going to send her to a great college in a few years after paying for Princeton? They said it would be fine, that we would all find a way to do it. But saying yes to that felt like being Walter Lee Younger from *A Raisin in the Sun*, selfishly and blindly assuming that the money available was for my dream and my dream alone. That distribution of savings was clearly what Princeton had in mind if the amount of financial aid they offered my upper middle class family was any indication.

My dream, quite literally, had a price tag and it wasn't on sale. It was disheartening to see the school I'd worked so hard to possibly attend become a selfish choice.

And yet, everyone seemed to think I was just going to ignore all of that and dive right in. No, I knew I shouldn't and that I couldn't.

It felt like a decision had been made when I had that thought and I could already feel the sadness creeping through my veins like shards of glass, chipping away at my insides and inching closer to my heart.

What a missed opportunity this was going to be. A thousand great experiences and dreams cherished throughout high school lost in the simple act of checking "No" on an index card. Then I made my real choice and decided that my first adult decision was going to be to take a risk and do something that pushed me to become better, to earn more money, to study harder and make the opportunity I'd been given worth it for everyone involved, even Vicky.

That thought was all it took.

Ok, no. It took that thought, a blue pen, a checked box, a walk down the stairs, out the front door and across the wet lawn, an opened mailbox, the insertion of an orange, black and white index card, a lifted red mailbox flag and an excited whisper into a cell phone, breaking a long silence.

"I did it," I said, "I'm going to Princeton."

~Catherine Mevs

Making My Decision

*The person who sends out positive thoughts
activates the world around him positively
and draws back to himself positive results.*
~Norman Vincent Peale

I never used to believe the saying, "everyone ends up where they're supposed to be," in terms of college. It was hard for me to understand, even though I am an optimist. My mind was completely altered, however, when it came time to make my own college decision.

I was always known as "the college girl" among my friends, family, and classmates. I recall perusing www.harvard.edu in the sixth grade, but as I grew older I became more realistic. I read Fiske and US News & World Report guidebooks for fun and found schools that better fit my student profile. Once I entered high school, the pressure was hard to ignore; society tells you that not only must you attend college, but a "good" college. In time I realized that "good" should not be defined as a high-ranking institution, but a "good" fit for you as an individual.

I went through many facets of the college process: I hopped around from preferring city campuses to isolated campuses, Boston to New York City, and journalism to political science majors. I would instantly fall in love, put all of my efforts into one university, and then change my mind. There was one school, however, that always remained consistent on my list of colleges. I loved it since my middle school years, and could always see myself going there. It was easy to forget about, however, when I was caught up in the moment at another university.

My senior fall was quickly approaching and teacher recommendations, activity lists, and college essays consumed my life. It was definitely the most overwhelming experience I have lived through yet, and I do not miss the days of headaches, anxiety, and sleep deprivation. With relief that it is all now over, I sympathize for the kids behind me, for I do not see this process becoming any easier.

With November came early action deadlines, and December was then accompanied by depression. Not only was I deferred from every single school I applied to, but one of them was my current favorite. Nothing can describe the feeling of being denied a chance where you think you belong; I would never wish it on my worst enemy.

With a broken heart, I did what I could to convince their admissions staff I was capable of success at their school. Months passed by, with letters from my safety schools—all good news. I reminded myself that my life would not be over and that I was college-bound. It was hard to forget, however, where my true enthusiasm was focused.

The next significant letter I received from an institution of higher learning was a rejection via e-mail—and many more followed. By April 1st, I had heard from all my colleges, and had not fared as well as I had hoped. I was rejected from all of my reaches and targets, except for two.

However, there was a catch. After being deferred early action and anxiously waiting for months to hear back, I was finally admitted to my "dream school"—for the spring semester. My reaction was still positive because I had achieved my yearlong goal. Initially there was not a question in my mind; that was where I was going to matriculate.

I went up to Boston with my parents for the day to visit, and we were impressed with the school's facilities, academics, and especially their Broadway-styled theater. I already had all of my courses picked out—none of which was mathematics, which to me would only happen in an ideal world.

There were little things, however, that started appearing on my radar. The campus is about two city blocks large; therefore it is easy to overlook the fact that you are on a college campus. I read an advertisement in the nearest Dunkin' Donuts that stated they gave away free iced coffee whenever the Red Sox won—I'm a Yankee fan for crying out loud, and it bothered me that I did not feel comfortable. Later on that same afternoon, my parents excitedly talked up the school over lunch, but I could not get excited. I had a weird feeling in the pit of my stomach, and questioned whether or not this was really where I belonged.

I then made the decision to visit Syracuse University. The drive upstate occurred in the middle of the night, and the first thing I laid my eyes on was the back of the campus, Crouse Hall specifically. The beautiful architecture of the traditional, Gothic building sent me a message along the lines of "we are a legitimate college, and we take education seriously." That was the moment that I knew.

I was forced to wake up early to attend admitted students seminars and other activities, and was thoroughly impressed with all of the day's events: a lecture from the Dean, clubs/activities fair, and lunch inside the Carrier Dome. I felt very comfortable walking around Syracuse on this beautiful April day—granted there will normally be a lot more snow—and could easily see myself making friends, joining "The Daily Orange," and succeeding academically. I finally discovered what it meant to find a college and be happy.

My initial reaction to my acceptance to Syracuse University was much greater than any other institution. The novelty wore off as I analyzed my options and realized there were a handful of characteristics I did not find appealing. But with that said, when I visited the school for my third and final time before making my decision, all of those components no longer mattered. I had "the feeling," and knew it was where I belonged.

It was hard to let go of the fantasy of attending my other option, especially after an entire year of being teased by deferrals and spring admission. But as much as I wanted to want it, I did not. This phase passed as did the others, and I sent in my deposit to the place that had been best all along—Syracuse University. I figured out that it was the better choice for me, regardless of past dreams.

I am now an advocate of believing everyone ends up where they are supposed to be, because despite all of my rejections, I am now officially a member of Syracuse University's class of 2012.

~Krystie Lee Yandoli

Waiting and Wondering

You can design and create, and build the most wonderful place in the world.
But it takes people to make the dream a reality.
~Walt Disney

Oh, the stress that comes along with applying to college—visiting the schools and deciding where you want to apply, seeking out the applications, and then filling them out. If only you could write one essay for them all. But no—the heartless admissions officers don't care. They don't realize all the homework we already get in high school. They aren't concerned that we have things to do and places to be. I mean, we're living the life; we're teenagers! And then, after you finally finish applying to all those schools—signature here, essay there, postmark on the outside... you wait.

After I struggled with writing twelve essays, for twelve different schools, I found the hardest part was waiting. However, it wasn't the twelve different schools I cared about hearing from, it was the one. Tufts University—the one with the plush green hills, students happily jogging early in the morning, fifteen minutes right outside the city of Boston, only four hours from home. What more could I want? I could see myself studying in the vast and bright libraries, full of walls and walls of books. I could see myself eating in that colossal cafeteria, dining with my new, smart friends from all over the world. Everyday I checked the mail at 3 P.M. waiting, hoping, wishing for my ticket into Tufts. And then it came—or something of the sort.

The envelope I received from Tufts was the size of an envelope my parents usually received for bills. The chances were small they would supply all the information an accepted student craved in such a small envelope. Deep down, I knew it couldn't be the answer I yearned for, but still holding onto some hope, I opened the envelope slowly.

It began, "We're sorry to inform you..." I didn't need to finish reading. But sorry couldn't stop the hurt, nor could it prevent my tears. I felt like I let my parents down, but more importantly, I let myself down. What would I tell my friends? They'd feel bad for me, or worse yet, think I was dumb. If only I'd done better in high school. I wish I'd studied instead of watching reruns of *Full House* or going to the movies on Friday night. My life was ruined, I thought.

Eleven more schools to hear from, and all I could do was wait. This time, though still anxious, I was also getting scared. I didn't get into Tufts—what if I don't get into any, I thought. Maybe I'll have to live with my parents or go to community college, when my dream was to live in a city and become my own person.

One by one I heard from the colleges, some rejections, some acceptances. With every acceptance came pleasure and happiness. No, none of them were my first choice. In the end it came down to three—Boston University, New York University, and University of Wisconsin—Madison. My three final schools strayed far from Tufts, the small liberal arts school I originally wanted to attend.

I'd visited Boston and New York and learned the advantages and disadvantages of each, yet I'd never traveled to Madison, since I applied there on a whim. A few weeks after I received the yes from UW—Madison, I packed a suitcase and boarded an airplane with my mom, so I could confirm my rejection of it and choose between two remaining schools. The flight was only about two hours and we arrived in Madison early enough to catch a tour of the campus and an information session.

A little while later, I fell in love. It was an overwhelming sensation, similar to opening presents on your birthday or going to Disney World for the very first time. I was excited because, although this school was the complete opposite from Tufts, in a way it was everything I wanted but never could have dreamed of knowing. Everyone on campus was smiling and willing to answer my questions. I'd never seen so many happy, pleasant people. I sat in on two classes and the professors were fascinating and simply enthralling. The campus had the plush green hill just like Tufts, but better and bigger, and with a huge stone statue of Abraham Lincoln on top. And right off campus was State Street, which included an array of restaurants, which gave off delicious scents. It had the campus life I yearned for, but also the city life perfect for a budding teenager. I had found my niche.

After my weekend in Madison, I went home with a smile on my face. Though it was far away from my home, and though it wasn't somewhere I initially thought I'd ever see myself, it ended up being perfect for me.

I am now a junior in the University of Wisconsin—Madison. The students here show their spirit at football games, their intelligence in the lecture halls, and their festivity at parties—and I couldn't be happier or more at home.

~Courtney Starr Sohn

Above and Beyond

It's nice to be important,
but it's more important to be nice.
~Author Unknown

My grades were good and my SAT scores were excellent, but still I was nervous as I strolled into the room. It was an Immediate Decision Day; I was to spend the whole day listening to faculty speeches and doing interviews. Then, at the end of the day, they would tell me if I was accepted.

Quickly I second- and third-guessed myself. What if these other students had better grades and personalities than me? How would that affect me? Why did I write my essay about the time a really pretty girl gave me her phone number when I was out with friends?

Then they started pairing candidates with their interviewers. I looked at the group of interviewers standing at the back of the room and felt a little intimidated. I knew I would have no problem articulating myself with these people, but making an actual connection with these formal-looking, older people seemed out of the question. Then they introduced the last interviewer, a young guy named Sean who walked in later than everyone else. I said to myself, "That's who you need to talk to in your interview." Lucky for me, that's the way the administration saw it too.

My interview with Sean went extremely well, and he told me he loved my essay. At the end of the day, he told me that I was accepted, but that the school couldn't offer me any scholarship money. My high school class was very small and competitive, and even though my rank was respectable, my class percentile wasn't within the scope of the school's scholarship window. He told me that if I wanted a scholarship, I would have to raise my SAT scores 30 points.

I was dejected. I didn't want to take the SATs again. I had gotten a great score and had told myself that I was only going to take them once. Now if I wanted to get any financial aid from my top choice school, I was going to have to take them again. I was frustrated and upset.

Three days later, Sean left a message at my house saying to call him back at his office. When I called back, he told me that he had talked for quite a long time with his boss after I left. The two of them agreed that it was unfair not to offer me a scholarship because my class size was so small. He was on the phone to tell me that they could, in fact, offer me the scholarship money.

My mouth hit the floor. I feebly tried to form a "Thank you" but I couldn't seem to string the words together. When I got off the phone, I was overwhelmed with emotion. He had stuck his neck out for me. He had gone above and beyond for me, and he didn't even have to. Nowhere in his job description does it say, "Stand up to your boss and fight the system to help the underdog." Yet he had done it all the same. I started to cry.

I immediately decided that this would be the school I was going to attend. I was already accepted, and now with a scholarship, but that wasn't the important part. I felt that any place that wanted me so much that they were willing to do that, is a place that I want to be. And you know what? When I came to school the next fall, I found myself surrounded by people who had similarly inspiring stories. More so then than ever, I knew this was the place for me.

Two years later, when one of my close friends was looking into college, I suggested my school to him. When he went to an Immediate Decision day, my friend had the same interviewer I did, so he asked him an offbeat question. Yes, Sean replied, he still remembered me.

~Ian Zapcic

Chapter
11

Teens Talk
GETTING IN...
TO COLLEGE

Disappointments and
Silver Linings

Disappointment to a noble soul is
what cold water is to burning metal;
it strengthens, tempers, intensifies,
but never destroys it.
~Eliza Tabor

I Didn't Get In Anywhere

Suspense is worse than disappointment.
~Robert Burns

Late one evening at the end of March, I realized, all of a sudden, that the impossible worst-case scenario that my friends and I had joked about might actually come true. I was only waiting for one more admissions letter and I still hadn't gotten into any colleges. It had been a rough week so far. Harvard—waitlist. Princeton—rejection. Brown—waitlist. Dartmouth—rejection. Georgetown—waitlist. I had one more letter to receive, from a school where I had no chance anyway—Stanford.

While preparing my college applications, I was fully aware that safety schools were conspicuously missing from my list of prospective universities. But I had been told that I had very strong prospects at a number of top schools, notably my first choice—Harvard. I hadn't even bothered to visit four of the six schools I applied to. My theory was that I would be perfectly happy to take a gap year, so why not apply only to schools that I really wanted to attend? What was the sense in applying to a school I wasn't excited about if, rather than attend, I would prefer to take a gap year and reapply to a more comprehensive list of schools a year later? Anyway, my application was strong enough that I was sure I would get in to at least one of the schools I applied to....

Unfortunately, the worst case scenario did come true... Stanford—rejection. That was a pretty interesting moment. Although

I'd always talked about how not getting in was built into my plan, actually experiencing it was jarring.

That night marked the beginning of a strange fourth quarter for a senior in high school. While my friends were slacking off on homework and blowing off steam because they were "in," I was continuously sending "update" letters to Harvard, Brown, and Georgetown (the schools where I still had a shot) and working frenetically to show good grades for the final few weeks of school. I was frustrated that I had to continue working hard like I had during the past two and a half years, but I expected that in the next six weeks, I'd either get rejection or acceptance letters from the three schools I was still waiting on.

I kept studying hard and received more letters telling me that I was being kept on the waitlist, even as other kids were receiving rejection letters from the same waitlists. That was just frustrating. I wanted an answer, even if it was no, so that I could figure out what to do next. Instead of giving me closure, they kept saying, "Thanks so much for waiting, and now just wait a little longer."

By the end of the school year, I had come down with a strange strain of senioritis. I had moved decisively from frenetically working to get in, to rebellious, disillusioned apathy. AP exams were... interesting. I had five. I didn't study for any. I managed a 5 for Calculus because it came down to whether you understood the material more than whether you had memorized enough. Physics was a different story. It would have taken a lot of studying to prepare adequately for that exam and I was in no mood to do that. What good are AP credits if you're not going to college? I think I got a 3 out of 5 on that one. History and Spanish were about the same story.

English was certainly my most memorable performance. The exam consisted of two parts: multiple choice and essays. Before the exam, I resolved to do my best despite the circumstances. My good intentions lasted through the multiple choice section. And I must have done pretty well on it because I got a 2 on the exam and I couldn't have gotten any points on the essay section. Upon reading the first question, my determination started dissolving quickly. My

Huck Finn essay deteriorated into a diatribe about how I resented that my school made us take an AP exam for every AP class we took. I used the writing space for the *King Lear* essay to transcribe lyrics from my favorite band at the time, Free. I left as early as you were allowed to. I wanted to go to the beach. A year later I wrote an e-mail to my English teacher apologizing. I knew the AP board had sent him our essays.

After AP exams were over, my classmates and I left school to do five-week internships (my high school's creative response to under-motivated fourth quarter seniors). I was still waiting. I didn't have much hope left that I'd get in anywhere, so I started making plans to study abroad in the fall. Just before graduation in mid-June, I finally received the thin letter from Brown.

When the summer started, I was in a pretty reckless state of mind. I saw no reason to be responsible. After all, I'd spent the better part of my high school career making sure that I'd have a strong college application and that hadn't gotten me very far. I actually didn't think too much about the two waitlists I was on during the first half of the summer. I was intent on enjoying my last summer at home with all my friends. And, I was waiting to actually get rejection letters before I started working on college applications for the second time.

On July 20th I went out to get the mail and found the last two thin letters. I was pretty accustomed to this routine and was ready to throw them out unopened. You can only read, "Due to the strength of the applicant pool this year..." so many times. My mom sadistically insisted that I open them. I complied. I opened the letter from Harvard: "We regret to inform you that..." But that wasn't enough for my mom; she made me open the Georgetown letter too. This was the first congratulatory college acceptance letter I'd ever seen. But, it still wasn't what I had expected. Georgetown offered me a one-year deferred acceptance, forcing me to take the gap year I'd been talking about.

The relief was enormous. Nine months had passed since I had sent in my first college application and, now, I was finally done. The process was brutal at times, but I wouldn't change the result. Being forced into a gap year turned out to be extremely lucky. A gap year isn't right for everyone, but it was exactly what I needed. I wound up spending nine months in Spain, where I studied for a few months, and then worked. It was a formative experience. And when I finally got to Georgetown almost two years after sending my early application to Harvard, I realized it was the right place for me.

~Michael Damiano

I Made Lemonade

If we will be quiet and ready enough,
we shall find compensation in every disappointment.
~Henry David Thoreau

itting in my seat during my high school graduation, I wasn't even thinking about the past four years. I was so excited about summer that I practically ran across the stage to receive my diploma. I pictured laying on the beach with my friends, swimming in the neighbors' pool, shopping for decorations for my dorm room n the fall. While daydreaming in that humid auditorium, with my parents and sister proudly watching, I never once considered the fact that I would not be able to pay for the life I so badly wanted.

For years I had been dreaming about going to Northwestern University. The campus was beautiful. The trees swayed in the breeze, the perfectly manicured gardens sparkled in the sunlight. Their academic program is one of the top in the country. It was only twenty-five miles away, making it close enough if there was an emergency, but far enough away so that I'd have my freedom. There was only one setback; the tuition was $40,000 a year.

My family had never had a lot of money. My dad was the manager of a pipe company and my mom was a secretary. We weren't poor either, though. We never went without the things we needed. We just had to watch what we spent.

Because my father made a considerable amount of money, I did not receive financial aid. However, he did not make enough to pay for college tuition and all the bills we had to pay. It seems like an ironic joke the government was playing on us. In order to receive the money I needed for school, I would have to take out loans. But here, there was another catch. I needed a cosigner because I had not established any credit. I couldn't use my parents as cosigners because they had previously cosigned for a loan that was not paid back, through no fault of their own.

It seemed hopeless. Day after day would go by, and I wasn't any closer to being able to pay for school. Each day that passed meant I was one day closer to the beginning of school. I searched the Internet for ideas and scholarships, but there wasn't anything to be found.

I became very anxious and scared. My friends were talking about all the things they got for their dorm rooms, and it just made me even more upset. I was too embarrassed to say anything to them. They had all been able to pay for the college of their dreams, but my family could not. I felt poor and out of place. I began to stay in at night and avoided my friends. I did not want them to know about my financial situation and I couldn't stand to hear them talk about college. I was afraid that I wouldn't be able to go to college and I would be an outcast who was too poor to do anything.

There were only three weeks left until the start of school and I had not come up with any solutions. My dad came into my room one morning and asked if we could talk. He was not a very verbal person and I knew it had to be important for him to want to talk. He told me he was so sorry that he couldn't give me what I wanted and what I deserved. He said he knew how much Northwestern meant to me, but maybe I should consider the other places I applied to.

After he left I felt so ashamed. During this whole ordeal, I had never once thought about how this was affecting my parents. It can't be easy to watch your child go through this, let alone not be able to help in anyway. I realized I was being very selfish and pouty.

After he left, I started looking through the acceptance pamphlets I had stacked on my dresser. None of them compared to what I wanted. However, I found one closest to what I imagined life at Northwestern would be like. The pamphlet showed students walking to class, smiling, with the wind blowing through the trees behind them. The campus seemed beautiful. The buildings were all red brick, with beautiful trees and flowers surrounding them. I guess it didn't look so bad, I thought. Also, the tuition was nowhere near what Northwestern's was. That's it, I thought, it's settled. I was going to Purdue University.

A couple of weeks later, my parents and I made the two-hour drive to the West Lafayette, Indiana campus. I was still very upset that I couldn't go to the college of my dreams.

However, this campus was very beautiful. We got to my tiny dorm room and moved in all the stuff I brought only to realize I had more than I needed. My parents packed half of what I brought back into the car, and hugged me. My dad told me that things don't always work out as planned but that doesn't mean it still isn't great. I smiled but didn't believe him. I turned around and walked back to my room unhappily.

A year has gone by, and I have absolutely no regrets about my decision to attend Purdue. While my life would definitely be different if I hadn't, I have made so many friends and so many memories that I don't care what life would be like at Northwestern. As I was packing my stuff to move out at the end of the school year, I was very sad again. However, this time, I didn't want to leave. I had so much fun that the thought of going home over the summer was horrible. My friends promised to keep in touch over the summer, and I knew I would see them again in the fall.

I realized that my dad was right. Things don't always work out as planned, but that doesn't mean it still isn't great. I had been so upset that I didn't get what I wanted that I didn't even think about the great things that could happen to me elsewhere. I learned that the cliché "when life gives you lemons, make lemonade" was completely accurate. If I hadn't gone to Purdue my life would be completely different and who knows if I would have been as happy as I am today. I cannot wait to go back to Purdue in the fall. From now on, I promise to look at all the options in any given situation to decide what is best for me. I promise to take the good with the bad and make my own happiness wherever I go, even if it's not what I originally planned.

~ Jacquelyn Gillis

71

Four Minutes

PRESENT, n.
*That part of eternity dividing the domain of disappointment
from the realm of hope.*
~Ambrose Bierce

"April," I asked, "Are you okay?"

She was crying. I helplessly watched the tears well up in her blue eyes as we sat down to history class, wishing I had never asked her how her college application process was going.

Our history teacher was getting up from his desk and bopping over to the board. I say "bopping" because he was not the kind of teacher who strode or stood still. Mr. Hesterson resembled a leprechaun on crack, hopping and yelling as he took us through a PeeWee Herman-esque version of European history. And because he was so crazy, we remembered every lesson.

I tried to turn my attention to him just as April's muffled sobs got worse and she ran out of the room. And in an impulse of sympathy I never would have followed as a freshman, I went after her.

An hour later, April and I sheepishly returned to History to collect our backpacks and give Mr. Hesterson some kind of explanation. Talking fast and looking at our shoes, we poured out the story of why we ran from his class without explanation, that college audition stress had gotten to us, and we'd spent the past hour in an empty band practice room, trying to stop hyperventilating. We were a bit worried about how he would take it. We expected yelling or at least dramatic sarcasm.

But the short man looked at us with unprecedented seriousness, his pink-faced features twisting into father-like sympathy. "You really don't have to worry like that," he told us. "It will all turn out fine."

We stared at him in disbelief. He didn't understand. No one understood, not even our guidance counselors.

April and I hoped to attend B.F.A. programs in theater (an Acting program for me, and a Musical Theater program for April). B.F.A. programs focus exclusively on one art. The info sessions I attended described years of courses, each dedicated to a different acting style, instead of college standards like math, history, and lit. I practically salivated at the prospect. I was the kid who had started putting on plays for my parents the moment I learned to talk, who couldn't remember a period of time when I wasn't in at least one community theater show, who had always dreamed of becoming a star.

The problem is that B.F.A. programs are incredibly small, and you have to audition if you want to get in. So in addition to the standard essay-writing and test-taking, April and I had spent the past few months selecting and preparing monologues. Two two-minute monologues, that's all the time we would get to distinguish ourselves from literally thousands of fellow auditionees.

I spent afternoons at Borders going through monologue books, trying to find something that would both fit me and blow away the judges with its brilliance. Nothing seemed brilliant enough. The monologues had to be age-appropriate. After a lifetime of playing quirky little kids and mothers, I could find no monologue for a high school age character that wasn't incredibly stupid.

The worst part was that no one except April understood the process. I made good grades and lived in an achievement-obsessed area, so when I told people what colleges I was applying to, I only got puzzled looks. Sure, the schools may not have limited themselves to the valedictorians of our nation, but in the theater world, they were top tier. Thousands of students aspired to study acting at schools like Syracuse, UConn, and of course, the Holy Grail of acting schools, the Tisch school at NYU. "You're a shoo-in," my guidance counselor assured me. He failed to understand that my GPA, essay, and extracurriculars were minor details compared to those fateful four minutes.

The true futility of it all didn't hit me until my Ithaca audition. Being in the college auditorium with what must have been over one hundred other students, I couldn't really focus on the man onstage who was preaching about the merits of a B.F.A. education. I just kept looking around at the sea of nervous and cocky expressions, of gorgeous girls and goofy-looking guys, thinking, "Twelve students. They're only accepting what amounts to, like, half of the first row." And this was just one round of auditions. Rumor had it that the total number of students who auditioned was nine hundred. Twelve out of nine hundred. I had a 1% chance of getting in.

But I had the dream, right? That was what mattered, or so they say, all those famous people who say they succeeded because they never stopped believing. I squinted my eyes like I was wishing on a star and tried to believe hard enough.

It didn't work.

During March and April, I moved around school like the walking dead, only coming alive when I got to the mailbox that would spit out a verdict on my future, which increasingly seemed to not exist. I would choke back tears to appease my mom until I found April in school, who had equally bad news to report.

"I got rejected from Ithaca."

"I got rejected from University of Minnesota."

"Tisch waitlisted me."

"BU rejected me."

One day I opened the mailbox and there sat an envelope from Emerson, an unassuming, thin little envelope. It had been my past experience that thin equalled bad. I stood there in the driveway, unsure whether I should even bother to open the envelope that I'd been awaiting all year.

Feeling dizzy, I opened the envelope and read the words "We regret to inform you...."

My sobs were huge and heaving, like someone died. How could

I ever be an actress? I couldn't even get into school to learn acting. I figured that must have no talent and no one had ever bothered to tell me, that all the roles I'd gotten up to that point were pity parts, or else I had gotten them because no talented person had auditioned. I saw myself winding up as one of those bitter, disappointed old people who never lived their dream. I called April, and she didn't know how to reassure me. She'd just gotten rejection letters from two other schools.

I wound up going to Hampshire College, the only school I'd applied to that didn't offer a B.F.A. program. I was not excited to be at a school that made me take core classes instead of exclusively study my dream.

Know what, though? Those classes were kind of interesting. I found myself getting into areas I'd never considered, like philosophy theories and social action. I performed in plenty of shows, I took theater classes, and I was on the college Theater Board. But I also studied playwriting, fiction writing, storytelling, education, child psychology, and children's literature. Through those studies, I found more dreams.

April went to a state school for a year, dropped out, and went through the whole college audition process again using different monologues and songs. She got into plenty of B.F.A. programs. Upon graduation, she got an acting job.

Despite my mere B.A., I also got an acting job right out of college. But I wound up leaving the job early. I found acting professionally to be an all-encompassing lifestyle, and there was too much else I wanted to do.

High schools push you to make up your mind so early. "Decide what you want to do," grown-ups say, "so you can get into a good school for your future major." The fact is, most people decide what they want to do way after college. It's great if you know already, but my point is, keep yourself open to opportunities.

Like Mr. Hesterson said, it'll all turn out fine.

~Valerie Howlett

Five Fantastic Rejections

If I had my way, if I was lucky enough,
if I could be on the brink my entire life—
that great sense of expectation and excitement
without the disappointment—
that would be the perfect state.
~Cate Blanchett

I expected to get in to every college I applied to. I knew, statistically, this was a ridiculous assumption, but deep down, I thought, "How could they possible reject me?"

On paper, I looked like the perfect candidate: Valedictorian at a competitive private school, President of the Student Body, Cross Country Captain, State Champion runner, produced playwright, newspaper section editor, frequent community service volunteer... I was everything I thought they wanted from an applicant.

When April rolled around, and with it the promise of decision letters, I found myself calm amidst my anxiety-ridden peers. I received my first acceptance at a state college with little more thought than a mental checkmark—my safety was taken care of. I received my second and third acceptances at Carnegie Mellon and Georgetown University with relatively little excitement—these were the fallbacks, the safe bets.

My thoughts were draped in Ivy...

I imagined myself deciding between Princeton, Harvard, Yale, The University of Pennsylvania, and my top choice, Columbia. In my head, I saw the pro and con lists I would draw up to advance the deliberation process. Which had the smallest student-faculty ratio? The safest campus? The most vibrant city life? The most enticing cafeteria food?

But then the envelopes came in the mail. And not the big ones. First came Princeton—"Thanks but no thanks," was the general message. Then came Yale—"Better luck elsewhere." And then, all on the same night, I saw my future plans come crashing down: Harvard decided I was not worthy to wear Crimson, and the University of Pennsylvania and Columbia put me on their waitlists.

My memories of that night consist of many tears, an overdose of hyperventilation, and a healthy helping or two of trademarked teenage freak-out.

On top of it all, the previous day, I had been rejected by the boy of my dreams, "Josh." We'd essentially been dating for a few months, but one major obstacle prevented things from really getting off the runway—his girlfriend. As of the night before, he had officially chosen her over me.

I was used to this type of rejection. I never had much luck with the opposite sex. I should rephrase: I had zero luck with the opposite sex. The most successful relationship I had had up until that point had been a two-month stint of "going out" in seventh grade with a boy I barely talked to. I was uncomfortable in my own skin, and didn't even think I deserved a healthy relationship. Part of me thought I deserved romantic rejection.

But school? School was my domain. I was used to succeeding as a student, athlete, and artist. And I deserved to—no one worked harder than me. I prided myself on my diligent work ethic, my desire to learn, my need to ask questions and further my understanding of the world around me. I wholeheartedly believed I deserved to go to one of the best schools in the nation. Because who would work harder than me? Who was more qualified?

Apparently, thousands of other graduating seniors.

My parents were shocked. But they were the shortlist: My entire extended family was extremely surprised that I would not be attending an Ivy League school. It was torture to tell them. Each time was like re-admitting my ultimate failure.

I saw my rejections as a personal attack. Just as Josh had decided that another girl was better than me, Columbia had decided that 1500 girls were. I simply wasn't good enough. I had fallen short in some way. Four years of arduous labor and sacrifice suddenly seemed like they'd gone unnoticed.

I enrolled at Georgetown University in the fall of 2006. I wasn't too excited about it. But that soon changed.

I just finished my sophomore year, and I am absolutely in love with my college. It's a great fit for me academically, artistically, athletically, and socially. I am so happy with my life right now.

I realize that I spent so much time and energy being upset over what I didn't have, that I forgot to appreciate and be excited about what I did have. I had the opportunity to attend one of the top universities in the country. The opportunity to go to school in our nation's capital, with a plethora of urban resources at my fingertips. To come face-to-face with political leaders on my campus and to become friends with some of the nation's brightest students. I had the opportunity to be very happy, and I have finally not only seized that opportunity, but become aware and deeply appreciative of it.

More than anything, I have learned not to measure my self worth in terms of what someone else thinks, whether it's a man I'm interested in, or an Admissions Officer. The college I attend does not define me or anyone else. Neither does the boyfriend of the hour. They are unimportant details compared to the content of a person's character. And that's a far trustier way to measure someone than by their SAT score or how attractive their significant other happens to be.

Over the course of my life, I have come to believe that every rejection I have received—whether it's been in my personal life, my academic endeavors, or a dramatic audition—has been a blessing in disguise. Each rejection has closed one door, but opened another. I am so happy today, and I have five Ivy League rejections to thank for it.

~Emma Lee Goode

Chicken Soup for the Soul

Perfect

When you aim for perfection,
you discover it's a moving target.
~George Fisher

I spent my eighteenth birthday sitting in front of a computer with my best friend, who was celebrating her birthday as well, waiting with bated breath to see what we were going to do with the next four years of our lives. We had spent a tense day giving each other presents and carrying balloons through the halls of our public high school, the whole time wondering what the computer screen would tell us when we logged in and entered our passwords.

Yale University and Brown University had finally made their decisions. Would we be able to call ourselves Yale students or Brown students at the end of the day? We looked at each other, fearful and excited, and clicked.

It turns out I couldn't call myself either of those titles. A week later, I couldn't call myself a student at Tufts or Wesleyan. That same month, I found out I wasn't going to be sporting a Johns Hopkins sweatshirt or drinking from a Columbia coffee mug any time soon. I was currently the top candidate for Valedictorian in a class of 450 people, and I had only gotten into one school. One. And it wasn't an Ivy.

Everyone has at least one thing that they're good at, something that becomes their hobby or passion, almost part of their identity. When I was little, I wanted that. I wanted people who knew me to describe me easily, to say, "That's Natalie. She's good at..." Whatever. But for me, that one thing wasn't easy to find.

I was a good athlete, but only when it came to certain sports. I was meticulous but I wasn't very crafty. Sure, I could color neatly in the lines, but my doodles were lifeless and boring, nothing particularly special or creative. You can imagine my relief when we moved from pasting macaroni pieces to counting them—math was something I learned early on that I could totally do... and do well.

In middle school, I learned that I was an expert studier. I could make myself do schoolwork for hours on end. I could ace my tests. But it wasn't enough to just study and get As... lots of people do that. To really make school my "thing," I would have to be perfect.

For the next few years, I pushed myself harder than I ever had. In a math class of twenty-five kids, I needed to get the 100 percent. On AP exams, I wouldn't settle for less than 5. The word perfection resonated in my head with every 97 I got on a test or every essay my teacher edited and changed. Almost perfect, but not quite what I wanted. The only person I was consistently letting down was myself.

Senior year of high school rolled around, and I was (once again) striving for perfection. My qualifications were impressive. Accomplished Irish dancer. Black belt in karate. Flutist in the marching band. National Merit Commended Scholar. I was ready to apply to college and see my hard work finally pay off, to have a college acceptance or two as proof of what I was good at.

The waiting was torturous. I sat in my classes looking at the other students who applied to the schools I did and my competitive nature would cloud my vision. "Look at her," I'd think in calculus, staring down a competitor. "Does she really think she has the grades for Wesleyan?" I was scared and miserable, but I knew it wasn't because people had applied to the same schools as I had. It was because of the nagging voice in the back of my head that wouldn't shut up, no matter how hard I tried to muffle it. What if you're not good enough? It asked. What if nothing you've ever done is good enough?

And then that voice won out, as the rejections and waitlists came pouring in. I sat in biology class as a guy who had also applied to Yale talked about how he'd been accepted, owing mostly to the fact that his father worked there. I looked down at the impeccable test grade I'd just gotten back and knew, instinctively, that his was lower. His grades were always lower. That feeling in the pit of my stomach, the anger mixed with sadness and a dash of "What the hell am I going to do now?" only worsened the more he spoke, a great big smile on his face. Had I really worked as hard as I had to be told I wasn't good enough? My entire identity had revolved around my being (or trying so desperately to be) perfect. Now who was I?

Bit by bit, life slowly started to improve. I was Valedictorian of my class, and gave a speech to my 450 classmates about new beginnings. I got off the waitlist at Haverford College, a tiny but good school in Pennsylvania. But Haverford, it turned out, was not the right fit for me. I felt smothered by the smallness of it, the homogeny of the personalities surrounding me, and the isolation I felt from the world outside the campus. Only then did it hit me, a truth that I had known deep down all along: the prestige of the school and the Dean's List didn't matter if I was not happy.

I transferred to Barnard College for sophomore year. Ironically, I was finally attending a school with a name I could tack on to "Valedictorian" and "straight A student" with ease, things I did not care about anymore. I was just happy to be in an environment I enjoyed, around people I could connect with.

The whole college application process exhausted me. But it also forced me to confront the part of me that needed to be perfect. Because as much as it made me who I am, it made me constantly pressure myself to reach the highest standards. It turned out that admissions officers may know more than I thought they did at the time. They knew I needed to learn a few things about myself to be happy... and not just perfect.

~Natalie Howlett

The Best Disappointment

You have to leave the city of your comfort
and go into the wilderness of your intuition.
What you'll discover will be wonderful.
What you'll discover is yourself.
~Alan Alda

"Are you sure you don't want the sweatshirt?" my mom asked one final time.

We were standing in front of a rack of red and white sweatshirts in the McGill bookstore. I had started to collect clothing from each college I visited—a pair of pajama pants from Rutgers, a T-shirt from Boston University—as I made the college tour up the East Coast and across the Canadian border. Now my closet was crammed with more clothing than I knew what to do with, and I was beginning to wonder what would happen to all of my purchases.

"I mean what am I going to do with, like, twenty sweatshirts from the schools I don't go to?" My mom shrugged and hung up the sweatshirt.

"Fine," my mom replied. "Do what you want."

Although McGill, a large international university in Montreal, was one of my top choices, I wasn't ready to buy one of their sweatshirts just yet. Since the start of my college application marathon, I had been torn between NYU and McGill. My parents and I spent countless hours around the dinner table weighing the relative advantages and disadvantages of each school.

Both had good reputations, but the price tag for NYU made my father cringe; McGill was a far friendlier alternative for his wallet. But NYU was only an hour from home, while McGill was four hundred miles away in another country altogether. Going to McGill would mean packing up my small town suburban life in New Jersey and moving to Montreal, where I didn't know a soul. I would have to leave behind my friends and family, and, as a self-proclaimed home-body, I wasn't sure if I could sever my ties with home that quickly.

The next day, after spending eight hours in the backseat of the family car, we arrived back home. My family had been away for a week for this visit to McGill, and I was sure that NYU's decision had arrived during that time. As soon as my dad pulled into the driveway, I bolted from the car, dashed through the front door, and began sifting through the tower of mail that a neighbor had left in the kitchen. Midway through the pile I found it — a small white envelope stamped with the NYU logo. My heart sunk. I knew that an envelope that tiny only contained bad news, a letter of rejection.

By the time my dad carried the first of our suitcases into the house, tears were welling in my eyes. I was being told "no" after all the AP courses, the hours of SAT prep sessions, and a wastepaper basket filled to the brim from my struggle to write the perfect college essay. A handful of sentences that took only few seconds to read ended a dream that was four years in the making.

I felt gloomy for the next few days, like one of those characters in a cartoon that has a black rain cloud follow him wherever he goes. Memories of meetings with my guidance counselor haunted me. I vividly remembered sitting in her office and sorting through a list of colleges that might be the right fit for me. We were discussing NYU.

"Your SAT scores are good and you have excellent recommendations," she said one afternoon. "I'm sure you'll get in."

I had taken her words as a guarantee and that only made the rejection all the more unbearable. My confidence was shot; if I couldn't get into NYU, why would McGill take me?

After what felt like an eternity, the day for McGill's decision finally came. The school posted their admissions information online, so that morning I rolled out of bed in a sleepy stupor and nervously clicked through the website. When the page finally loaded, I had to read it twice to make sure I wasn't dreaming. It was a yes.

I ran into my parents' bedroom with a grin that stretched from ear to ear.

"I got in! McGill wants me!" I shrieked.

"That's great," my mom said, giving me a hug. "I guess you should have bought that sweatshirt after all..."

After all the tears and angst and sleepless nights, everything worked out just fine. Today, with four years of hindsight on my side, I've realized that being rejected by NYU is one of the best things that ever happened to me. McGill was absolutely the right match for me; I can't imagine going to any other school. But if I had the option of going to NYU, I don't know if I would have ever had the courage to move to Montreal. I think I would have chosen NYU, where I could come home for the weekends, visit the same places, see the same people. I might have been happy, but I also know I wouldn't have grown up.

Being so far away from home gave me a crash course in confidence and self-sufficiency. I mastered the fine art of laundry, learned how to pay bills, and met people from across the globe. I took ski trips with friends, tasted poutine, and paid rent. Four hundred miles from home, I blossomed into a better, worldlier person and became the proud owner of two McGill sweatshirts. And it's all thanks to that small envelope NYU mailed me one day.

~Rebecca H. Cramer

It's a Sure Bet

Things turn out best for the people
who make the best out of the way things turn out.
~Art Linkletter

I t's a sure bet to get in... to get money... to succeed.

But to like it? Have it be the right decision? That I was not so sure about.

The long, thick white envelope stares at me from the kitchen counter. It's from the University of Florida, my safety school.

"Well, what does it say?" Mom looks up excitedly from the papers she's grading.

I feel the weight and shrug. "I got in."

"You didn't even open it!"

I sigh. "I don't really need to." Movies, books, guidance counselors—they all have prepared me for this moment. Big equals the thin words "you're in." Small and thin equals "Big fat no."

My fingers unhinge the flap from the glue and I dump the many different colored pieces of paper onto the counter.

"Britt Leigh, is that how you treat your college acceptance?" Mom whines from the couch.

I roll my eyes. I sift through the registration forms, the schedule of classes, the dates-to-remember memo, and find the letter. "Yep, they're giving me that scholarship."

Mom does this weird shoulder shake. "Ooh. When do they need to hear back from you?"

I push the papers back into a pile intended for a spot on my cluttered desk. "Um, by May?"

Mom gets up from the couch. "Here, I want to see them." She yanks them from my grasp. "Here it is." It's the verification form. "You can sign this tonight and have Dad mail it out in the morning."

I bite my lip to keep my tone in check. "It's only November. I haven't even sent in the applications to the other schools yet." I have some essays to write for Northwestern, Dartmouth, Yale, and Swarthmore.

"But what if you don't get in, and UF has given your spot away?"

"Oh please, like they'd really tell a National Merit Scholar, no, sorry we don't want you to boost our ratings."

"Br-itt. Anything can happen. But, OK, miss. Say you do get into those fancy schools? How are you going to go? Because your father and I are not going to pay for it."

"I don't know! Anything can happen!"

I grab the papers and trudge to my room. I slam the door. The University of Florida isn't so bad. It has more trees than the University of Central Florida campus. And less emphasis on the technology programs. Plus, the scholarship and promise of early registration dates showed that the Gator Nation was throwing itself at me shamelessly, and I didn't even play a sport. It was the very definition of a "safety" school. I guess they figured since I was smart, they were safely assuming I was going to do research. But I longed to write.

That spring, I eagerly awaited fat envelopes from my "dream" schools. I ignored the much-touted formula of two dream schools, two reachable schools, and two safety schools. I wanted to wear the purple colors of Northwestern because it had one of the best Journalism schools in the nation. Not to mention it was the go-to school in any Chicago-set movie. Failing that, I happily would trade in my flip-flops for snowshoes if I got into Dartmouth. Notable students included Dr. Seuss and Don Shula's grandson. The latter guy made my mom more open to the idea of me going there.

If we won the lottery, of course.

My third choice, Swarthmore, had the prettiest (and only) out-of-state campus I visited. I liked discussing the role of women in *Pride and Prejudice* with my interviewer. And of course, I had to apply to an Ivy, like all the other smart kids in my uber-competitive high school. I chose Yale because it had a Nobel Laureate in English as a professor, and not applying to Harvard seemed like a really cool non-conformist statement to make.

As the fat letters from Northwestern and Dartmouth arrived, I did not think about the fact that I had never done any real journalism before, and Dr. Seuss did not major in children's literature. That major didn't exist at Dartmouth, and still doesn't. When I got the waitlist envelope from Swarthmore, I was terrified at the loss of a pretty Pennsylvania campus with a real fall season, and not the amazing liberal arts education. When the thin, big fat no came from Yale, I naively thought I was losing the chance to study under Toni Morrison—which happened in the 1970s, as it turns out.

UF was looking more and more like a foregone conclusion. To me, the fancy names of the other schools translated into a secure future; the "safety" of UF was just in being able to get in. Would a state education really give me what I needed to succeed?

I was forced to find out. My family never did win the lottery. So in August, my parents dropped me off at the hospital-looking corridors of Hume Hall at the University of Florida. Within a week, I had a brand new circle of friends. Within a month, I had the love of football. Within a semester, I had academic plans to go to Europe and get degrees in both English, specializing in children's literature, and in Journalism.

Walking across the large field in front of the library, where the leaves had fallen (albeit in January), I finally figured out what the "dream" and "safety" words should really mean. My real dream for college was to find forever friends, balance school and play, and pursue my passions with full support. Maybe I would have gotten those things at the other schools. Maybe not. But ultimately choosing UF meant choosing to give myself the tools to secure my own future, regardless of the name of the school.

Right before I graduated, the University developed the "Go"

commercials. One line said "Go write the great American novel." When I moved up to Boston after getting accepted to my dream Masters program at Simmons College, I would hear that line and say, "Okay! That's exactly what I'm here to do." And since UF gave the opportunity to do so, I have to add, "Go Gators."

~Britt Leigh

Chapter
12

Teens Talk
GETTING IN...
TO COLLEGE

Hey, I Totally
Changed My Mind

Change always comes bearing gifts.
~Price Pritchett

My Mistakes

The most successful people are those who are good at plan B.
~James Yorke

I sat in my seat, squinting as the sun rose over the top of the clouds, searing my exhausted eyes. God I was tired. I had a love-hate relationship with planes — part of me was always desperate to get on, partly to relax my aching shoulder from carrying all my stuff, partly to not worry about anything being stolen, but mostly the feeling. Walking down the unheated ramp that led to the airplane door, I felt such a twisty thrill in my stomach.

This time had been no different. All the ads on the gangway might as well have said, "New life ahead," "Excitement, This Way," or, "For the Change You Need, Choose 37A." It was all the same. This particular plane, this particular journey, signaled a new and thrilling time in my life. I couldn't even begin to understand the profound changes it would make in my life.

So I boarded my plane of dreams and I sat in 37A and I hunkered down for the long flight. I was not prepared. It had been four years since I last took a transatlantic flight, and I forgot one crucial detail: I don't sleep on planes. Ever.

I had stayed up all night packing before boarding, thinking I'd zonk right out. I brought a book, but nothing to distract me, like puzzles. I didn't bring enough water to support eight hours of being awake and bored, nor enough munchies. And I forgot that I hated plane food. And I forgot that, unlike most people who got very cold on planes, I got wicked hot. The sweatshirt wasn't a good idea.

So it was that the sun found me, sweaty, grumpy, bored, and so exhausted my eyeballs felt like it would be a relief to bleed. I stumbled off one plane and onto my connection without really thinking, rolled off that connection and managed to find the school-sponsored bus. I wasn't sure which dorm I was actually going to, so I had to perk up a bit to find the info.

Once dropped off at my dorm, I threw my stuff in the room and locked the door; flying transatlantic, anything cheap and easily replaceable was not included, so toiletries were left at home. I cornered an RA and asked how to get into town, and I began to haul my butt up a huge hill that stretched behind my dorm.

At the top of the hill, I paused—more from necessity than I'd like to admit—and in so doing, I looked out.

The countryside unrolled before me, one natural golf course of lustrous green after another, lined on one side by the tumultuous North Sea. Everything was touched by the golden light of the midday sun, and it took my breath away. I made it. I was there, in St Andrews, Scotland, about to start my year abroad. Though I didn't know it then, I was about to start my whole life. And I couldn't believe how I got there.

You have to know something about my high school. Like any high school, there was a social struggle of cool being waged between all the students—but unlike most high schools, the battlefield was filled with only women, and rather than looks and boys, it was grades and confidence that mattered most.

I really wanted to go to Georgetown. I was a legacy—I should have been a sure bet. But when it came down to it, my grades weren't all that great and my potential, at that point, was difficult to see on paper. But it didn't make it any easier when I got a pretty snooty rejection letter, that basically implied that they really wanted to accept me, based on the legacy thing, but I just sucked that badly.

Girls posted their rejection letters on the wall in our locker room as a private rebellion, but I couldn't even do that. I got into Goucher

College in Maryland—it was nice and I met some nice people visiting there, and within minutes I convinced myself it was the only place I would go if Georgetown didn't want me.

So I wore my Goucher sweatshirt to school and I told everyone how thrilled I was—until the second campus visit. My dad took me this time, and I was staying the weekend. He doesn't like to walk much, so we drove around the campus together.

And it took barely a minute.

"This... this is it?" I asked him. "I could have sworn it was bigger before."

He shrugged, beginning to offer some consolation, but I didn't listen. Instead I opened my quick fact sheet from admissions and made a startling discovery—the school was about the same size as my high school.

"Dad," I said softly. "I made a big mistake."

"What do you mean?"

I showed him the numbers. I hated my high school's size, because it prevented it from offering as much as the local public school. Fewer AP classes with limited class size, fewer languages offered, fewer programs. I couldn't do the same for college. "I can't go here."

He stopped the car and sighed. "Well, did you get in anywhere else?"

I nodded. "Mount Holyoke. But do I really want to do another all girl school?"

"It's your choice," he told me.

I chose Mount Holyoke, especially after being reluctantly dazzled by their community-enriching traditions, like everyone gathering at night for milk and cookies (hello freshman fifteen), the dorms that looked more like beautiful homes, and the breathtakingly gorgeous campus with little quirks like a stone amphitheater and a Japanese tea house—but most of all, I was enraptured by the huge percentage of their junior class that went abroad.

For a year, I loved it helplessly, but I felt a little out of place. I loved the variety of friends I had, but I didn't really like the environment. The fierce competition that drives women had melted down into a campus wide catfight; instead of support and community, I felt animosity and jealousy, everyone fighting everyone else instead of creating a strong female network.

Junior year came none too soon. I was off; I was carefree, I was on a cultural learning experience, a flight of fancy for one year.

Only, I never went back.

I ended up transferring to The University of St Andrews in Scotland, and I ended up doing another degree, staying three years in total. When I got there, when I climbed that first hill and took my first walk into the historic town, little fireworks went off. I felt the magic, the thrill of being well and truly home. As I write this, I have a ticket beside me—in a few months, I'm moving to Scotland for as long as I can swing it.

The thing with college is that it's like life, and sometimes, your first decision isn't your best one. You make it for all the right reasons, but sometimes it just doesn't fit. And you might not know it for a year or even two—or you might even know the second you set foot on campus. For me, it happened both ways, first with Goucher, then with Mount Holyoke. But in the end, college, like life, is all about the journey I took, the false starts and the magical endings. Don't be afraid to mess it up.

~AC Gaughen

A Pittsburgh Rose

Trust your hunches.
They're usually based on facts filed away just below the conscious level.
~Joyce Brothers

"Did anyone get the mail yet?" I shouted.

"No, honey. You can go check it," my mother replied. As I bounded out the door, and raced down the driveway, the cold January air stung my lungs with each breath. I opened the mailbox and all I saw at first was junk mail, but there it was—a letter from the Admission Office at James Madison University. I raced back inside to open it.

As a high school senior with good grades and plenty of extra-curricular activities, I decided to apply "early admission" to James Madison, my first choice school. I applied to several other colleges for regular admission but I wasn't particularly inspired by any of them. I really wanted to go to JMU. I loved the campus. It just felt like a place where I would belong.

My heart was racing as I sat at the kitchen table with my mother over my shoulder. I tore open the envelope and started scanning the letter. "We regret to inform you... you will be deferred... general applicants..." My heart sank. I ached. Tears welled up in my eyes. My mother hugged me. "Oh honey. I'm so sorry. It'll be okay. You'll get in during the next round of admissions."

"No, it's not okay," I insisted through the tears. "What if I don't get in during the next round?"

"You will. And if you don't, you'll get in to one of the other schools where you applied."

"You don't understand! I don't want to go to any of those other schools!" There was no way I could go to those other schools. They had been fine to apply to but I couldn't actually see myself attending them. They were just supposed to be my "safety" schools. I had to go to James Madison. It was the only place I would be happy. Oh why God was this happening to me?!

The next morning, I marched into our guidance counselor's office. "Mrs. Edwards, I need some serious help. I wasn't accepted to James Madison through early admission and I don't want to go to any of the other schools I applied to," I said in an emotional explosion.

"Okay, take a deep breath. Calm down and have a seat." I spent that whole morning in Mrs. Edwards' office. Ultimately we decided it would be best if I started applying to some additional schools.

When I had first structured my college search, I limited myself by tuition expense, geography, student body size, and one other thing. I insisted that I would not attend any Catholic colleges. Having spent the last twelve years in Catholic school, I wanted to experience secular education. Mrs. Edwards reminded me that I was now applying to colleges late in the application process and that I should be open-minded about schools.

That night I came home and my parents helped me apply to five additional schools. We agreed that we would wait and see if I was accepted before we made trips out to visit them. I felt good. I had a plan of action.

As the winter turned into spring, I began getting acceptance letters. I was accepted at every college I applied to from my first round of applications, except I still had not heard from James Madison. Then I started getting acceptance letters from my later round of applications. I was accepted into two schools in Pittsburgh, Pennsylvania, including Duquesne University. So my mom and I packed up and headed to Pittsburgh.

We started the morning at Duquesne, even though it had a strike in my book because it was a Catholic university. As we set foot on the campus, I was filled with a euphoric feeling. "Isn't it just gorgeous here?" I asked my mom.

Duquesne has a charming campus in the springtime. There are flowers everywhere and fountains flowing. Students were studying outside and playing around on the athletic fields. Duquesne is situated at the top of a mountain which overlooks downtown Pittsburgh. It is absolutely one of the best views of the city.

After our tour of the campus, we went and met with an admissions counselor. It turned out Duquesne really wanted me. They were willing to give me a scholarship! My mother was beaming with pride.

As soon as we left the admissions office, I excitedly called my dad. I told him how much I loved the school and that they were going to give me a scholarship. We decided that our whole family would head back up to Duquesne that weekend so that my dad and sister could see the school as well.

"Natalie, let's stop in and make a visit to the chapel before we leave," my mom suggested as we were heading to our car. We walked inside and my breath was taken away. It was the most understated and gorgeous chapel I had ever been in. We took time to say a prayer. I prayed to God to lead me to the school I was meant to go to. I asked for a specific sign. I asked God to send me a rose if this was the school for me. As we left the chapel, I was filled with emotion. I felt in love, and at peace, and so very, very happy.

And so that weekend my mom and I returned to Duquesne with my dad and sister in tow. I flitted around campus eagerly showing them the sights. I was already picturing which dorm I would live in. I found myself with an immense sense of pride in the university. My father commented on how happy I appeared. I told him I wanted to show him the school's beautiful chapel.

Before I was completely in the sanctuary, it caught my eye. There on the side altar was a single pink rose in a vase. Tears welled up in my eyes. I turned to my parents and said, "I have to go here."

The following week, as my parents prepared to send a deposit to Duquesne, my mom reminded me, "You know Natalie, you still haven't heard from James Madison. We can wait to send in this deposit."

"No, go ahead Mom. I know I want to go there. It was meant to be." My mom smiled at me and gave me a hug as she mailed the check that would register me as a Duquesne student.

A few days later, the envelope I'd been waiting for arrived. I was accepted into James Madison. I was happy to receive validation that I could have gone there. But I was thrilled to end up instead where I was supposed to go.

~Natalie Embrey Hikel

78

The Horsey Girl

Horses lend us the wings we lack.
~Author Unknown

There were two things that set me apart from most of the kids I went to grade school with: I rode horses very well and I was a pretty lousy student. Not a troublemaker or stupid necessarily, but very shy and somewhat lazy and distracted. My teachers hated me.

My school had a riding team, however, and my riding coaches loved me. I had been riding competitively since I was seven years old, and I knew my way around a show ring. I had no fear on a horse. I would ride any animal in the barn and could compete with riders of any age. My schools were small and private, and both (I switched in the sixth grade for academic reasons) had high school riding teams. I rode on the varsity teams from the fifth grade on.

Kids in my class didn't know what to think of me. Mostly, I doubt they thought of me at all. I was the weird, quiet kid who rode horses. I may have had my very own high school varsity letter in the fifth grade, but it didn't get me out of gym class. That was all anyone really needed to know.

I progressed through my school years this way, riding horses and being shy. I stumbled through my classes and got in trouble for not finishing my homework. In tenth grade, I got an average score on the PSAT and people started rumbling about college, largely pressing me to bring up my grades. In my junior year, I took the SAT and people started outright harassing me to work harder in my classes. I kept riding, kept bringing home ribbons, and tried not to think too much about the college issue.

Eventually the day came that I had to sit down with my school's guidance counselor and come up with a plan.

"Well, you want to ride, of course," she said, flipping through her file.

"Yeah," I nodded, head down. "Not really."

"You don't want to ride?"

"Yeah, no. I mean, it's not that important."

It's fair to say that everyone was shocked. Actually, even I was shocked. What was I without a horse? Everyone assumed that a series of large, four-legged animals would bear the entire burden of my academic career. When all was said and done, I would end up teaching riding at a small, private school very much like the one I was about to depart. Possibly, if I could bring my grades way up and survive college, I might get into veterinary school one day. No one, least of all me, thought I could do anything even remotely notable without four legs underneath me.

There was, however, a problem. Over the years I had lost the drive. It wasn't that anything else seemed all that important; it was just that I had developed this itch to be someone else. I began to feel like I was faking it, and I noticed that I was wrestling with horses instead of riding them. However, I also didn't know how to stop. Who on earth was I if not the girl on the horse in the yearbook?

"I just want to go somewhere different," I said to the college counselor. "I want to go away."

My counselor selected several small, liberal arts colleges for me to look at, mostly in upstate New York and Ohio. I suppose she considered this far enough away from my home in Maryland, but not so far as to be completely foreign. Their common thread was that they were pretty remote and not particularly selective academically. After all, take away the varsity riding, and I was an unmemorable C student with a very awkward personality. There weren't going to be that many options, clearly.

"Okay," I said. "I'll look."

I did everything she told me to do and prayed that I would be accepted somewhere. I wrote my essays about books I liked. In my interviews I talked about wanting to experience the broader world in general, if uninformed, terms.

All these years later, it's hard to remember actually being accepted to college. I'm reasonably certain my acceptance letter came with as much panic as relief. Relief that I had somewhere to go, panic that there would not be a riding program to disappear into if I changed my mind. What I do remember is arriving on that first day wearing a long green skirt and a neat new white blouse. I remember walking down the path to the student center like an actress going to accept an award, determined to present a different me. A me who would not be shy. A me who did not have a saddle on my hip. A me without a fall schedule of competitions and daily riding practices. I was good at nothing, open to everything, and hopelessly naïve about the rest of my life.

It was the best feeling ever.

I turn forty years old this year and haven't ridden horses since high school, other than a few trail rides on vacations just for fun. Do I miss it? Sure, sometimes. Was giving it up the right thing to do? For me, yes. The things that have filled the void—great friends, a career, a passion for reading and writing, a husband and children—are beyond any expectation I ever allowed myself to have in high school. Shedding the life of a horsey girl was what I needed to do to allow myself to grow into me, which was the most important gift my four years of college had to give.

When I think about my middle and high school years and the horses that carried me through them, I sometimes feel as though I was brought to the gates of adulthood by some mythological beast, a beautiful animal who cared for me when I was afraid and guided me when I was lost. When we parted ways, we looked each other in the eye and wished each other well. And then I turned toward that little campus in the center of Ohio and began the rest of my life.

~Christina Kapp

Road of One Thousand Bends

Nothing in life is to be feared.
It is only to be understood.
~Marie Curie

W hen I graduated from high school in Scotland everyone assumed I would go on to college. I really dropped a bombshell when I said that was not going to be the case. My aunt, the most outspoken of our family, sat me down and asked in her own subtle way, "What the hell is going on with you?"

I met her steely-eyed gaze and said; "It's a long and far too difficult road for me."

My aunt Paula studied me and exclaimed, "Havers!" (a good old Scottish word implying I was talking absolute rubbish).

"No," I replied. "It's all the years ahead of me — days full of learning and nights full of studying. My friends will be out playing sports or going to the movies, and I will be at home with my books. No weekends of boyfriends or going dancing, because I won't have the time. I'll have no money to buy music or clothes and my life will be a misery."

I expected Paula to be taken aback at my grand, and I have to admit, well-rehearsed reasoning. I was not prepared for her snapping at me, "This all goes back to Tossa de Mar in Spain and that so-called "Road of a Thousand Bends" of yours."

I stared at her amazed. "I don't see the connection with that and my not going to college."

"Oh," she responded, "then maybe you are not as bright as you like to think!"

I had always been car sick, so when I went on my first flight at the age of twelve, my family expected the worst, but I loved it. Landing in Gerona, in northeastern Spain, we boarded a bus to take us to Tossa de Mar. At first, I was fine, but as we got closer to Tossa, the road began to bend and twist, and just kept on winding. They stopped the bus twice for me to be sick, and I nearly died! I was so bad that on the return journey we took a taxi so that it was easier to make stops for me.

It took my family two years to persuade me to go back to Tossa. If it weren't for the fact that it was such a beautiful little Spanish town, and I had fallen in love with it, nothing would have made me go back. This time we hired a car and drove along what I had by then christened "the road of a thousand bends!"

I dreaded it all through the flight, I steeled myself for the bends to start, and then I was sick most of the way to Tossa as usual! I declared on that holiday I would never go back.

Giving me time to remember, Paula continued, "Why do you always have to focus on the one thing you dislike, when it is surrounded by things you do like?"

"I don't do that!" I denied hotly.

Paula waved a hand. "Of course you do. If you concentrate on the negative, it will take over your life. This whole college thing is your "road of a thousand bends" all over again."

"What?" I asked. "It has nothing to do with that horrendous road?"

"The road is not horrendous and it does not have a thousand bends," she pointed out. "Actually there are fifteen of them, steep, I admit. I can understand they made you sick the first time, but after that, it was all you focused on. You have to put things in perspective; everyone has to accept the things they don't like along with those that they do!"

I took that in and got a bit tearful and she sighed, "It's part of growing up. You have to learn things about yourself, good and bad. If you give up on your education now, it's yourself you are letting down. You could at least give it a try and stop moaning about the bad things and think of all the good things."

"What good things, that I will get certificates and be regarded as brainy, but lose out on my youth?"

Paula walked towards me in an almost threatening manner at that outburst. "Do you think every kid who goes to college leads such a dull and tragic life as you anticipate for yourself?"

I decided it was best to stay silent to that question, and besides, I had no answer.

"You will make lots of new friends, share your studying with them and obviously, you can play your sports at college. You can get a part-time job and earn money to buy all those things you think you will never be able to afford. You can choose subjects that interest you and find endless things full of enjoyment and fun that every other student seems to manage. If you can't find a boyfriend during all that, then you probably never will, so why worry on that score?"

Fortunately, I listened to what my aunt said to me that day. I made friends for life at college, fell in love and out again a few times, had a number of weird and wonderful jobs and studied hard, yet I enjoyed it all. I can honestly say they were some of the best years of my life and though there were some bends, there were nothing like a thousand, and the journey was just as exciting and special to me as my destination.

~Joyce Stark

Choose Wisely

Good decisions come from experience,
and experience comes from bad decisions.
~Author Unknown

I t's a day everyone looks forward to, some with feelings of anxiety and dread, others with excitement and anticipation. I, personally, could not have been more excited.

It was my first day of college, and not a regular, run of the mill college, but one in downtown Chicago. After living in the suburbs my entire life, the idea of becoming a "city girl" was polluting my brain. I would take the subway and hail cabs. I would know all the trendy little spots and be a regular at their functions. I would be cool and mysterious at times and open and flamboyant at others.

This was it. This was the beginning of the rest of my life. It's amazing how quickly what I considered a most promising beginning could turn into what was, by my standards, one of the most traumatic events of my life.

I should have made some assumptions from the weather. It was like one of those way too obvious foreshadowing scenes you read in books. It was overcast and dreary. It was late August, and despite being only 7:00 A.M., it was already hot to a stifling degree, and the humidity was oppressive. There was a stench of staleness in the air. Obvious overtones aside, I was still optimistic.

I drove my brand new car to the train station in an excited hurry. The train ride seemed to drag on indefinitely, like when you were younger and the week before your birthday could not pass fast enough. Looking back, if I had known what awaited me at the end of that ride, I would have appreciated the slow train.

It started right as I stepped off the train, or should I say, tumbled off the train. As soon as I set my foot down, I knew it wouldn't be good. As I felt myself falling, my arms flailed out searching for anything to help me regain my balance. My left hand caught hold of something, and out of reflex, I clung to it with every ounce of strength in me.

Unfortunately, what I had caught onto was another passenger's bag. Not only did I fall completely out of the train, but I brought an innocent bystander down with me. My initial state of shock quickly turned to complete mortification as several passers-by glanced, snickered, and continued on their way. I stood up, by this time a quite unnatural shade of red, offered a hand and a quick apology to my unfortunate companion, and scurried on my way.

Continuing on, I found myself in an unusually empty subway car. After looking around, I knew why. The ground had several random wet spots in an array of colors, some complete with unidentifiable chunks and pieces. The ads that lined the top of the car were for services such as 1-800-AM-I-A-DAD and cheap legal services with slogans like "We'll come bail you out." The graffiti that decorated the plastic seats and dirty windows was from killing, stealing, ruthless gangs. I was slowly beginning to see exactly how out of my element I was. I could not get out of there fast enough. When my stop finally came, I all but ran out onto the platform.

As I looked around, I could physically feel my excitement turning to dread. I had no idea what I was doing or where I was going. I had been to freshman orientation, but I was too busy socializing to really pay attention. I followed a group of fellow students up a small flight of stairs ready to be greeted by the school I had been looking forward to attending for several months. Instead, I was greeted with one of the most depressing sights of my life. During orientation, I realized the campus was far from attractive, but then it was sunny.

Now, in the gloom of the approaching storm, the place seemed to be crying out to some all powerful force to take it out of its misery.

The landscaping was wilting in the sweltering heat. The mismatched brick of the buildings, ranging from white to almost black, stood out against the green-tinged sky. The windows, on the select few buildings that actually possessed them, were all of a foot wide, tinted dark brown, and in desperate need of a washing. The skeletons of a complex system of skywalks that had been long ago removed remained attached to some buildings, boarded up with plywood with ominous phrases such as "Danger" and "Positively No Admittance" spray-painted across them in faded orange paint.

I hurried to class, and opened the door to lecture hall F3. Because I knew lecture hall A1 was for the largest classes, I purposely chose the section in F3 in an attempt to get a smaller class. I was ten minutes early, and there were already well over 100 people waiting. I tried not to look stunned and give away my freshman status. I took a seat at the end of a row near the middle of the room. As the class grew, so did my astonishment. A math class with roughly 200 people was above and beyond my expectations.

I have been described as a social butterfly, and with so many opportunities to talk, I almost didn't know where to start. I decided to try the girl next to me. She reminded me of a friend from back home so I felt a sense a familiarity.

I started simply. "Hi!"

She looked up and looked back at the picture she was so intently drawing on her desk. Still, I tried again. "Um... have you bought this book yet?"

This time, the look she gave me spoke volumes. She returned to drawing on her desk, and I dropped it. I attempted one more conversation with another kid and it went much the same way, only this time, instead of finding vandalism more enticing, he chose the imaginary lint on his shirt. I was stunned. Never in my life had people so rudely rebuffed my attempts at conversation. I looked around, and slowly and sadly came to the realization that none of the 200 people were talking with one another.

I wanted to cry. I continued through the day just going through the motions. My two other classes were strikingly similar to the first.

Even the one hour cafeteria break didn't show any promise of the year I had envisioned. I rode home in a daze. I was too disappointed for words, like a child who has just found out the truth about Santa Claus, the Tooth Fairy and the Easter Bunny in one day.

As soon as I got home, I started looking into transferring schools. Some might think I was overreacting, claiming everyone has a bad day and that just happened to be mine. I had a gut instinct, though, that I could not ignore. That was just not the place for me, and I knew it.

I was frustrated with myself because I knew it was a mistake that I did not have to make. There was a long list of steps I could have taken to prevent spending a year at a school I could not stand, including a visit to the campus or an evaluation of my real reasons for choosing that school, but because of that day, and several others like it, I can truly appreciate the path I set up for myself when I made my decision to transfer. It made me realize the importance of being in the right atmosphere and the right environment. After I transferred, I was happier than I had been in a long time, I can honestly say I owe it to that first horrible day of college.

~Megan Foley

Chapter
13

Teens Talk

GETTING IN...
TO COLLEGE

Gap Years and
Other Alternative Paths

Do not go where the path may lead;
go instead where there is no path and leave a trail.
~Ralph Waldo Emerson

Gap Year Missionary

Life is either a daring adventure or nothing.
~Helen Keller

I blinked once, twice, trying to make sense of what was happening. My eyes, bleary from more than twenty-four hours of constant travel, flitted over the surroundings of my new home in the YMCA of Lima, Peru. I took everything in: the spartan room filled with steel bunk beds, the giant crucifix above my bed, the enormous yellow "Jesus Lives!" banner below my window, the piles of pocket-sized New Testaments by the closet door. My stomach dropped six floors. What had I gotten myself into?

I was eighteen years old when I set off for a totally new world. Among my middle class suburban friends, I was one of the only ones who didn't go straight to a four year college. While they were buying comforters and trash cans at Bed, Bath & Beyond for their new dorm rooms, I decided to invest in a green hiking backpack, get my passport ready, and take off for the horizon.

My high school was pretty typical among the area high schools. We grew up with the understanding that college was the only route after high school, no questions. But I wasn't ready to go to college. I didn't know what I wanted to do or what I wanted to study.

People call it a year "off," the year I spent between high school and college, first milking cows on a commune in Israel (a kibbutz), then on the other side of the world volunteering with the YMCA in Lima, Peru.

But this wasn't a vacation — my gap year was the best decision I ever made. I learned to speak two languages, worked outside under the Mediterranean sun, and salsa danced in the shanty towns of Lima.

High school seniors often don't consider taking some time on the relentless march to a bachelor's degree. Hey, man, slow down! Going to college is an amazing opportunity, one that you should take advantage of when you are totally ready, not just because your friends are doing it. So many people around the world and in America would love to be in your situation, so make sure you are mature enough to really get everything out of the experience.

A gap year isn't expensive — you'd be surprised how little money you need to survive when you're living abroad, if you don't mind roughing it a little. There are so many programs out somewhere on the Internet where you can work in exchange for room and board, both in the States and around the world. All it takes is some flexibility and an open mind. Work, volunteer, travel, live somewhere new. The experiences you gain will be priceless.

I know my experiences were certainly interesting. Before I left on my whirlwind adventure, the International YMCA office in New York reassured me that a nice Jewish girl from suburban Boston had nothing to worry about, working with the Young Men's Christian Association. Yes, Peru was 98% Roman Catholic, but don't worry, you'll be fine, they told me.

The opposite turned out to be true. Me, Melanie Lidman, with ten years of Hebrew School under my belt and the biggest Jewish nose you've ever seen, suddenly found myself in a foreign country singing songs about Jesus and planning skits about the Holy Trinity. It sounds implausible, but it's true: I had accidentally become a Catholic missionary.

Surviving those five months in Peru was the most difficult and most rewarding thing I have ever done. Among other things, it gave me an incredible sense of self and pride in my identity. I learned quickly how to adapt to a culture completely foreign to what I knew. Though I disagreed with some of the religious messages, I felt passionate about the social work we were doing in Lima's poorest slums.

We brought weekly recreation programs to these plywood shack neighborhoods, tutored child street workers, and collaborated with local teens to start a community nutrition group. The poverty I saw was shocking, arresting: something I never could have learned in the classroom. The days were hard, but I knew these experiences were the reasons I put off college in the first place.

I started college the next year a completely different person. Confident, relaxed, more mature. I decided to study journalism, something that would enable me to continue traveling and learning about different places, and writing about other people's stories. At my large university, I found some amazing friends who also took alternative routes towards graduation. I stayed in touch with my friends around the world and even led a short YMCA spring break trip back to Peru the following year. In short, I was ready to be in college.

Taking the road less traveled is always scary. There were times that I was lonely and homesick and missed my friends, who regaled me with stories about college keg parties and crazy Saturday nights, while I got ready for the sunrise milking at 4 A.M. in Israel.

But I wouldn't change a thing about my crazy year when I was eighteen. Working on a farm, being a missionary—I wouldn't be the same person today without those experiences.

So, high school senior, congrats on graduating and good luck in whatever you do. But think about deferring for a year or two. The college of your dreams isn't going anywhere, but you can. And just think about it, you'll turn twenty-one before all your classmates.

~Melanie Lidman

A Different Kind of "Higher" Education

God provides the wind,
but man must raise the sails.
~St. Augustine

I was sixteen years old when I fell in love. It was the kind of amazing and wonderful first love that makes your head spin and your heart race. My thoughts and feelings were consumed by this new and exciting relationship. There were gifts of flowers, shared sunsets at the park and late night conversations that brought us even closer.

Since I was so young when it began, I'm sure most people would have dismissed the relationship as a "crush," an infatuation that would disappear with time and maturity. But I was certain this was going to last forever.

The hardest part was keeping the relationship a secret. But I had to. I knew my parents would never approve and my friends would never understand. I had fallen in love with God.

I come from a Catholic family so I had spent many years attending Sunday Masses, singing in the Church folk group, participating in Christmas Nativity scenes, May Crownings, and Holy Thursday processions. I had years of religion classes in the Catholic School I attended. But at sixteen years of age, the relationship with God became personal. In God I found the love, acceptance and belonging that seemed to be missing from the relationships around me. And soon I knew that I wanted my life to be about developing an even stronger personal relationship with God through prayer and service. I was going to be a nun.

A vocation or calling was something I had often heard about. But who can really explain something so mysterious? Maybe if God used cell phones, pagers and the Internet, God's invitation to me would have been much clearer. All I had to rely on was the conviction in my heart that no one else could ever fill my life in the same way. Isn't that really what everyone relies on in finding the love of their life?

My junior and senior years of high school were filled with classes, extra-curricular activities and friends. My girlfriends and I did everything together, but it was actually a boy I met named Jimmy who became the friend I could confide in. I learned more about the life of a religious Sister through an affiliate program. And all the while my relationship with God grew stronger and deeper.

I anxiously awaited my graduation day but I looked forward even more to August 29th when I would enter the convent. Friends planned and prepared for college, while I planned and prepared for my first year in the convent as a postulant.

Toward the end of my senior year, I could no longer avoid the unavoidable. It was time to tell my parents of my decision to become a nun. I imagined they would be upset. My parents' idea of the convent was a place of sacrifice and hardship. They thought they would never see me again. It was too much to expect them to be supportive of a decision that they couldn't possibly understand.

I would tell my mother first. I was secretly hoping she would then tell my father for me. I spent a great deal of time trying to find the perfect words and the perfect moment. They never came. So one warm day in June, when my mother and I were together in the kitchen, I blurted out "I'm entering the convent in August." Her response was unexpected. She said, "What about Jimmy?"

"Well, I don't think they'll let him come with me," I said jokingly, hoping humor would lighten the conversation. The humor fell like a lead balloon as my mother began sobbing and asking why I would do this. I knew there was no answer I could give that would make this decision acceptable.

I was more fearful of telling my father. It was probably not the best idea to bring it up when he was driving me home from school one day. "I'm going to become a nun," I said. In his anger, he yelled, "If you do that, you're not my daughter any more!" I cried the rest of the way home. There are some words spoken in defining moments that change a relationship forever.

The topic was off limits in my parent's house for the rest of the summer. I'm sure they were expecting and hoping that I would change my mind before August came. If you ignore something long enough, it will go away. They painted my bedroom and bought a new mattress for my bed. I joked that they were preparing the room to rent it out after I left. In reality, it was their sweet yet silly attempt to entice me to stay, and to deal with their sense of loss in accepting that I wouldn't.

My friends were supportive in a disbelieving kind of way. Wasn't I the girl who in a huge lapse of good judgment drank a bottle of cheap wine with a boy and returned home to throw up repeatedly on my father's beautiful rose bushes? Wasn't I the girl who was voted by the senior class as "most likely to try anything?" I certainly wasn't anyone's stereotype of who a nun should be. The amazing thing was not that I was in love with God but that God was in love with me.

That summer, my brother got married a week before I would leave for the convent. What different paths our lives would take. My parents were beaming with pride. I imagined their disappointment in me. They would never see me in a beautiful white gown on my wedding day. My father would never walk me down the aisle. I would never give them grandchildren to spoil in their old age. God was definitely not who my parents had in mind for a son-in-law.

August 29th finally arrived. I was packed and ready to go long before the afternoon ceremony. I was happy and scared and nervous and excited. My mother made spaghetti for lunch, my favorite meal. My father washed the car that he would use to drive me to the convent. These were small signs to me that my parents were beginning to accept that their dreams for my life were theirs, not mine.

My father parked the car outside the convent chapel. Before getting out, my parents asked one last time if I had changed my mind. They assured me that I could always come home. "Just call and I'll pick you up," my father said.

I walked to the chapel door confident and excited about living my dream. The Sister who greeted us at the door pointed to the reserved seats up front. And so I walked my parents down the aisle knowing that the dream we shared was for my happiness.

~Maria Zawistowski

My Great Gap Year

One's destination is never a place,
but a new way of seeing things.
~Henry Miller

After a drawn-out and often painful college application process, I received a deferred acceptance from Georgetown in the middle of the summer. This forced me to take the gap year that I had always contemplated.

I didn't see any rush to graduate from college. And, inserting a year between high school and college seemed like free time to me. After college, I'd probably get a job that would turn into a career. When else could I take a year to travel, to do something different, to learn something about myself? Whatever the possible merits of a gap year, I never got to make the decision. I had a year and a month before freshman orientation and I had to do something.

I wound up in Salamanca, Spain in September. I went with a company that organizes study abroad at universities. So my companions in the program were mostly college juniors and seniors. After an orientation weekend in London at the end of August, we flew to Madrid and boarded a bus to Salamanca. One of my clearest memories on that bus trip was spotting the ancient cathedral of Salamanca rise up over the Rio Telme from a distance.

When my roommate, Mike, and I got off the bus, Luisi, a spunky four-foot ten-inch Spanish woman greeted us. It turned out that we would be living in a boarding house rather than a family's home.

This was a lucky break. We lived with an international group that, in November, wished me a happy nineteenth birthday in seven languages (each of which someone spoke fluently). Apart from Luisi, I made three great friends who I am still in touch with three years later: Mike is from Texas, Rainer is from Bavaria (in Southern Germany), and Victor is from Vitoria in the Basque Country of Spain. We talked about girls, politics, music, travel and anything else, in our steadily improving Spanish. Victor always helped us along.

About halfway through the semester, I realized that three and a half months in Salamanca wasn't going to be enough. I decided I wanted to spend the second semester in Spain as well. I started pitching half-baked ideas to my parents, who gently pointed out my plans' logistical flaws. One particularly fanciful scheme was to spend the winter and early spring as a ski bum in the Pyrenees. It took quite a bit of constructive criticism to get me to let go of that idea. Eventually, after developing and rejecting a handful of ideas, I found a job in Madrid.

I went home for Christmas and headed back to Spain in January, with no idea where I would live. After a week of running around, I found a place on the outskirts of the city near the office I'd be working in. It was far away from the city center but it was cheap. And my two new roommates, Vicente and Paco, were great and spoke absolutely no English, which was a big plus for me.

I spent my five months in Madrid working full time, but I got plenty of time off per the norm in Spain, where every obscure religious holiday is celebrated, seemingly always with a three or four day weekend. I spent my long weekends and vacations traveling around Spain haphazardly. I'd leave Madrid with a one-way train or bus ticket and a rough idea of an itinerary. I never knew exactly where I'd stay or how I'd get back, but things always worked themselves out.

One time while traveling in Andalucía (in Southern Spain) during Easter week, I was unable to find a room in a hostel in Sevilla. So, I caught a late night bus to Málaga, several hours away, and slept in a tent on the beach. On a trip to Mallorca (a Spanish island in the Mediterranean), I wound up on a secluded part of the Northern coast after the buses stopped running. I managed to hitchhike back to Palma where I slept in the ferry station for a few hours before heading back to the mainland on an early morning departure.

Experiences like these were fun and they make good stories. However, the most valuable thing I got from traveling on my own was the confidence that came from being responsible for myself, with no safety net.

Everywhere I traveled, I made a point of visiting art museums. I was kind of surprised at myself for this. Before going to Spain, I had been pretty indifferent to art. I didn't dread field trips to art museums, but they were hardly my favorite way to spend a day. In Salamanca, I had taken a course about Renaissance and Baroque Spanish art because I needed one more course and it was the only one available that fit into my schedule. By the time I got to Madrid, I found myself excited to visit the Prado and even reading about art in my free time.

Art has turned into one of my primary interests. (I'm writing this story in Spain, where I'm spending the summer doing research on a contemporary Spanish painter.) Since my gap year in Spain, I've noticed how my interests and priorities have changed. Spending so much time by myself in a different setting forced me to reassess a lot of assumptions I had about myself.

When I got back to the U.S. and enrolled at Georgetown, I felt more comfortable with myself than I had in high school. I was more confident that when I became interested in something, it was worth pursuing. Conversely, when I left an interest or activity behind, I was more comfortable with that decision. I think that while in Spain I went through a sometimes-uncomfortable process of introspection. I reevaluated my values and interests. I realized that some things I'd actually thought were important to me weren't. Other times, I concluded that certain interests or values really were important to me after thinking about them critically for the first time. This made me more confident that they were worth keeping.

Overall, getting a deferred acceptance was one of the luckiest things that has ever happened to me. I graduated from high school a little confused about who I was and entered Georgetown a lot more sure of myself. A gap year was exactly what I needed. Taking a year off isn't right for everyone, but it might be perfect if you want to learn a bit about yourself before embarking on the next phase of your education.

~Michael Damiano

Don't Give Up Before You Start

*Many of life's failures are men who did not realize
how close they were to success when they gave up.*
~Thomas Edison

I couldn't help smiling as dogs—black, white, and brown, some as high as my waist and others no bigger than a small rabbit—launched themselves at the cage mesh and barked. The noise was deafening, but to me, it was also music—the soprano, alto, and bass voices of eager animals excited to see us as we entered the vet tech school kennels.

"I never even knew this was up here," my mom said.

I didn't either. I'd never really imagined there were animals living four floors up from the city streets. It wasn't just the dogs, either—here were sweet, wobbly puppies, cats and fuzzy kittens, rabbits, squealing guinea pigs. Students in blue scrubs cleaned cages and cuddled animals. They seemed so professional—and lucky. Everything I saw made me long more and more for the chance to go to school here.

I could just see myself filling food dishes and giving medications—or sitting right there, in the anatomy lab, or taking notes in that classroom. Becoming a veterinary technician had been my dream since middle school, but actually being here for the interview and tour made it seem so real. And way more exciting than my daydreams.

As we trailed after the admissions director on our way back to her office, I whispered to my mom, "Now I want to go to school here more than ever. I'm going to really work to bring my grades up."

But the interview part of the day wasn't exactly encouraging. The admissions director told us there weren't very many certified vet tech programs in the whole country. The school only took ten students from the surrounding counties, so they could leave slots open for students from across the state and out-of-state. They didn't want to graduate a whole bunch of local students who couldn't find jobs.

I kind of gulped. I wasn't a bad student, but I was definitely not an outstanding student either. Plus, during my sophomore year, I'd gotten a bad case of mono that caused a whole lot of other problems. I became so sick I'd ended up in the ICU for a while. I missed months of school, and it was a miracle I passed at all—never mind my grades that year.

The director talked a lot about how hard the program was, and how many people wanted to get in, because there just weren't a lot of other places to go. She told us, "Apply right away, because if you wait, there definitely won't be a spot." I left with my feet dragging, and my heart felt like it was down there with them.

I was supposed to follow up by sending the school my high school transcript, and completing a formal application. I did go ahead and send the transcript, but I just never got around to filling out the application. My mom mentioned something, and I told her I hardly thought it was worth it. My whole life, I'd been scared to take a chance and fail. Life is hard enough without making a fool of myself. We discussed it a bit, but in the end, she didn't push me.

A couple of weeks went by, and one day the director called. "Maria! How come we never got an application from you? I'm looking at a transcript here, and it doesn't look bad at all. Did you change your mind?"

I was shocked. I thought they would look at my C- average and I'd be out the door, but she remembered me from our interview and liked me, and she understood about my being so sick. She said,

"Don't quit before you even get started. You send that application in — promise?"

After that, I did go ahead and apply, and was surprised to receive an acceptance packet soon afterward. But my next hurdle was trying to decide whether to tell them I'd attend. The director's warnings about how hard the program was had shaken me up. Finally, I told Mom that no matter how hard it was, I wanted to try. This was my dream, and if I never tried, I knew I'd always regret it. Better to try my best and fail than to never know if I could have done this.

The program was hard. It was the hardest thing I'd ever done in my life, and more than once, I came close to failure. But the proudest moment of my life was when I finally stood there in my graduation gown and became a veterinary technician — it was almost as thrilling as the first time I put on those blue scrubs! The best part is that now I spend every workday taking care of animals, and my family and friends know they can always call me when their pet is sick, or hurt, or just acting funny. I like feeling competent and professional, and I sometimes think about what life would be like if I had been too scared to try.

~Maria Wright

85

My Gap Year Plans

Twenty years from now you will be more disappointed by the things that you
didn't do than by the ones you did do.
So throw off the bowlines. Sail away from the safe harbor.
Catch the trade winds in your sails. Explore. Dream. Discover.
~Mark Twain

Some nights during my junior year I lay in bed late at night, stressed out by my U.S. History textbook, *The Enduring Vision*, which rested on my desk, demanding to be annotated and underlined, read and understood. I lay and thought about the freedom that supposedly flourished outside the walls of my dormitory room and the fences of my boarding school, Deerfield Academy.

Summer came after anti-climactic final exams, and I looked at a few colleges before I left for a month in Guayavi, Costa Rica, to do community service work for the one hundred inhabitants of the tiny mountain town. We arrived in San Jose and drove eight hours south, towards the Panamanian border, on paved roads that quickly turned into rocky roads embedded with deep ruts from the daily rainfall. When the sixteen of us arrived, we were met with wide eyes and seeming admiration; our next door neighbors Josué, ten, and Antony, six, ran from their small house with dirt floors and a tin roof. They were curious to meet Americans for the first time.

We fell into a routine quickly. We woke every morning at 6:30 and climbed out of our sleeping bags, dressed in the same clothes we had worn so many hot and humid days before, and walked down the rocky, scarred roads to the *salon comunal*. There was always a layer of fog that hovered quietly, almost apathetically, above the ground and as we walked we could see down into a deep valley walled in by blue-forested mountains that rose emphatically just half a mile away. The land that lay beyond was too far to see, but I thought it might be the Pacific that rested behind those mountains.

Collectively, we lost ourselves in the landscape, the mountains and the jungle, and in our jobs, whether teaching English or painting a schoolhouse. My friend from Tampa Bay was able to forget her best friend's eating disorder, and my other friend, from New York, could postpone dealing with his parents' rough divorce. In the company of fifteen other high school students, we were all able to take a step outside the stresses of our everyday lives and understand how we wanted to deal with them when we returned home.

It was Peter, our group leader, an International Relations major and graduate of Tufts University, who first planted the seed of a gap year in my mind, a seed that would soon flourish like the freedom it entails.

"I took a gap year in Nicaragua," he told us. "I didn't know any Spanish and went there planning to stay for three months. I ended up staying for the year. It was an unbelievable experience. I was alone with my own thoughts for weeks, until I had the language skills to meet people. Did you know that it's possible to remember your dreams?" he continued. "I used to write down my dreams every morning, and by the end of the year, I could not only remember every insignificant detail from any dream, but also write eight pages about it every morning in a journal I kept next to my bed."

Enthralled, I listened to Peter's stories from Nicaragua, stories that it seemed an eighteen-year-old would rarely have the opportunity to be a part of.

The next spring, I got into college with a sigh of relief; nevertheless, I kept telling everyone that I was going to take a year off, without giving it much thought. One day, I talked to a friend who hadn't gotten into any schools and on a whim we decided to live in Argentina together and teach English.

My parents fully supported my decision to take a gap year because my mom has researched it, finding articles that wholeheartedly endorsed the idea.

"Did you know that Princeton is requiring 10% of its students to take a gap year next year?" my mom asked.

"No," I responded, almost uninterested, for I had already made up my mind.

I knew that I would stay in touch with high school and middle school friends, although they would be a year older than me in college. In college, age doesn't really make a difference. I decided that a year traveling was the type of education I would learn from the most the next year. I sent in a deferral letter.

My month in Costa Rica was the first opportunity I was given to leave the bubble of American high school and my American way of life, and I am excited to go and experience the real world for a full year this time.

My group leader, Peter, suggested that we work in the National Park Service in Patagonia while we are in Argentina, and warned us not to plan on making money. The idea evolved and now four of us will be teaching English next year in Buenos Aires, learning how to manage our own money and relate to people in a foreign language.

Until I leave for Buenos Aires, I will be in the Himalayas for three months on a similar program to the one I did in Costa Rica, without anyone that I know.

My mom and I both laugh when she tells me some of her friends' concerns. "What will you do if Bo comes home from the Himalayas with a wife and family?" "What happens if he never comes home from Argentina?"

I would be lying if I told you my family isn't worried, but I am grateful to them for giving me the freedom to choose what I want to do next year.

I am now reading *Three Cups of Tea*, by Greg Mortenson, who tried to summit K2, failed, and is now building schools in rural Pakistan. At the beginning of every chapter there is a quote and at the beginning of Chapter 7 entitled "Hard Way Home," the quote reads:

This harsh and splendid land
With snow-covered rock mountains, cold-crystal streams,
Deep forests of cypress, juniper and ash
Is as much my body as what you see before you here.
I cannot be separated from this or from you.
Our many hearts have only a single beat.

~from The Warrior Song of King Cezar

I hope to experience this "single beat" over the next year in the Himalayas and in Argentina, whether in the vastness of Patagonia, the crags of the Himalayas, or the concrete expanses of Buenos Aires. I hope to surrender myself to my surroundings, to the people and the places, yet also to remember my dreams every morning. And I look forward to returning to the mountains, with only the landscape and my own thoughts, pursuing the enduring vision, without expectations and with nothing to lose. As Peter says, "You can't even imagine how much you will change."

~Bo Swindell

86

Chicken Soup for the Soul

A Long but Ultimately Very Rewarding Road

Always bear in mind that your own resolution to succeed
is more important than any other one thing.
~Abraham Lincoln

I didn't go straight to college after high school. I thought, "Why should I, anyway? I've been trying to get out of school for twelve years now; why would I want to go back?" I wasn't the first eighteen-year-old boy to have that thought, and I won't be the last. So, instead of going to college, I got a job.

Telemarketing was my first, full-time job as a high school graduate. At first, it was almost thrilling. The intensity level at the company's offices was very high. And it felt professional to put on a tie every day. I even thought that I could build a career for myself—garnering accolades and smashing sales records, my meteoric rise through the company ranks serving as a model for future employees! My enthusiasm waned sharply after about six months of repeating the same, lengthy sales pitch every couple of minutes and hearing the same objections from angry customers:

"You know I'm in the middle of dinner, right?"

"I don't want what you're selling!"

"Take me off your list! Now!"

"Get a real job!"

That last one always hurt the most. Looking back, I think that

I was using that job as an insufficient surrogate for the things I was missing. The telemarketing office was near the University of New Hampshire campus, and most of the coworkers who were my age were only working part time while they were in college. I always felt a little left behind knowing that they would be off to lead interesting and fulfilling lives while I was told to "get a real job" fifty times a day.

In order to alleviate those feelings, I got a different job. I became a line cook at a busy restaurant. It was a refreshing change of pace: from air-conditioned office to searing hot kitchen; from quiet civility to loud, high-energy mayhem; from telephones and computer screens to fire and sharp knives—after the cubicles and the nonstop rejection, it was a kind of heaven. I got a free dinner every night and even some overtime pay on busy weeks. Best of all, nobody ever told me to "get a real job." And there were no more ties, which was good because I was sick of wearing them by that point, and I had promised myself I would never wear one again.

That job, in many ways, purified me. The heat of the kitchen and the hard, hard work. Long days and longer nights. Staying up all night and sleeping all day. Burns, cuts, bruises, sore back and sorer feet, all beat me down to the point where I had to find the strength to get back on the line. Day by day, week by week, for two years I seared steaks, fried chicken, grilled fish and prepped salads. I got invested in the tiny, infinitely complicated world that the kitchen offered, and it took me in, burned away the parts of me that couldn't stand up to the pressure. It helped to silence forever that facet of my person that had thought that a career in telemarketing was even remotely feasible. I had no delusions of grandeur or a future in the kitchen, only the food and the fire, one night at a time.

While I was working in the kitchen—losing the little weight I had to lose and gaining a sense of skepticism and a sizeable set of burn scars (the ghosts of which I carry to this day)—I kept in contact with my best friend, who was in school at that time. Sometimes, I would visit him at his dorm. We would hang out, catching up on the time we'd been apart, catching up on each other's lives. He would tell me about his school, his classes, and his friends. I even went to his school a few times, to investigate the building and the people who took classes there.

His world was everything mine wasn't. My existence as a cook was a single-minded life that let me shut my mind down and focus on one exceedingly narrow thing. For my friend, his life at school was the exact opposite. It was all about the massive influx of stimuli that the college atmosphere generated all around him. I realized that there was more going on in that one environment than anything I had ever experienced before—and I was just a peripheral observer! I grew pretty jealous of my friend, and I told him so one evening while we were talking in his dorm room.

"You know," he said, "you could go to school. There's really nothing stopping you."

It sounds silly, hard to believe, certainly not to my credit, but I honestly hadn't thought of that. I hadn't even given myself the chance to think of that. I had stopped thinking about "the future"—that big, scary, shapeless mass of time sprawling out in front of me—in any real or practical way, so college had just never seemed like an option.

"Nah," I told him, "that's not for me."

But what he said got me thinking, a lot. I turned the possibilities over in my mind, weighed the pros and cons, and finally decided to give it a shot. My friend was overjoyed in an "I know you can do it" way. I went to my parents' house (since I didn't have a computer at the time and I was staying with my grandmother because I couldn't scrape together enough money to get a place of my own) to do some research.

Everywhere was closed. Application deadlines were long past. It was mid-February and I was losing hope. I checked all the schools I could think of, but it was too late to apply for admission in the fall semester. Despairing, I called my friend to tell him that I'd given it my best shot but it was hopeless. He told me to keep trying and he recommended that I check with a small, liberal arts college of which he knew. He had some friends who went there.

It turned out that they accepted applications through the end of February. At the eleventh hour, I found a school to which I could apply. Needless to say, I applied, and I was accepted. Getting that letter in the mail, the one that began "Congratulations," was probably the most significant thing that has ever happened to me. Getting into college, and the decision to go, of course, turned out to be exactly what I needed. It wasn't exactly all easy from there, naturally. It turned out that school was a battle for me. But, since it was one entirely worth fighting, it was never too hard or too much. The biggest challenge by far was taking that step and getting in. Hard won battle that it was, it is one thing about which I have never had so much as a single, brief regret.

~Ian Pike

87

Chicken Soup for the Soul

What I Learned at Community College

*In this day and age, some turn 18 and think they're a
man or a woman and that's it, but that's just not true.
You have to establish your manhood or your womanhood with actions.*
~Orlando McGuire

My college career began with a flood of tears. Nothing in the world could make me want to stay at home and commute to NOVA—the community college nearby which had the street reputation of being "where the 'N' stands for knowledge." In other words, no self-respecting, 4.0 student like me would ever go to community college. I was quite sure that I was a genius, and not only that, but that the world owed me something for being a genius. So when the world did not give me what I was so sure I deserved—namely, a scholarship so I could afford to move out and go to a "real college"—I cried. Life wasn't fair. And that was Lesson Number One.

I worked full time through a tear-filled summer, reluctantly accepting my fate, which of course, was worse than anyone else's. Looking back, I laugh at what I now see as just plain egocentrism. I never once thought about how blessed I was to live in a country in which going to college was possible; the focus was on the fact that things had not worked out the way I had planned. Besides, how was I going to get along at a school where I was the smartest person?

And then came the first day of Calculus class. I knew that this would be challenging, even at NOVA, but of course I would succeed—there was no doubt in my mind that I would do well. That was how it always was before; sure, math was hard, but as long as I did my homework, I always got an A. So when the professor spent the first day explaining just how difficult this class was, and how everyone needed to have a very clear picture of what they were getting into, I just smiled. And when the following week, I noticed that half the class had dropped Calculus, I just smiled again.

That was the most difficult class I have ever taken. I did everything a student could possibly do: I went to class faithfully, I did my homework religiously, I asked questions daily, and I even went to see the professor for help—something that impressed even my professor, a man who was not easy to impress. I spent late nights studying, something I had never had to do before. Because of the lack of sleep, I caught more colds in that first semester than most people catch in a year. Still, my first semester ended the way it had begun—when I saw that all my work had gotten me only a C, the floodgates opened again and I cried the whole day, blaming it on the teacher rather than my own shortcomings. But I soon realized that the balloon of my inflated ego had been filled with only hot air—I was no genius.

But if I was not a genius, then my self-worth had to come from somewhere. Maybe that is why I signed up for a weight training class in the spring. And while I might have had somewhat distorted goals in mind, that decision was one of the best I had made up to that point. Taking this class was a bit of a risk for me. In high school, any time I wanted to join a club or try out for a team, I always had to have a friend try it with me. If none of my friends wanted to, then I just would not do it. Being at community college and not really having met any friends, forced me to do what I wanted to do, and not worry what other people thought. But this class not only taught me confidence, it also taught me lessons about fitness I will remember throughout life. I became a healthier person physically, committed to an exercise program that, had I not gone to community college, I never would have attempted. Besides, I had my own personal trainer:

now I was motivated and able to go to the gym with my dad. After that spring, and all those weekends I was able to spend at the gym with my dad, I was no longer envious of my friends who had gone away to school.

And maybe that is when my real growth began. Living at home afforded me extra time, and I responded in earnest to that "youthful idealism," which I think really is the impulse that comes when you finally start to outgrow the selfishness of childhood—in other words, when you finally start to grow as a person. I taught religious education at a local church, and learned just how difficult teaching really is. I suppose that I always knew that teaching was not easy—but it is true that until you experience something, you do not really understand. I also volunteered for an organization that helped pregnant women. I came into contact with people who were truly in need—a population whose existence I had largely ignored. In both of those jobs, there was a period of disillusionment, in which I came to realize that the work I did was not exactly saving the world. Yet, what followed was a realistic view of the small amount of work that I put in. Mother Teresa said that God doesn't ask for success, just faithfulness. An hour a week was not going to save the world; I realized that. I also realized that an hour a week which I dedicated to other people—well, it just might save me.

Having just finished my time at community college, things are looking up. I was just accepted to the University of Virginia in the fall, studying a major I am truly excited about—English. Good things can happen to those who go to community college. My story is proof of that, but most of all, my story is for every high school senior who wonders if his or her self-worth comes from the answer to the question: "What college do you go to?"

~Barbara Jane Wheeler

Teens Talk
GETTING IN...
TO COLLEGE

A Few Words from the
People Who Pay the Bills

*Lucky that man whose children make his happiness in life and not his
grief, the anguished disappointment of his hopes.*
~Euripedes

Live Your Dream

There's a long, long trail a-winding into the land of my dreams.
~Stoddard King, Jr.

When well-meaning friends and relatives heard that our son, Mark, had applied to only one college, the statements were generally like these:

"Shouldn't he apply to at least one other college, just in case?"

"What's he going to do next year if he doesn't get accepted?"

"I know he's smart, but look at the odds."

Even though my husband, Ron, and I had some of those same thoughts, we never wavered in defending his decision and supporting him all the way. After discussing the situation at great length with him, we knew no other college would do. It was Washington University in St. Louis, or nothing!

Mark always had been an intelligent student and college was certainly in his future. Exactly when he became so intent on Wash U, we're really not sure. Some time during high school, he heard it was the best university in the St. Louis area for mathematics, and math was his passion. He enjoyed reading math books the way many people enjoy reading light fiction. I would pick up one his books, flip through it, and only see numbers and symbols that looked like Greek to me.

Ron and I joked about where Mark might have acquired such a mathematical brain. I claimed it was from my side of the family! My deceased father had once been a math teacher at a small local college and studied aeronautical engineering. The "math gene" seemed to follow only the males in my family, because I understood only the simplest math and barely passed Algebra I in high school. My brother, Mike, was quite good at it and he tried numerous times to help me with my homework until he finally gave up in exasperation.

In July of 2005, the summer between his junior and senior year in high school, Mark e-mailed David Wright, Chair of the Math Department at Wash U. He introduced himself and asked if the professor could possibly speak with him, either in person or by phone, for help and advice in his pursuit of advanced math knowledge. Professor Wright promptly replied and invited Mark to visit him the next week.

The day of the visit, Mark collected some notes he'd written, brought a pencil and note pad, and I went along, too. I wanted to meet Professor Wright and let him know that Ron and I were behind Mark one hundred percent. What transpired that day will stay with me for the rest of my life. I watched and listened as Mark spoke in math terms I'd never heard before. I was mesmerized by the entire situation, especially when Mark stood at the blackboard and wrote out a huge equation he'd been working on. It covered the entire board, and it reminded me of a scene in the movie *Good Will Hunting*. It was truly a surreal moment.

Professor Wright was impressed with Mark's calculations and amazed with his desire and ability to work them out. He was kind and gracious and immediately put him at ease. After their discussions, he browsed through his bookshelves with great consideration and suggested some titles and authors for Mark to read.

As we left his office and walked down the beautiful, old halls of such a distinguished place of learning, I know neither Mark's feet nor mine ever touched the floor. I looked up at my handsome son who towered a foot over me. He appeared to be in the same state of pride and happiness as I was. We talked excitedly about the events that just occurred, each wanting to make sure the other heard the same praise and compliments. My son's dream seemed as if it just might be within reach after all.

The next few months were demanding. Mark continued to do very well in high school, and he read every book he could get his hands on about math and physics. His thirst for knowledge branched out to psychology and philosophy. While he was idealistically confident about his acceptance, Ron and I were the ones worrying, knowing how devastated he would be if he did not get in.

A setback came in December. Mark received the news that his early application had not been accepted. It was not a rejection letter, but a deferral stating the admissions department wanted to wait another semester and obtain more information about him before they made their decision. My thoughts were these:

"Okay... they are very interested, but they want to know just how serious and intent this young man is, in his quest to become a student at Washington University."

So, there was more work to be done. Mark continued to excel in his classes. He put together a composition about himself, which highlighted his accomplishments and interests, and stressed his desire to be a student there. Ron hand delivered the packet to the Admissions Office, just to make sure it made it into the right hands!

During those months of waiting, I came across a quote by Henry David Thoreau, which I have hanging in my office. It was also printed on Mark's graduation party invitations. It has been my mantra ever since:

"Go confidently in the direction of your dreams! Live the life you've imagined."

We finally received the tremendous news in mid-March, two months before Mark graduated with honors from high school. He indeed had been accepted to the one and only university he wanted to attend. The acceptance letter also stated an amazing fact: There were 22,000 applications for a class of 1,350. Some dreams do come true, especially if you work hard enough and walk in the direction of those dreams.

~Becky Povich

89

Endings and Beginnings

Star-spangled happiness and banner waves of pride.
~Cherishe Archer

The night my son Christopher said, "Mom, I want to apply to the Air Force Academy," is etched in my memory. Chris was a freshman in high school and an active member of Civil Air Patrol. The CAP senior commander's son had attended the Air Force Academy and the commander had encouraged the cadets to think about it.

It seemed like an impossible goal. We were a Midwestern family with no significant military influence. But my husband, John, had been in the Air Force and had shared his admiration for that military branch and general aviation with Chris. We were determined to help Chris succeed.

We began researching the lengthy academy application process and what the commitment to join the military would mean. Chris didn't seem intimidated by the stringent requirements, such as survival training during boot camp. He continued to attend CAP camps and meetings, as well as speaking opportunities to talk about his role as Cadet Commander of CAP. He was also involved in school sporting events, club competitions, and church youth events. These would all be looked at favorably when listed as activities on his AFA application.

Often Chris was busy every night of the week. Through discipline and good study habits, he maintained high grades, held high leadership positions and stayed active in multiple school and church activities.

Chris finished the lengthy application process in the fall of his senior year of high school and submitted the paperwork. His Congressional interviews were scheduled for early December. Every cadet has to be nominated by a member of Congress, or the President or Vice President of the United States, to be considered for an academy. We believed Chris' years of interaction with CAP senior members (adults) had prepared him well for the poise and quick-thinking skills he would need for the interviews. The liaison officer had said the letter of acceptance or denial from the Academy would probably come in January.

The liaison officer also mentioned that a Letter of Assurance (LOA) was sometimes issued from the Academy. It was the academy's notification to a cadet that the AFA wanted him or her as a cadet if the Congressional nomination came through. Most cadets apply to more than one academy to increase their chances of acceptance (Chris applied to three). However, these LOAs were rarely issued, the liaison officer said, so we should not expect one.

Instead, we placed our prayers on the upcoming Congressional interviews.

Then, one day in mid-November, an envelope addressed to Chris came from the AFA. Chris had a basketball game that night so John and I knew it would be late before he arrived home. To be honest, we thought about steaming open the letter before Chris returned, but we resisted.

When Chris opened the letter, hours later, it was what we had hoped—a Letter of Assurance from the AFA! They wanted Chris for the Class of 2007!

The three of us and our younger daughter, Lindsay, whooped and hugged for several minutes. Then we called our college-age daughter and told her the good news. The whooping began all over again!

I was happy knowing the months of waiting were over. Chris had been chosen among 12,000 applicants to attend one of the finest colleges in the country. He would meet people from all over the world, learn discipline, independence—and hopefully to pick up his clothes.

Chris did receive his congressional nomination and chose to attend the AFA. The day he and all of the other cadets reported for Processing Day at the beautiful AFA grounds in Colorado Springs was a confusing, emotional time. When the new recruits were told to go upstairs for more processing, everyone knew that was goodbye.

The literature we had received from the Academy advised parents to hold back the tears when saying goodbye. "It is hard on your child to have this last view of you in their memory," the book stated.

So I forced a big smile while John snapped a photo of Chris and me. A quick exchange of tight hugs and he was gone.

Chris came home twice a year during the next four years—at Christmas and in the summer for two weeks. Each time I could see changes from the little boy I had raised to a young man—a straightening of the shoulders, good eating and exercise habits, an ease in greeting and talking with people.

In June 2007 Chris graduated from the AFA and was promoted to Second Lieutenant in the Air Force. He is now in pilot training.

At times we still can't believe it happened. Our son found the courage and determination to apply for and graduate from one of the finest colleges in the nation. He now has his eyes set on being an Air Force pilot. I have no doubt if he uses that same courage and determination he will reach that goal, too.

~Kayleen Reusser

90

Totally Awesome

You are my sonshine.
~Author Unknown

I t's not that we don't have anything in common, but he's seventeen going on eighteen and I'm twenty-nine going on fifty-something, and we are a few generations apart. We are supposed to have different perspectives and different outlooks on things. That's the way it goes. However, when my son and I are in the same vehicle, assuming none of his friends pass by in their vehicles, call him on his cell phone, and interrupt our bonding moments, sometimes we hit upon a subject we can talk about without one of us losing patience with the other.

Several Saturdays ago, my son had his senior pictures taken. I went along for the ride to make sure he showed up. He had to sit for approximately three minutes while a photographer took six photos of him. We were going to pick the best photo to go into his high school yearbook.

Other parents have children who like having their pictures taken and look forward to this. Some kids even agree to photo packages where the kid poses wearing a letter jacket, a band uniform, or formal attire. That's just not my kid. If I were seventeen going on eighteen again, it wouldn't be me either. My son would rather be taking the pictures himself and the pictures would never be of a person wearing a letter jacket or a band uniform. Somewhere in the photo, he would have a sunset or a tree or something which stirred his creative spirit. Or maybe he'd just take a picture of a cat. But it wouldn't be for a yearbook, especially a yearbook he says he doesn't want but I'm getting for him because maybe someday in his future, he'll want to remember when he was a kid. Or not.

I'm not sure why he was so easy-going about getting up early to do this photo thing. I think it had something to do with him wanting to grow his Mohawk back over the summer. I think he's smart enough to know that a Mohawk in his senior picture was just not going to fly with his parents. Anyway, my husband gave him a sports jacket, a shirt, and a tie to wear. I said nothing about his earrings. He is who he is, and if he wants to look like a Ubangi, well, there are worse things. When he came out of the dressing room and his black T-shirt was sticking out of his white shirt collar because he didn't want to take it off, I did the mom thing and helped him tuck it in more so it wouldn't be so evident. He was frighteningly cooperative. It scares me when he's frighteningly cooperative because I'm always waiting for the other spiked boot to drop.

The thing is—I like my son. He is smart, funny, and a little bit quirky, even if he is stubborn. He must have inherited that stubbornness from my husband because I am certainly not the stubborn type. He has thick skin and puts up with a lot of my jabs most of the time. He even lets me write about him as long as I refrain from being too honest.

While driving in my son's black pickup truck with his punk music being played at a surprisingly bearable volume, out of the blue, my son said, "I hate what they've done to the word 'awesome.'" Well, it wasn't really out of the blue. My son doesn't do blue; he just does black. I had just made a comment that the word "cool" was a word that has been used by many generations, but other words have been single-generation words. I was scribbling down ideas in my writing notebook which I carry with me wherever I go.

"Like 'groovy' and 'far-out' were just for your hippie generation," he said, which required me to correct him and tell him that I didn't know anyone, except for maybe Simon and Garfunkel who actually said they were "feelin' groovy" out loud so others could hear them.

I also corrected him because I am not old enough to be part of that hippie generation.

That's when he made the comment about "awesome." It was something I had never really thought about, but once again, my son said something very mature and astute—which is why I ignore the Mohawk, the earrings, and his boxers sticking out from his sagging ripped black pants.

What he said was this: "Since everything has become totally awesome, the word 'awesome' has lost its ability to express anything profound. How can something that takes your breath away be awesome, if what Josh said in class was awesome, and what happened at the park was awesome, and if Jen's new haircut is awesome, and if parents and teachers are using awesome just to connect with their kids? Describing an Arizona sunrise or sunset as being awesome is minimizing it."

I thought it was pretty awesome that my kid came up with that.

Then he reached behind his seat and showed me a catalog he had gotten from a college he had been thinking about applying to. "Read what I highlighted on the page that's folded down," he said.

"When I go home, I love telling everyone where I go to college. This is an awesome school, and it's totally awesome being a student here."

"I can't go to that college," he said.

I understood. I also understood that my son is still learning and has a tendency to maximize that which should be ignored, so I suggested he take things from their source. "For instance," I said, "just because some people overuse the word awesome, doesn't mean everyone does. If you hear me use it, understand that I am referring to the real thing."

• • •

The other night my son called on his cell phone. He was in his bedroom. I was in the family room. He didn't want to get up.

"I need you to come in here and read what I just wrote," he said.

"I'll be there after this movie is over," I said.

A few minutes later, my phone beeped, telling me I had a text message. We recently negotiated a deal with my son that, if he paid for it in advance, he could have the 1,000 text messages package offered by our cell phone company. The cell phone companies are very smart doing this. First, they know kids communicate in school with these text messages, and second, they get paid for them twice—once outgoing and once incoming. It's a regular racket. I gave in because it also keeps my son in contact with me—even when he doesn't actually want to talk to me.

The text message said, "pleez comeer & c what i wrote."

When I ignored that message, a second came in: "i wuv u, mommy."

I put the movie on pause and walked to the scary room at the end of the hall. The pet tarantula was in his cage sleeping after a three-course dinner consisting of crickets and mealworms, and my son was sitting in the chair he bought at a thrift shop for ten dollars because he said it spoke to him.

"It's summer vacation," I said. "Why are you writing?"

"I just felt like it," he said. "And I need an essay for my applications."

"Okay," I said. "Read it to me."

"The brilliant crimson sun peaked its crown over the horizon and all that could be heard were the birds rustling in the trees, waiting to meet the coming day. However pristine, the serenity was soon shattered by an echoing scream, "Steven, what did you do to my alarm clock? I am going to be late for work. Why did you take it apart?"

He continued with a very poignant essay describing his need to know how and why things work and why things happen the way they do. I was impressed. It was simple yet profound, and I kept thinking, "Am I being a biased parent or is this as good as I think it is?"

When he finished, he asked, "Well, what do you think?"

"Awesome," I said. "Totally awesome."

~Felice Prager

91

The College Application Meltdown

Teamwork divides the task and multiplies the success.
~Author Unknown

O ne of the delights of my life has always been enjoying the musical talents of my children. Early on, my son Jack displayed a particular penchant for musicianship, picking out simple melodies on the piano as soon as he could reach the keys. Later, he took up the saxophone, and as he improved, he was a frequent soloist in All-State band and other select ensembles. So when it came time to choose a college, it was only natural for Jack to look at universities with reputations for turning out talented instrumentalists, conductors and teachers of music. The good news was that his ability made him an attractive candidate for those schools.

And that was also the bad news. As my son "narrowed" his search to five colleges, he realized that in addition to applying to each university, he also needed to apply to each college's school of music. That meant filling out ten applications instead of five. It meant double the number of contacts, e-mails, online passwords and essays. It meant twice as many deadlines. It meant multiple recommendation letters from multiple sources. Each music school also required an audition, in person. That meant scheduling out-of-town trips during what was already the busiest time thus far in his seventeen years of life.

Jack had always been an easy-going child. In high school he

somehow managed, with the energy of youth, to juggle his school-work with his near daily after-school rehearsals and private lessons and still find time for an active social life.

But the weight of activity in the winter of his senior year became immense. It included All-State auditions (for both band and chorus), weekend trips for both state concerts, additional local concerts, and even a week-long visit to Ireland leading his marching band as drum major in Dublin's St. Patrick's Day parade. His regular class schedule that semester was not an easy one; the senior calculus class was especially challenging. Add to that the weight of college application deadlines and auditions, and the inevitable occurred.

One evening my wife and I confronted our son with the importance of his upcoming college trips. Jack was lagging behind in the application process. We felt he needed to practice his instrument more often. He needed to think about how he would answer interview questions. In our overall opinion, he wasn't taking enough ownership of the countless getting-into-college tasks. As we talked, and as he began to realize the magnitude of the work that still awaited him, our conversation with him became one-sided. He grew quiet and unresponsive.

My wife and I should have read the warning signs and stopped questioning and prodding him, but, we thought, he needed to understand what was at stake. The more we tried to wrench words from him, the gloomier he got. Finally he could take no more. He got out of his chair and climbed the stairs with his head hung low as we continued to pepper him with questions, like reporters following a defendant into a courthouse.

When those questions were at last greeted with a closed bedroom door, we realized, too late, what had happened. Our son was on overload. And the resulting meltdown was acute and paralyzing. Our easy-going, positive young man was replaced by a melancholy and tearful teenager. Earlier, he had been so excited about college, but now it seemed a colossal burden. The looming application deadlines appeared to him as ominous as a terminal illness. Even his assurance that music was his chosen field came into doubt. Music, a major source of our son's joy, had turned into a source of fear and anxiety.

My wife and I put our heads together. How were we to relieve Jack's stress while spurring him to jump through the necessary hoops to get into college? We talked. We prayed. Mostly we worried. Why can't he finish his application essays? Why won't he practice harder? Doesn't he realize a C in calculus could jeopardize a scholarship? The questions were endless. That is, until finally it dawned on us that our son's stress was simply a reflection of our own. And no wonder. The three of us might as well have been trying to eat an entire Thanksgiving turkey at one sitting. In fact, we were trying to force our son to swallow it in one gulp. True, the big picture was enormous. Could the two of us learn to take one task at a time? Perhaps if we could, Jack could too.

So we began to break off smaller pieces, setting one or two-day goals. We directed him first to a single essay in a single college application, then to one more, then to one appointment, and then another. And we made progress. Sometimes it came slowly, other times in major leaps forward.

Jack became more realistic, deciding that there were not enough hours in the day to apply to five universities and their corresponding music departments. The field was narrowed to four schools, and only two of them out-of-state. That February we made one trip, then one more. They turned out to be adventures—leaving our snowless Georgia soil to visit the winter wonderland of Minnesota and the heartland of Indiana, enjoying the tours of college campuses, vibrant with activity. Our son talked with students; he met with professors. As he dealt with one portion of the college search at a time, Jack's spark was reignited.

The interviews came and went; our son performed his auditions beautifully. He met his deadlines. He played his concerts. He got his homework done (well, most of it). All this happened not in one week, not in one month, or even two.

And in March, when Jack returned from his marching band's thrilling trip to Ireland to find he had been accepted by all four universities, with scholarship offers from three of them, he was energized anew. The process had been arduous, but not life-threatening, and not without reward. And when his whirlwind of a senior year in high school came to an end, our son looked forward to continuing his education, a little more experienced in prioritizing and planning, and his parents a little more schooled in patience, in the benefits of baby steps, and in the enjoyment of the moment.

Jack, bless his heart, even got an A in calculus.

~Nick Walker

92

Joy Will Come

Every evening I turn my worries over to God.
He's going to be up all night anyway.
~Mary C. Crowley

C hris's 6:00 A.M. knock on the bathroom door surprised me. I opened it to see our son with a shocked look on his face. Chris said in anguish, "I didn't get in."

I didn't understand, so he repeated, "I didn't get in." Then the tears came. Our high school senior hadn't cried in years.

"What am I going to do now?"

Chris had checked on the website and found that he was denied entrance into his number one college choice. In fact, it was his only choice. Chris was crushed and broken hearted! He had only applied to one school.

When we visited the college a few months earlier, everything seemed to click. We found a great parking spot; the tour guide even mentioned the Fellowship of Christian Athletes play Ultimate Frisbee (one of our son's passions) every Thursday night! I was thoroughly convinced this was the college Chris should go to. My husband wasn't so sure. "Just apply to a few more, just to cover all your bases," John said. But I assured him it was a done deal.

The evening after Chris found out the news, John took him upstairs to the computer and proceeded to apply to two more colleges—I stayed downstairs, out of this application process! He got waitlisted at college number two, but number three quickly accepted him. Needless to say, he was not overjoyed about starting college at a "third choice" school in the fall, but he felt it was in the plan somehow, so he agreed to go.

After we visited the college in the spring, Chris decided this might be a good fit for him after all (the joy was beginning to come). As the summer went on, he actually became excited about going to the school and looked forward to beginning classes in the fall.

Chris got married this past summer. He married a wonderful young woman he met at that third choice college, which was the best choice after all. He graduated with honors and was accepted into his number one graduate school selection for the fall.

If you asked Chris if he is joyful now, he would quickly say yes! Was he joyful that early morning over four years ago? The answer would probably be no. He did tell his classmates, that stressful day when he received the news, "that God had a plan." He didn't understand it, but everything would be okay. Chris just needed to obey and wait to see it all unfold, which took four years.

"In this you greatly rejoice, though now for a little while you may have had to suffer grief in all kinds of trials. These have come so that your faith—of greater worth than gold, which perishes even though refined by fire—may be proved genuine..."(1 Peter 1:6-7-NIV). This verse has proven true in our son's life.

Chris now understands why things happened the way they did and he is joyful about the outcome. His faith was tested, but he was rewarded for his obedience. True joy came many mornings later as Chris followed the plan uniquely designed for him, instead of charting his own.

~Gail J. Veale

93

Chicken Soup for the Soul

Give Him the Money

Money is better than poverty, if only for financial reasons.
~Woody Allen

The attractive blond anchor was interviewing twins, a brother and sister, whose parents could not afford to send both of their children to college. The twins said they were never honors students, nor had they excelled in any sport or extracurricular activity. Yet, between the two, according to the news story, they had received over $100,000 in scholarships.

I was sitting on the couch with my younger son at the time. It was early in the morning, and early in the morning is not a good time to talk to him. Lately, neither is late in the afternoon, early in the evening, or late at night. This is not unusual for a seventeen-year-old high school junior. Sometimes I think to myself, "Well, he IS sitting on the same piece of furniture as I am! We are in the same room." That alone is progress. There is hope, that beyond the horizon, this son will grow out of this stage just as my older son has. For now, I take advantage of our couch-sharing moments and perfect my nagging skills.

"Have your guidance counselors started talking to you about colleges and scholarships yet?" The nagging part is that I already know the answer to my question. I know the counselors have begun because it was written in the monthly newsletter. It was also the topic at several PTO meetings.

Unless you consider a grunt and a look of disdain a reply, my son ignores me.

I consider this a sign of affection. There is acknowledgment that the words were heard.

We moms have to take what we can get.

I know a bit about scholarships because I've researched it before. In fact, several times a year, news programs and magazines cover the topic. It's not difficult to find the information. The Internet is filled with information about ways to get money for education, and not all of them are scams.

My favorites are the weird scholarships.

For instance, in addition to the usual academic and athletic scholarships, Juaniata College in Pennsylvania gives grants to needy left-handers. In addition to corporate, community, and university funds, Loyola University in Chicago offers a four-year, full-tuition scholarship to Catholic students with the last name of Zolp. There is also the Scarpinato scholarship at Texas A&M for students who have the last name of Scarpinato. Stopping right there, unless my son changes his last name to Zolp or Scarpinato, becomes Catholic, or practices writing with his left hand, this money is not earmarked for him.

Bucknell University has a scholarship for students who do not use alcohol, tobacco, or narcotics and do not participate in strenuous activities. My son does wheelies and flips on his BMX bike and that's pretty strenuous, so that eliminates another source of funding. I have seen my son limping into his room with bruises on his arms and a lump on his head, not telling me about whatever injury he has sustained because he doesn't want to hear, "Were you wearing your helmet? I told you to wear a helmet."

The Little People of America for people under 4 feet 10 inches, Tall Clubs International for women over 5 feet 10 inches and men over 6 feet 2 inches, and the New England chapter of the National Association to Advance Fat Acceptance all have funds available for qualified candidates. My kid is a relatively thin 5 feet 11 inches. He also works as a Sandwich Artist at SUBWAY(r), and according to the ads, Jared Fogle lost 245 pounds by eating two SUBWAY(r) submarine sandwiches a day, so I don't think my kid is going to all of a sudden become overweight by having a part-time job.

The David Letterman Telecommunications Scholarship is for students at Ball State University and awards a $10,000 prize for an "average" student with a creative mind. My son is way above average. The kid does his homework, studies, and gets great grades.

The Icy Frost Bridge Scholarship, named for the sister of DePauw alumnus Jack Frost Bridge, goes to female music students who can play or sing the national anthem "with sincerity." Even if they opened this scholarship up to males, my son is into ska music and plays the guitar, but the sounds I hear coming from his band when they practice in our garage for their shows hardly sound like the national anthem. They may think they sound sincere, but it's so loud, it is hard to tell.

There is the Chick and Sophie Major Memorial scholarship for duck-calling. My kid is into eating chicken and turkey, not duck. Plus, he took three years of French, but they did not offer Duck at his high school.

The national Make It Yourself with Wool organization offers a $2,000 reward to students who work with wool. My son wears one sweatshirt and will not let me wash it. In seventh grade, he had to take a Life Skills course, and in that course, the students learned to sew. He had to make a pillow. He started the pillow, but let the truth be known: I finished it for him. The boy just wasn't gifted with a needle and thread.

Up to four students may collaborate on an invention for the Collegiate Inventors Competition with a potential value of $50,000, plus $10,000 more for the college advisor. My son has an inventive mind, but usually it is inventing ways to manipulate his parents into saying "Yes" to a tattoo. And he hasn't been very convincing yet.

Several colleges offer special scholarships, discounts, or two-for-one deals for twins. I was there at his birth and can confirm that he is not a twin. I don't think I would have survived two of him.

A $25,000 scholarship to the Culinary Institute of America is available to a student with the best apple pie recipe. He eats a lot of pie, but his best recipe to date has been a mixture of Pillsbury Dough, brown sugar, and powdered sugar that he and his buddy put in my microwave one night. A lot of it is still stuck to the inside of my microwave.

There is also the Patrick Kerr Skateboard Scholarship. He's a biker, not a skater. There is a big difference between the two. Just ask a biker... or a skater.

The American Society for Enology and Viticulture gives scholarships to students studying grapes or winemaking. Not a good match. He eats grapes but doesn't like them enough to turn them into wine.

The makers of Duck Tape brand duct tape hand out cash to the best-dressed couple at a high school prom if they are wearing duct tape costumes or accessories. When my son was in fourth grade, he made a Duck Tape wallet, and for awhile, a Duck Tape belt held up his pants, but he's not the prom type. Or so he says—this week.

It's frustrating as a parent to watch a child who just doesn't fit the mold. It would be wonderful for him to qualify for a weird scholarship, but I'm afraid he will have to find a more conventional way to get money for his education. Perhaps his grades will open up a few doors. He does work hard and is at the top of his class. But then again, maybe some kind philanthropist will decide to give his money away to a bright kid who likes to sleep until noon, wears unusual hairstyles and gauged earrings, listens to ska music very loud, and still, with his hard exterior, loves kittens. Then, I would have a perfect candidate.

~Felice Prager

The Dress and the Dream

Follow your passion, and success will follow you.
~Arthur Buddhold

In late 2005, my daughter Pallavi and I went shopping to buy a formal dress for her Year 12 Formal. We decided to buy the dress during Christmas as we knew that the festive season would offer more choices, and also because my daughter did not want to spend time shopping during her final year. We searched high and low and finally bought a beautiful floor-length pink silk gown.

Pallavi was ecstatic when she tried it on. As a mother, I thought my daughter was the most beautiful girl in the world.

The summer holidays ended soon after that, and Year 12 began in January. We knew it was going to be a busy year for all of us. Pallavi was attending a selective school and we were proud parents. We knew that she was a very high achiever since primary school—very diligent and a conscientious student. At parent-teacher conferences her teachers often told me about her exemplary character and that she was an asset to the school; it was a pleasure to hear her teachers talk about her. On one occasion, however, a teacher mentioned that our daughter was working overtime with her extracurricular activities and that she had to slow down.

As June approached, Pallavi was studying hard for her midterm school exams. One Sunday afternoon, I observed her fiddling her fingers in the air as if drawing shapes in the air. When I curiously asked her what she was doing, she said she was preparing for UMAT.

The Undergraduate Medical Admission Test is an intimidating exam required for Australian medical schools. I just looked at her proudly and was impressed with her discipline.

A couple of months later, the school confirmed the Formal for September. Pallavi wanted to try on her dress again to ensure she had not gained weight! All the girls at her school were talking about their dresses, jewelry and shoes. Pallavi would come home daily with detailed descriptions of what each of her friends had bought.

The next week, my daughter decided she would not go to the Formal, as she wanted to attend a UMAT preparation workshop which began early the morning after the formal. I was disappointed. I had imagined my little girl with the beautiful gown; her hair and make-up done grandly and wearing those lovely designer silver heels. I really wanted her to go to the Formal, but it just wasn't her priority. She explained that after a late night at the party, she would not be able to make the most of the workshop. I commended her for that, and knew that she was a very determined young lady.

Life soon brought a new exciting phase: applications. When Pallavi asked me to edit her written applications for various medical schools, I was honoured by her request. We carefully read through them together and I was amazed at how well she had written. I did not do much as an editor, but as a mother I was getting emotional. If anybody deserved admission to medical school, it was Pallavi.

When she went to the UMAT, she came home admitting the exam was extremely difficult. My husband, who was overseas at the time, called that night and I relayed the message. We had all known that the exam was challenging, so we did not make much of Pallavi's reaction, and for the next few weeks there was no talk of the UMAT.

Then, late one night, my husband and I were watching television in our bedroom and Pallavi walked in with tears in her eyes and her laptop in her hand. One of the top medical schools in the country had offered her an interview and informed her that she had scored extremely highly on the UMAT. While we both sat crying with happiness, my husband, who has the habit of reading things multiple times, was dissecting the information and trying to ensure we had not misunderstood the e-mail! We still did not know her test score, however. I called my sisters in New Jersey and San Francisco early the next morning to tell them the good news.

My husband and I went to watch our son play his clarinet one night. Though Pallavi and Pranay are normally inseparable, she did not want to leave her computer; UMAT results were supposed to be out. Having waited all day with no sign of the results, we left for the concert. Seven minutes after we left, Pallavi called her dad's mobile phone and asked us to call her back. We turned on the speakerphone and we heard our little daughter yelling with excitement. The numbers were surreal—281 out of 300—and we were so proud of her. However, this did not guarantee admission to a medical college. This was just the first hurdle.

Pallavi started getting interviews from other medical schools. She called me every day during her long train ride home and asked if anything came in the post for her. After watching so many episodes of *Gilmore Girls*, Pallavi routinely asked if the envelopes were big or small. According to the show (and therefore, her) if the envelopes were big, they brought good news. We live in Australia, though, and things are different over here. Regardless, I would wait by the door with the envelope in my hand. Pallavi would rush to open it and scream that she got another interview.

On the 14th of January, a year after we bought her Formal gown, I did not get any sleep at all. The university placements were due on the morning of the 15th. My husband and I woke up early that morning, and all I could think to do was pray to our God.

At 9 A.M., Pallavi said that she would use her dad's computer to check the university offers. Suddenly there was a deafening scream. Pallavi was shouting out that she had been offered entry into the Bachelor of Medicine/Bachelor of Surgery course at the university that was her first preference. Her little brother was yelling and I rushed downstairs jumping two steps at a time to the computer. By this time my husband had to read the whole thing again "just to make sure it is right." In the days following, Pallavi went on to get multiple offers from other medical colleges.

I am a very proud mother today not because my daughter got into Medical School but because my daughter is living her dreams. She is a great role model for her little brother, who wants to be an orthopaedic surgeon.

Oh, and that beautiful pink gown that was unworn? Pallavi is planning to wear it to her medical school ball this year.

~Sumana Prathivadi

Chapter
15

Teens Talk
GETTING IN...
TO COLLEGE

See Ya...

Parting is such sweet sorrow,
That I shall say good night till it be morrow.
~William Shakespeare

Flying Solo

To do anything truly worth doing,
I must not stand back shivering and thinking of the cold and danger,
but jump in with gusto and scramble through as well as I can.
~Og Mandino

I don't see a light upon this path.
I can't find the footprints in the snow.
No one holds the door open for me.
No one's here to tell me where to go.

I've got to find my own way in this world.
I can't depend on anyone but me.
I've got to accept the person I am.
I've got to know what I want to be.

But I'm afraid that failure will prevail.
And I'm not yet ready for this.
I'm terrified I'll shoot for the fullest moon,
And for all the stars,

And miss.

So I've got to wait till the sky is clear.
Wait till the climb gets steep.

Gather my courage, take a breath, close my eyes...

And leap!

~Renee Adair

The Last Night Home

How lucky I am to have something that makes saying goodbye so hard.
~Carol Sobieski and Thomas Meehan,
Annie

I have many photographs tacked to the corkboard above my college desk. One of my family, one of my cats, a few of favorite musicians and concerts, and one giant picture of twelve kids piled on a couch, several caught unaware and mid-laugh as others pulled goofy faces with arms draped over shoulders and limbs tangled in a teenage heap.

That moment, captured on my last night in my hometown with my high school friends, occurred only a few short hours before the night ended and I retreated to my room in tears. After an entire summer of excitement and dorm-shopping, a summer spent anticipating college freedom, I suddenly looked at my packed belongings and reality hit me like an 18-wheel semi—I was leaving.

I was one of those sheltered kids, the first-born and only girl, who never went to sleep-away camp, had never traveled alone, and had never spent more than two or three nights away from her parents at a time. Born and raised in suburban Ohio, I had convinced myself that what I desperately wanted was an escape from the Midwest cornfields. So why, on the brink of leaving for our nation's capitol, was I terrified out of my wits?

In all my excitement over college and everything it stood for (freedom, novelty, adulthood, independence), I had forgotten the sacrifice

I made when I chose Georgetown over universities closer to home — I had chosen to leave my friends and family behind. Too shortsighted to remember that I'd be home soon enough for Thanksgiving break, I bid my friends farewell that night as if I were on my deathbed, and began to sob uncontrollably when I shut the front door behind the last of them. Withdrawing to my room, I cried until there was nothing wet left inside me, and then wandered aimlessly and zombie-like under the pretense of packing my last few possessions.

Soon enough, I heard my mom's soft knock at my door. I sat still and waited for her to leave, reasoning that hugging my mother and seeing her sympathy would only make it harder to say goodbye to her later. Predictably, she didn't go away, and I turned away in a (poor) attempt to hide my tear-streaked face as she let herself into my room and sat down on my bed.

"What's wrong?" she asked gently.

Rather than attempt an intelligible and thought-out response, I simply began to sob again and buried my head in her shoulder. Somewhere in between my blubbering, I managed to choke out, "I'm... not... r-ready...."

My mom stroked my hair until I calmed down enough to listen, and then held me by the shoulders and looked me in the eyes. "I know you're not ready, Michelle... none of us is until it actually happens. I'm not ready to say goodbye to you either. But, you know what? I've seen how capable you are. I know how smart you are. And I'm absolutely positive that you'll be fine. You know why?"

I shook my head slowly, squinting as hard as I could to keep fresh tears from burning their way down my cheeks.

"Because I've seen how far you've already come. I know you can do this. It's hard, I won't deny that, but you know that I'm here for you, and that I'll be right there with you every step of the way." She brushed the tears from my face and stood, darting into the hallway and calling, "Stay right there... I'll be right back...."

I waited on my bed, looking at the boxes and bags surrounding me in an empty room I barely recognized as mine. Finally she returned with a bag, handing it to me and explaining, "I had been waiting to give this to you when we got there, but you look like you could use this right now instead."

I opened the bag, and inside I found an old and tattered stuffed rabbit that I had clung to throughout my childhood. He was always my favorite and my most battered, and I had thought he was lost for the last several years. Alongside it was a DVD of a *My Little Pony* movie I had almost forgotten existed. We had rented that movie so many times in my younger years that it surprises me we didn't simply buy it — we must have paid at least ten times what the movie is actually worth in rental fees.

I stared at these gifts, two simple yet central parts of my childhood, and couldn't find words. Instead, I let new tears escape as my mother wrapped her arms around me once again, rocking me like she would when I was younger.

"I just wanted to give you these to let you know that, no matter how old you get, it's always okay to still be a little girl."

In that moment I knew that she understood and I realized that the world was not going to end when I moved into my new dorm. With a new mix of sadness and excitement, I prepared myself to enter this new world, knowing that I was finally ready to leave.

~Michelle Vanderwist

The Best Kind of Farewell

Don't be dismayed at goodbyes.
A farewell is necessary before you can meet again.
And meeting again, after moments or lifetime,
is certain for those who are friends.
~Richard Bach

M y best friends and I had been waiting for the evening to come, putting it off in our heads until the last possible moment, when it was inevitable that we'd have to say goodbye. Of course, that inevitability didn't stop us from tiptoeing around the situation with the sneakiness we had probably learned together in high school. It was there that we became close, going to the Chinese buffet during lunch hour, driving in each other's cars to no particular destination, and skillfully mastering the art of cutting class whenever a substitute teacher was present.

Our last summer together was filled with late nights at house parties, day trips to Belmar Beach, and obsessing over the impending separation that we would undergo as a group at the end of August. And it was now apparent that our time together was indeed drawing to a close—not forever, but until our first Thanksgiving break as college freshmen, a long, scary, three months away. It seemed as if every clichéd high school movie was suddenly coming true. Visions of tearful goodbyes and overloaded minivans driving into the unknown future played over and over in my dreams. It was all becoming real, and it was all very dramatic.

Instead of getting pizza from our favorite place, where the owners greeted us by name, we made reservations for a tiny, stuffy, and highly priced bistro. As we picked at our fifteen-dollar salads, we felt forced to muffle our exclamations and hold back our normally boisterous conversation. The girls wore dresses, and the guys wore khakis and button-up shirts, signifying the importance of the occasion.

As we conformed to the staid ambiance of the restaurant, it was evident that our quest for closure had not succeeded. There was no sense of normalcy, little spontaneity, and certainly not enough laughs. In fact, sitting in the cramped restaurant, surrounded by chandeliers and paintings of Rome, it became difficult to conjure up any conversation at all. We found ourselves quiet for the first time in four years.

As the evening drew to a close, it was apparent that we were unfulfilled, so we remedied the situation in the best way possible. Though we could try to mask our anxiety through tablecloths and impeccable service, it wasn't what any of us wanted. For the past year or so, we had resolved that someday we would watch *The Big Lebowski* while drinking milk shakes along with the title character. Though many of our other similar goals had been fulfilled throughout senior and that summer, this was one we hadn't yet carried out. Of course, our last night was the perfect time to complete this final mission. After our disastrous dinner, we went to the video store to pick up the movie and then to the grocery store.

We had gone to the nearby grocery store countless times in the past, purchasing a breadth of items for strange uses. We often did this, buying supplies for the night and settling in to stay at Jenny's house until daybreak. Setting out our final evening, planning to buy only ice cream and milk, we somehow managed to return to Jenny's house with these ingredients, as well as a jumbo-sized bag of Milky Way bars, way too many flavors of ice cream, and an assortment of plastic martini glasses in outrageous, neon colors, procured for ninety-nine cents each.

Setting up shop in her familiar, messy basement, we poured our drinks into the bright stemware, played some ping pong, and turned on the stereo. Eventually, we decided to start the movie, but didn't really pay much attention to it. Whenever we sprawled ourselves on the blue couch in Jenny's basement to watch a movie, we never could summarize the plot by the end, let alone recall the names of the lead characters. We had far more fun joking, gossiping, and doing whatever we did, with the movie as a mere excuse for structured activity.

Even though we had no expensive meal in front of us and even though we had changed into shorts and T-shirts, this was our real, formal, farewell. As the movie progressed, I looked around at my friends and smiled. This was what we wanted, and this was what we really needed, I thought. Sometimes the moments devoid of anything special are the ones that truly mean the most.

~Oren Margolis

Long Road

I learned that the richness of life is found in adventure...
It develops self-reliance and independence.
Life then teems with excitement. There is stagnation only in security.
~William Orville Douglas

Heart beats,
Dry lips.
The road never seems to end.
The hours crawl by
With a hypnotic eerie slowness.
Tap my fingers
And wonder, worry and wander
In and out of random snatches of thought.
Leaving home, leaving friends, leaving the security
Of years accumulated in a little room
In a little town.

Finished paperwork, gone through red tape,
Packed my bags, went to bed.
Didn't sleep at all.
Ready to leave, wanting to change,
Worried about it all.
So far from home.
Did I make the right decision?

Did I choose the right school?
Am I doing the best I can do?

Heart beats,
Dry lips.
Tap my fingers on the wheel.

Leaving home,
But home is with me.
Leaving family
But they will never leave me.
Leaving security,
But finding strength
And confidence, and dreams
Within me.

Heart beats,
Dry lips.
Tap my fingers on the wheel.
Take a breath.
And a smile starts on my lips.

Finding dreams, finding love
In what I create, in what I do.
And forever,
Growing, growing, growing.

And I am no longer afraid
Of what lies ahead.

~Clara Nguyen

Dōrm Rōōm Distress

Great perils have this beauty,
that they bring to light the fraternity of strangers.
~Victor Hugo

I remember driving to K-State for the first time with my parents on an early, very early, August morning. My parents drove our minivan full of my clothes, shower supplies, food and other personal belongings, which I knew would never fit in the dormitory, but couldn't bring myself to discard. I followed behind them eagerly in my car. The reality of the situation, of leaving home, never really set in until I found myself in the driver's seat cruising down the highway and I realized that there was no turning back.

It was finally time to move away from the safety and comfort of the mother's nest and venture into the unknown and sometimes dangerous world of college. I was anxious, nervous, excited but mostly scared. I was leaving behind many of my friends from high school, leaving behind everything I knew to be familiar and safe in order to pursue the coveted and prized bachelor's degree in a field that I was convinced would make me a lot of money once I graduated, if I graduated. I felt as I am sure many other freshmen felt that morning—my life will forever change, for better or worse by this experience they call college.

My parents and I arrived on campus, and as I looked around, my feelings of anxiety and fear rapidly evolved to pure panic. What lay before my eyes was a chaotic menagerie of parents and new students scurrying around like rabid squirrels, endlessly searching for the last acorn before a cold winter set in. It was a race to see who could move their child in the fastest, who could conquer the endless crowd first. They had assigned me a potluck roommate and a dorm room on the seventh of eight floors in the dormitory.

Needless to say, I was one of thousands of people trying to move into a building that had only two elevators. After countless trips to the parking lot, which was not so conveniently located a quarter mile away from my building, and endless hours of riding one of two elevators, both of which I was convinced would plummet to the basement at any given moment, we lost the race. It was then that I felt a little bitter for waking up at four in the morning to make a simple, non-threatening two-hour drive across the state, only to have my plans of an easy and quick move-in thwarted by thousands of others who had stolen my idea. For me, dormitory move-in day was reminiscent of Black Friday during the Christmas shopping season; everyone was tired, angry or on edge, and we were all spending a lot of money on things we might later deem useless, unwanted or simply not worth the money.

After I had moved in and settled down, it took nearly a week before I met my roommate. He wasn't around much; I think his name was Carl. That week gave me a lot of time to sit alone and wonder why I had decided to leave everything and everyone I knew behind. My dorm room felt like a prison cell, with windows that never quite shut and carpeting that screamed of years of abuse. While everyone was running around with their friends, eager to see what this new city had to offer, I trapped myself in my room unable to conquer my fear of rejection in the eyes of my peers. So I sat in my room, unwilling to put my shyness aside, and patiently waited for someone else to make the first move toward friendship. I remember that I cried myself to sleep the first two nights I was there. I was furious with myself for jumping so recklessly outside my comfort zone and being overly confident that everything would fall into my lap. I felt utterly alone.

It took nearly two weeks for me to muster up enough courage to break out of my self-induced house arrest. It was a Thursday night and I had just finished eating my seventh or eighth helping of Easy Mac that week. I looked outside my window and all I could see was a massive group of people gathered outside a house across the street.

I decided that it was now or never. I knew that the first few weeks at school were critical to meeting people and developing friendships that would hopefully last throughout my college career. So, I took a chance. I realized that there was much more to gain than to lose from the situation. The risk versus reward weighed heavily on the side of reward once I sat down and really thought it through.

I played it out in my head and came to the conclusion that the worst case scenario would go something like this—I would walk over there, try to meet some people and at the very worst I would leave in the same position that I was already in. If by some chance things went well, then maybe I wouldn't have to feel so alone; maybe I would actually meet some people who accepted me and would welcome me into their group.

Walking over to the party and leaving my shyness, if only momentarily, in the dorm room was the best decision of my college career. At the party I met a guy named Brian. We started talking about this and that, where we grew up, what our major was and how we felt about the little city of Manhattan, Kansas. Brian was a member of a fraternity and after I told him I had yet to meet any friends, he convinced me to come by his fraternity house and meet the rest of the guys.

The next day he called me and invited me over for dinner at the house. I was nervous at first, but I came to realize that there was no need to be nervous—they obviously wanted me there if they took the time to call me and invite me over. The hard part was over. Later that week, I moved out of my dorm room, with the help of a dozen new friends and moved into the fraternity house.

If I had never left my dorm room that night it would have been the biggest mistake of my life thus far. I chose to face my fears and put my emotions aside by taking a chance in a new place. I found a group of friends who I will remember and treat as brothers for the rest of my life. Fraternities aren't for everyone, but the point is that you have to take control of your life. You cannot depend on somebody else to make it easy for you. If I had given in to my shy tendencies that night, I wouldn't have any of the friends and memories that I do today.

~Aaron Ewert

Homesick

Home is not where you live but where they understand you.
~Christian Morgenstern

"I know I told you that I want to go to Michigan for college, but I think I'd rather live at home instead," my son told me, his eyes glazing over as he looked at one college catalog after another.

"How come?" I asked.

"Well," he replied, "it would be easier. And cheaper." He hesitated a moment before the real reason tumbled out. "Besides, I think I might get homesick."

Homesick. I knew that affliction all too well. But I have to admit that I was a little surprised that my son was aware that he might miss being home when he was away at school. I never considered that I might be homesick before I went away to college. I'm not too sure I thought about anything during my last year of high school. From the first day of school senior year, all I thought about was the crush of time hanging over me, intruding on every thought and pushing its way into every conversation. That final year of high school was the last time I'd get to be with my friends and I never wanted it to end. So I applied to one college five hundred miles away from home and when I was accepted, I didn't bother applying anywhere else. After all, I didn't have the time.

Senior year seemed go by at warp speed. One day it was Homecoming and it seemed as if the next day was June 14th and we were graduating. Summer passed in a blur and then it was time to leave for college.

The moment my parents drove off, leaving me surrounded by suitcases, blankets, and books, a suffocating wave of homesickness swept over me. What was I doing so far from home? Why had I chosen to go to a college where I didn't know a soul and no one knew me? Why hadn't I stay where I belonged and done something easier, like work at the local hot dog stand or deliver newspapers, for the rest of my life? I would have been home and I wouldn't have been so miserable. Homesickness enveloped me like the thickest and darkest of fogs, making it impossible for me to see more than a foot or two in front of myself.

But I couldn't crawl into bed and wait to feel better. And I wouldn't walk around crying all day long, even though that's what I felt like doing. All I could do was force myself to act as normal—and as un-homesick—as possible. Oh, and transfer to some place closer to home ASAP.

The first few weeks of college crawled past in a homesick daze. Some inner safety guard warned me that a familiar voice over the phone would unglue me faster than wallpaper in a steamy bathroom, so I forbade my family and friends to call me. Instead, I spent my free time writing long letters to everyone I knew.

Autumn trudged along. Slowly, oh-so-slowly, I made friends with some girls on my dorm floor. Then I made a few other friends in classes and the cafeteria. I started finding people to walk across the huge campus with. And the more I found familiarity in what had first been such a strange, scary place, the less of a grip homesickness had on me.

Finally, it was Thanksgiving, my first chance to go home in almost three months. I spent the entire vacation eating, going out with my high school friends, and amazingly, missing life at college. Sunday morning, my mom drove me to the bus stop. "I know how hard it's been on you to be away from home," she told me as we waited for the bus to arrive. "I must have wanted to call you and tell you to come home at least a dozen times over the past few months."

"Why didn't you?" I asked.

Mom shrugged. "Coming home was the easy answer. And what's easiest isn't always what's best."

I thought about her words now, as I looked at my son, struggling as he tried to figure out where he wanted to spend his freshman year of college and leaning toward the easy answer, the safe one. "What's easiest isn't always what's best," I repeated, some twenty-five years after my mother had told me the same thing.

"What's that supposed to mean?"

"It means, go to Michigan if that's where you want to be. Sure, you'll get homesick but you'll also survive."

"You think so?"

I smiled at him, a smile of experience. "I know so."

"How do you know for sure?" he questioned.

"Because I've been there. Besides, homesickness is miserable but it's never fatal."

My son smiled back at me. "That's good to know."

But it struck me as I put the catalogs away in a cupboard, how was I going to handle being homesick for him?

~Nell Musolf

A Year in the Life of a College Freshman

The more we do, the more we can do;
the more busy we are, the more leisure we have.
~Dag Hammarskjold

I vividly remember the intensely stressful two-to-three month college acceptance waiting period, when it felt like each trip to the mailbox could determine The Rest of My Life. But, unfortunately, the anxiety didn't end when I received that glorious thick-enveloped college acceptance letter. Oh, no—far from it. In a way, the stress had just begun.

So many questions, so few answers. Sure, I'd visited my college campus, but it's not the same as actually going to college, living there, twenty-four hours a day, seven days a week, nine months a year. Sure, I'd seen movies—but the Hollywood version of high school and the real-life version of high school were two birds of a different feather, so how was I to expect the Hollywood version of college would be anything like the real-life version?

Thus, the questions remained, whirling around inside my head, anxiety tainting the excitement of my approaching independence. But here's the good news, now, as I look back on my freshman year of college. I cannot imagine a better experience. Read on to follow my transformation from a nervous eighteen-year-old girl into a confident young woman full of school pride.

August: I can't believe how much energy there is on campus—there is always so much going on, I never want to sleep! This whole month has been full of new experiences—moving into my dorm room, signing up for classes, making new friends, getting my first checking account, eating in the dining halls, getting used to a college lifestyle of late nights and breakfast at noon.

September: My university has more than 600 student organizations, and it is difficult to pick just a couple to get involved with. I admit I overextended myself at first, but I eventually narrowed my involvement down primarily to two volunteer groups I really care about. Along with the joy I receive from helping others, I really enjoy being a part of these groups because I am making friends with other students of all grade levels, majors and personal backgrounds. And it's a great way to meet people.

October: I contact the Dean of the Masters of Professional Writing program at my school and set up a meeting to introduce myself. The Dean is a world-renowned poet, screenwriter, and director, but he takes time from his busy day to chat with me for more than half an hour about my writing endeavors and college experience thus far. I've discovered that professors are often only too happy to help you with questions or problems, or simply get to know you as more than a nameless face in the lecture hall. Go to office hours whenever you get a chance.

November: Six years ago, I created a nonprofit foundation called "Write On" to encourage kids to discover the joys of reading and writing through essay contests, read-a-thons, and my website (www.zest. net/writeon). My ultimate dream is to establish chapters of Write On in all fifty states. With the support of my new classmates and my school's alumni, my seemingly impossible goal seems much more attainable! I've learned how important it is to share your goals—you are sure to find other people at college who share your passions, and who are happy to offer advice and support as you strive to achieve your dreams.

December: Football games have been one of my favorite parts of the fall semester. A friend of mine from high school visited me for a weekend and came to a football game. I wasn't surprised when she didn't want to leave on Sunday! The definite highlight of the month was the annual week of festivities centering around the football game against our rival school. Friday night there was a bonfire, where the marching band played, cheerleaders performed, and the hugely popular band Jimmy Eat World gave a concert.

January: I had a wonderful holiday break at home with my family, but I was surprised at how much I missed my school friends and dorm-mates. I remember in high school dreading the end of holiday break, but this year I was so excited to come back to school—the dorm truly has become my "second home."

February: Giving back is encouraged as part of a well-rounded university education. In this spirit, I join a group of volunteers that hosts prospective students who stay overnight as part of the admissions program. Our job is to give them a taste of the college experience—dinner in the dining hall, a performance by one of the student improv comedy groups, and a night sleeping in the dorms with us. I vividly remember my visit to college as a prospective student, and it is surreal to think that an entire year has already passed since then!

March: I become a part of the "Joint Educational Project" (JEP), a program in which students take what they are learning in class and in turn teach it to others in the community. I am teaching a dozen seventh graders about topics including evolution, natural selection, and Charles Darwin that we are studying in my Biological Anthropology class. I also tutor a group of elementary school students after school once a week, and since many of them speak mostly Spanish, I'm able to use knowledge from my Spanish III class to communicate with them in their primary language and better help them with their homework.

April: I captain a team for the USC Relay for Life, a major fundraiser for the American Cancer Society. This full-day event entails "teams" of students collecting pledge donations from students, friends and family, and then taking turns walking around the track. Besides raising money, the goal is to raise cancer awareness and to have at least one member of each team on the track at all times for the full twenty-four hours. Hundreds of students camp out into the wee hours of the morning, and it really moves me that so many would give up an entire weekend—during the hectic pre-finals push, no less!—for a cause greater than themselves.

May: As big of a relief as it is to have final exams over with, I don't want to leave! My dorm hallway is filled with crying girls as we box up our belongings and move out of the rooms we have shared for the past nine months. It is hard to say goodbye to these friends, who have become my second family. We promise to keep in touch over the summer and are already making plans for when we reunite in August for the next chapter of our college journey.

~Dallas Woodburn

Meet Our Contributors

Meet Our Contributors!

Kristin Abrams received her Bachelor of Arts from the University at Albany in 2006. She writes as a journalist for a Travel Resource Website based out of Los Angeles, California. Kristin enjoys boating, swimming, traveling and being with her family. She is currently working on a novel that she hopes to have done by 2009. Please e-mail her at Kabrams5@gmail.com.

Renee Adair is a freshman at Northern Michigan University. She is planning a career in Special Education. She graduated from high school in 2008. She enjoys spending time with her friends and family, reading, swimming, writing and music.

Max Adler gained a Master of Letters degree, with distinction, from the University of St. Andrews in Scotland while studying on a Ransome Scholarship. He is an Associate Editor at *Golf Digest* magazine where he writes regularly and his original fiction has appeared in *Golf World*. He is also an avid skier and mountain biker. Contact Max at max.adler@gmail.com.

Amy Anderson is an aspiring chef who loves to write novels in her spare time. She plans to attend Johnson & Wales University to receive her degree in Culinary Arts. She enjoys ballroom dancing, volunteering in a local hospital, playing golf, and working in the children's department at church.

Lauren Andreano is a writer living in Clarks Summit, Pennsylvania.

Having successfully lived through her daughter Carolyn's getting into college, Lauren feels reasonably confident that she will survive her son Andrew's college search as well.

Aaron Bacall has graduate degrees in organic chemistry as well as in educational administration and supervision from New York University. He has been a pharmaceutical research chemist, college department coordinator, college instructor and cartoonist. His work has appeared in most national publications and he has been a contributor to several cartoon collections. His work has been used for advertising, greeting cards, wall and desk calendars and several corporate promotional books. Three of his cartoons are featured in the permanent collection at the Harvard Business School's Baker Library. He continues to create and sell his cartoons. He can be reached at ABACALL@MSN.COM.

Laura L. Bradford is a retired caregiver, who resides in Walla Walla, Washington, USA. She seeks to encourage others through her writings. Some of Laura's stories have appeared in: *Life Savors*, and *Cup of Comfort* books, in addition to the *Oregon Christian Writers* newsletter. Please e-mail her at llbradford@hotmail.com.

Thursday Bram is a freelance journalist with over six years experience. She studied Communications at the University of Tulsa and is currently working on her MA in Communication Design. Her work has focused primarily on entrepreneurial topics. More information about Thursday is available at www.thursdaybram.com.

Tawnee Calhoun will be attending Loyola University of Chicago this fall, double-majoring in Journalism and English. Writing is her passion. Her dream is to become a published novelist. She was published previously in *Chicken Soup for the Teenage Soul: The Real Deal Friends*.

Andrea Canale is a junior in high school maintaining high honor roll for the past three years. She writes for the school newspaper. She is a percussionist in the school concert and jazz band. She volunteers in her community and church. She hopes to pursue a career as a Physical Therapist.

Nacie Carson graduated magna cum laude from the College of the Holy Cross in 2007 with an honors degree in history. She is a member of Phi Beta Kappa and loves her work as a freelance writer. She is currently working on her first novel. Please e-mail her at nacie.carson@gmail.com.

Juan Casanova is a junior at the University of Connecticut, majoring in Finance. He was born in Argentina and enjoys playing soccer and spending time with his large family.

Aimee Cirucci is an educator, writer, and communications professional. A proud graduate of Wake Forest University, she now teaches at Temple University where she is also pursuing an MS in Communications. Aimee's writing focuses on the humorous aspects of families, relationships, and everyday life. Her website is www.cirucci.com.

Madeline Clapps is a student at New York University, studying Vocal Performance and Journalism, as well as an editor at Chicken Soup for the Soul. She enjoys singing, acting, reading, and writing articles, fiction, and poetry. Look for her on the stage, in books, and in periodicals in the future! E-mail her at maddychickensoup@gmail.com.

Rebecca Cramer is a senior at McGill University, where she is pursuing her B.A. in English Literature. She splits her time between the Jersey Shore and Montreal and hopes to pursue a career in writing after graduation.

Michael Damiano is an undergraduate student at Georgetown University. He is currently conducting research on a contemporary Spanish artist named Miquel Barceló. He plans to compile a collection of interviews about the artist during the first half of 2009. He enjoys triathlons, traveling, and playing guitar. Contact him at mjd79@georgetown.edu.

Ella Damiano is a pre-medical student at Georgetown University, specializing in health care policy studies. She is a volunteer EMT, a member of the Georgetown triathlon team, and is active in politics in her home town and in the Georgetown University College Democrats.

Michelle Desnoyer received her Bachelor of Science from the University of Wisconsin-Madison. She is a freelance writer. Please e-mail her at midesnoyer@gmail.com.

Alexsys Echevarria is an alumna of St. Johns University. Alexsys has been writing for years. She is currently a stay-at-home mom. Her daughter is her inspiration.

Aaron Ewert received his Bachelor of Arts of English Literature from Kansas State University in 2008. Aaron currently resides in Chicago and has plans of pursuing a career in writing. Please e-mail him at aewert85@gmail.com.

Molly Fedick is a student at Boston University studying Journalism. She has written for numerous publications including *CosmoGirl* magazine, and is currently completing her first novel. Molly loves traveling and scouring the racks at Filene's Basement. She is a member of the BU sailing team and Delta Gamma sorority. Please e-mail her at mfedick@gmail.com.

Seth Fiegerman has always believed in the power of words to inform and also to heal. He decided to become a journalist so that he could engage himself in writing full time. His work has been published in several newspapers and magazines. When he is not writing, Seth tries to be creative in other ways. Last year, he learned to play the banjo.

Megan Foley received her Bachelor of Science in Communications from Bradley University in 2005. After a brief career in Public Relations, she plans to return to school to pursue a new career path. Until then, she lives in Chicago and enjoys spending time with her family and friends.

Marie Franqui is completing her BA now, with an expected graduation date of December, 2008. She has been accepted into the MBA program with UNCW, contingent upon receiving her BA in December. She is married to a United States Marine and is currently living in Jacksonville, North Carolina.

Marcella Dario Fuentes attends University of Wisconsin-Madison, where she is a graduate student. She enjoys playing her bassoon, traveling, reading, and spending time with friends and family. She plans to move back to her native Honduras and play in an orchestra there.

Sue Lowell Gallion writes for children and adults. She is a graduate of Southern Methodist University with degrees in Journalism and History. She has a son in college and will be on the campus tour circuit again soon with her daughter. E-mail her at slgallion@sbcglobal.net.

AC Gaughen is twenty-three years old and a recent graduate of the University of St Andrews in Scotland. She writes all kinds of young adult fiction and hopes that one day her passion for writing will finance her passion for travel. She can be reached by e-mail at acgaughen@gmail.com.

Lauren Gibbons is currently a junior at Providence College. An English and Secondary Education major, she is studying to become a high school English teacher. It is her passion for reading and writing that has ultimately led her to this career. Please e-mail her at lgibbon1@providence.edu.

Alexandra Tracey Gierak graduated from the University of Notre Dame with a B.A. in English and Design in 2004. She currently lives and writes in Manhattan. Please e-mail her at alexandratracey@gmail.com.

Rachel Glickhouse received her Bachelor of Arts, summa cum laude, from George Washington University in Latin American Studies and Spanish in May 2007. She loves to travel and has spent a great deal of time abroad in the Dominican Republic, Argentina, and Brazil. She also enjoys ballet and teaching dance. She hopes to write her own book someday.

Andrea Gosling graduated from New College, Oxford University in 2005 with a BA Hons in English Literature. She lives in the South of England with her partner and many dogs. She spends her time writing and working with young people, silk painting, reading and being outdoors in all weather. Please e-mail her at andii@gmail.com.

Tina Haapala was a member of Phi Theta Kappa Honor Society for two-year colleges. She received her Bachelor of Science, with honors, from Arizona State University in 1996. Tina has worked in sales, marketing, and operations management. She enjoys writing, reading, yoga, and belly dancing. Contact her at tinahaapala@gmail.com.

Jonny Hawkins is a fulltime cartoonist whose work has appeared in *Phi Delta Kappan, American Educator, Harvard Business Review*, and over 400 other publications. His books — *A Joke A Day Keeps the Doctor Away, The Awesome Book of Heavenly Humor* and annual calendars — *Medical, Fishing and Car-Toon-A-Day* calendars are available everywhere.

Rachel Henry lives in Chardon, Ohio. She will be attending Miami University in the fall, where she plans to major in middle childhood education. Rachel enjoys traveling and spending time with her family. Please e-mail her at r.1.henry892gmail.com.

Elizabeth Herrera completed her Master's Degree in Educational Leadership from Northeastern Illinois University in 2004. She currently works as a career counselor at the University of Illinois at Chicago. She is passionate about working with adolescents and inspiring them to continue their education and explore career opportunities.

Natalie Embrey Hikel holds a J.D. from the University of Baltimore. She has a passion for litigation, community service, and creative writing. She dreams of making a living out of pursuing all three in tandem. She currently lives in Washington, D.C. with her husband. You can reach Natalie at nhikel@gmail.com.

Dennis Hixson grew up in the Northwest and has a Bachelor's degree from the University of Idaho, an Associate of Theology degree from Portland Bible College and a Master's degree from Trinity Western University. He is currently the vice president of Pacific Life Bible College in Surrey, British Columbia. His wife and four children are his greatest treasures. Dennis enjoys his yearly humanitarian trips around the world, fly fishing, and gardening.

Erika Hoffman received her Bachelor of Arts in English and French Literature from Duke University where she also received her M.A.T. in English Education. She taught in NJ, GA, and NC. Erika's non-fiction has been published in newspapers,magazines, and the anthology, *Cup of Comfort*. She can be reached via e-mail at bhoffman@nc.rr.com.

Valerie Howlett graduated from Hampshire College last year after studying creative writing, children's literature, and children's theater. She worked for a theater company and a law office before finding her wonderful position at Chicken Soup for the Soul! She loves show-tunes, chilling with her younger siblings, curling up with a good book and, of course, writing.

Natalie Howlett is a junior Biology major at Barnard College in New York City. Please e-mail her at nh2239@barnard.edu.

Liza Johnson received her Bachelors of Science in 2007 from Syracuse University, making the Dean's List four consecutive semesters. She majored in Advertising and Women's Studies and minored in Music Industry. She lives in Chicago with her boyfriend and dog, and works at a marketing firm. E-mail her at lizamjohnson@gmail.com.

Jennifer Lee Johnson is a graduate of The Johns Hopkins University. She is a freelance writer and editor based in Baltimore, Maryland. She runs The Next Rich Girl, a personal finance blog for young women, and is currently working on her first novel.

Susan Johnston is a graduate of Boston University. As a freelance writer, she covers career and lifestyle topics for a variety of print and online publications. Susan dedicates this essay to her dad for supporting her unconditionally in everything she does. Read more at www.susan-johnston.com.

Christina Kapp lives in New Jersey with her husband and children. She writes fiction and poetry and is currently finishing her first novel.

Tress Klassen lives in Edmonds, Washington where she attends Edmonds-Woodway High School. She loves to swim, read and write when she's not busy filling out college applications. She plans to major in Journalism, hopefully at a certain East Coast Ivy League college.

Mary Kolesnikova is working on her MFA in creative writing at the University of San Francisco, where she lives with her boyfriend and two cats. She is the author of the forthcoming young adult novel, *Coven*, and you can find her online at www.marykolesnikova.com.

Joan Lee received her Bachelor of Arts in English from the University of California, Berkeley in 2004. She lives in New York and works in publishing. Joan runs a writing group and plans to write books for young adults and children. Please e-mail her at joan@joanhlee.net.

Britt Leigh is earning her Master of Fine Arts in Writing for Children at Simmons College in Boston. She writes fiction for all ages and always imbues her work with faith, family, friends and fancy. Please e-mail her at beeleigh312@yahoo.com.

Melanie Lidman graduated from the University of Maryland with a triple degree in Spanish, Journalism and Ultimate Frisbee. A native of Massachusetts, Melanie has freelanced for a variety of international publications and dreams of living out of a backpack for the next ten years.

Michelle Lott is a writer in Houston, Texas. She is the chief entertainer, maid, and waitress for three cats and a dog who are all single-mindedly focused on their next meal, their grueling napping schedules, and the scourge of vacuum cleaners.

Oren Margolis is a student at New York University, majoring in Media, Culture, and Communication with a minor in Music. He is a student leader at school, in addition to actively studying classical voice and opera. Oren is originally from Lawrenceville, New Jersey.

Alexandra May received her Bachelor of Arts from Hampshire College, where she made a lot of friends, did a lot of work, and just generally had a great time. She currently works as a research assistant at Harvard University, and spends her free time writing the first chapters of novels and baking birthday cakes for her friends.

Catherine Mevs will graduate from Princeton University in 2009 with degrees in English and Creative Writing. Catherine enjoys playing tennis, reading, and listening to music. She hopes to write for magazines and someday publish a novel.

Kate Mishara received her Bachelor of Science, in Journalism, from the University of Colorado at Boulder in 2008. She loves the beautiful state of Colorado and is full of Buff pride! She enjoys traveling, skiing, writing, and spending time with her family and friends.

Beth Morrissey graduated Summa Cum Laude from Providence College, and the Providence College Liberal Arts Honors Programme, in 2002. She went on to earn a First Honours Masters degree in Library and Information Studies from University College Dublin, National University of Ireland in 2004. Today Beth is a freelance writer in Dublin, Ireland. Visit Beth online at www.bethmorrissey.com.

Valerie Muller received her Bachelor of Arts in English at Franklin & Marshall College and her Master of Education at The College of William and Mary. Currently a high school English teacher, she writes in her spare time. Please e-mail her at mercuryval@yahoo.com.

Nell Musolf grew up in Illinois and has lived in Illinois, Indiana, Michigan, Wisconsin, and currently resides in Minnesota. Nell enjoys writing about her family.

Hank Musolf was born in Wisconsin and now lives in Minnesota with his family. He plays the cello in his high school orchestra and is also on the Speech Team.

Joe Musolf lives in the Midwest. He enjoys music (almost all kinds), playing his bass guitar, working, friends, and school (sometimes).

Clara Nguyen is currently studying at East Carolina University for a Bachelor's Degree in Art History with a Studio Concentration. She enjoys finding new ways to re-create recipes, music, and painting.

Jacqueline Palma is a high school senior who will be attending the University of Michigan in the fall of 2008. She plans to continue taking many literature and writing courses in college. Jacqueline enjoys photography, reading, diving, and dancing. Please e-mail her at thatscooliguess3@yahoo.com.

Donna Paulson received her Bachelor of Arts from S.U.N.Y. Albany before moving to the island of Martha's Vineyard where she has lived for twenty-seven years. A mother of four children, she enjoys writing as well as reading novels, going to the beach and attending church. E-mail Donna at dpaulson31@verizon.net.

Ian Pike is a part-time and full-time writer living in Boston. He is the proud parent of an adorable guinea pig named Ignatius J. Reilly, who he loves very much even though the little guy can be unfriendly.

Stephanie Piro lives in New Hampshire with her husband and three cats. She is one of King Features' "Six Chix" (she is the Saturday chick!). Her single panel, "Fair Game," appears in newspapers and on her website: www.stephaniepiro.com. She also designs gift items for her company Strip T's. Contact her at: stephaniepiro@verizon.net or: 27 River Road, Farmington, NH 03835. Stephanie went through the college application experience with her (now married!) daughter, Nico, so she knows the craziness first hand.

Kathleen Whitman Plucker is a freelance writer living in the Midwest. Her work has appeared in both children's magazines and anthologies, including *Chicken Soup for the Kid's Soul 2*. A married mother of two, Kathleen enjoys organizing events, taking pictures, and scrapbooking. You may reach Kathleen at kplucker@earthlink.net.

Angela Polidoro received her Bachelor of the Arts, with high honors, from The College of William and Mary in 2006. She currently works in publishing in New York City and when she has the time, she enjoys traveling, reading, and (occasionally) pretending that she's still in college. You can contact her at arpolidoro@gmail.com.

Becky Povich lives near St. Louis, Missouri. Her stories have been published in previous *Chicken Soup for the Soul* anthologies, local magazines and newspapers. She recently began writing a column for the *Adair County Free Press*, in Greenfield, Iowa. Both sets of her grandparents and her parents are from there. She is currently working on her memoir. Becky can be reached at Writergal53@aol.com.

Felice Prager is a freelance writer from Scottsdale, Arizona with credits in local, national, and international publications. In addition to writing, she also works with adults and children, who have moderate to severe learning disabilities, as a multisensory educational therapist.

Pallavi Prathivadi is currently completing her medical degree at Monash University in Melbourne, Australia. She hopes to be a writer in the future, and would like to specialise in neonatology. Please e-mail her at pallup@gmail.com.

Sumana Prathivadi immigrated from India to Australia in 1991 with her husband and her daughter. Four years later they had their son. Sumana has a Master's degree in Economics and is now working in the health industry. She loves reading, writing, going for walks and spending time with her family.

Tom Ranocchia is a student at King School in Stamford, Connecticut. A senior, he hopes to go to college to study journalism after he finishes high school. He can be reached at tranocchia@klht.org.

Kayleen Reusser has published four children's books and has had more than 1,500 articles on travel, profiles, and essays published and accepted in books, newspapers, and magazines, including *Elks, The Lookout, Business, People Magazine, Grit, Farm and Ranch Living, and Indianapolis Monthly* magazines. She can be reached at www.KayleenR.com.

Morgan Richardson's hobbies are reading, writing, cooking, playing video games, listening to music, playing music, and watching videos and television.

Elaine Ernst Schneider is an accomplished writer for many audiences. Her children's devotional book, *52 Children's Moments*, is carried by Amazon. Other curriculum guided articles are available at www.lessontutor.com.

Maxwell Schulz recently graduated from Northtown Academy High School and is looking forward to attending the University of Illinois at Champaign/Urbana in the fall. Currently he is busy mowing lawns in Chicago. Max also enjoys playing baseball and hopes to major in Geography. Please contact him at Maxwellschulz@yahoo.com.

Courtney Sohn attends the University of Wisconsin-Madison, double majoring in Journalism and Political Science. Courtney hopes to pursue a career in broadcast journalism, public relations or law. When she's not studying, Courtney can be found reading, shopping or outdoors. She would love to hear from you at Courtneystarr@yahoo.com.

Joyce Stark left local government to write a book about her USA/European travels and a children's series. She has met so many interesting people that her mind is like a busy airport: ideas on the ground, about to land and many circling overhead. Contact her at joric.stark@virgin.net.

Alexandra Swanson currently attends Northeastern University where she is pursuing a Bachelor of Arts, with honors, in English. She helps run www.phoenixpenna.com and enjoys writing, singing, and learning foreign languages. She hopes to become a fantasy or young adult novelist. E-mail her at drea317@comcast.net.

Bo Swindell graduated from Deerfield Academy in Deerfield, Massachusetts in May of 2008 and will attend the University of Virginia in the Fall of 2009. He played water polo and was on the swim team at Deerfield and hopes to study International Relations in college.

Michelle Vanderwist is currently a student at Georgetown University. She loves to draw, paint, play the guitar, work with animals, and stay active. Michelle is a terrible cook but has a hidden talent for hula hooping. E-mail Michelle at mav49@georgetown.edu.

Sourena Vasseghi received his Bachelor of Science in Business from the University of Southern California in 2001. Undaunted by his handicap, he writes self-help books and inspires everyone with his motivational speaking message "Love Your Life and It Will Love You Back." Please e-mail him at sourena@loveyourlifeseminars.com.

Gail Veale is a wife, mom, and homemaker in North Carolina. She enjoys spending time with her two children and daughter-in-law, on and off the Ultimate Frisbee field. Gail likes to go fishing with her husband and leads a Women's Bible study group in her neighborhood. Please e-mail her at ncbeachbum@nc.rr.com.

Nick Walker is an on-camera meteorologist for The Weather Channel and author of *"Sing Along with the Weather Dude,"* a CD/Book to teach kids about weather. This is his second story in the *Chicken Soup for the Soul* series. You can contact him at his "Weather Dude" web site at www.wxdude.com.

Wendy Walker is the author of the widely acclaimed *Four Wives*, released in 2008. Her next novel, *The Queen of Suburbia*, will be released in 2009. Wendy is also editing *Chicken Soup for the Soul: Power Moms*, celebrating stay-at-home and work-from-home mothers, scheduled for publication in the spring of 2009.

Barbara Wheeler recently earned her Associate of Arts degree from Northern Virginia Community College and is now a junior studying English at the University of Virginia. Besides writing she enjoys hiking, running, reading, and playing the piano. Please e-mail her at bjw4p@virginia.edu.

Dallas Woodburn has published two collections of short stories and is currently shopping her first novel to publishers. Her writing credits include four other *Chicken Soup for the Soul* books, in addition to the magazines *Family Circle, Writer's Digest*, and *Cicada*. Learn more about her nonprofit literacy foundation "Write On!" at http://dallaswoodburn.blogspot.com.

Maria Wright received her associate degree from Vet Tech Institute in 2007, and works as a veterinary technician in an animal clinic. She has two cats, Tami and Sydney, and a naked rat, Maverick. She looks forward to having a house and big yard she can share with some dogs.

Krystie Lee Yandoli is a graduate of Greenwich High School and a columnist for both the *Greenwich Post* and *Greenwich Citizen*. Glad that the college admissions process is over, Krystie now attends Syracuse University. Someday, she hopes to be the kind of journalist who changes the world.

Ian Zapcic recently graduated from Ramapo College and is hoping to pursue a career in writing. He also enjoys music, theater, friends, family, animals, and discovering new things. He lives with his family on the New Jersey Shore.

Maria Zawistowski currently lives in Lewiston, NY. Maria has been an educator for many years and now works as an Assistant Principal of an elementary school. Her interests include photography, travel and writing.

Meet the Authors
Acknowledgments
More Chicken Soup

Chicken Soup for the Soul

Who Is
Jack Canfield?

J ack Canfield is the co-creator and editor of the Chicken Soup for the Soul series, which Time magazine has called "the publishing phenomenon of the decade." Jack is also the co-author of eight other bestselling books including *The Success Principles™: How to Get from Where You Are to Where You Want to Be*, *Dare to Win*, *The Aladdin Factor*, *You've Got to Read This Book*, and *The Power of Focus: How to Hit Your Business and Personal and Financial Targets with Absolute Certainty*.

Jack is the CEO of the Canfield Training Group in Santa Barbara, California, and founder of the Foundation for Self-Esteem in Culver City, California. He has conducted intensive personal and professional development seminars on the principles of success for over a million people in twenty-three countries. Jack is a dynamic keynote speaker and he has spoken to hundreds of thousands of others at more than 1,000 corporations, universities, professional conferences and conventions, and has been seen by millions more on national television shows such as *The Today Show*, *Fox and Friends*, *Inside Edition*, *Hard Copy*, CNN's *Talk Back Live*, *20/20*, *Eye to Eye*, and the *NBC Nightly News* and the *CBS Evening News*.

Jack is the recipient of many awards and honors, including three honorary doctorates and a Guinness World Records Certificate for having seven books from the *Chicken Soup for the Soul* series appearing on the New York Times bestseller list on May 24, 1998.

You can reach Jack at:

Jack Canfield
The Canfield Companies
P. O. Box 30880 • Santa Barbara, CA 93130
phone: 805-563-2935 • fax: 805-563-2945
www.jackcanfield.com

Who Is
Mark Victor Hansen?

M ark Victor Hansen is the co-founder of Chicken Soup for the Soul, along with Jack Canfield. He is also a sought-after keynote speaker, bestselling author, and marketing maven. For more than thirty years, Mark's powerful messages of possibility, opportunity, and action have created powerful change in thousands of organizations and millions of individuals worldwide.

Mark's credentials include a lifetime of entrepreneurial success. He is a prolific writer with many bestselling books, such as *The One Minute Millionaire*, *Cracking the Millionaire Code*, *How to Make the Rest of Your Life the Best of Your Life*, *The Power of Focus*, *The Aladdin Factor*, and *Dare to Win*, in addition to the Chicken Soup for the Soul series. Mark has had a profound influence in the field of human potential through his library of audios, videos, and articles in the areas of big thinking, sales achievement, wealth building, publishing success, and personal and professional development. Mark is also the founder of the MEGA Seminar Series.

He has appeared on *Oprah*, CNN, and *The Today Show*. He has been quoted in *Time*, *U.S. News & World Report*, *USA Today*, *The New York Times*, and *Entrepreneur* and has given countless radio interviews, assuring our planet's people that "You can easily create the life you deserve."

Mark is the recipient of numerous awards that honor his entrepreneurial spirit, philanthropic heart, and business acumen. He is a lifetime member of the Horatio Alger Association of Distinguished Americans, an organization that honored Mark with the prestigious Horatio Alger Award for his extraordinary life achievements.

You can reach Mark at:

Mark Victor Hansen & Associates, Inc.
P. O. Box 7665 • Newport Beach, CA 92658
phone: 949-764-2640 • fax: 949-722-6912
www.markvictorhansen.com

Who Is
Amy Newmark?

Amy Newmark is the publisher of Chicken Soup for the Soul, after a thirty-year career as a writer, speaker, financial analyst, and business executive in the worlds of finance and telecommunications.

Amy is a graduate of Harvard College, where she majored in Portuguese, minored in French, and traveled extensively. She is also the mother of two children in college and has two grown stepchildren.

After a long career writing books on telecommunications, voluminous financial reports, business plans, and corporate press releases, Chicken Soup for the Soul is a breath of fresh air for Amy. She has fallen in love with Chicken Soup for the Soul and its life-changing books, and is really enjoying putting these books together for Chicken Soup's wonderful readers.

The best way to contact Amy is through our webmaster, who can be reached at:

webmaster@chickensoupforthesoul.com

If you do not have access to the Internet, please contact Amy by mail or by facsimile at:

Chicken Soup for the Soul
P. O. Box 700
Cos Cob, CT 06807-0700
Fax 203-861-7194

Thank You!

We owe huge thanks to all of our contributors. We know that you pour your hearts and souls into the stories and poems that you share with us, and ultimately with each other. We appreciate your willingness to open up your lives to other Chicken Soup readers.

We can only publish a small percentage of the stories that are submitted, but we read every single one and even the ones that do not appear in the book have an influence on us and on the final manuscript.

We also want to thank D'ette Corona, our Assistant Publisher, who is the heart and soul of the Chicken Soup for the Soul publishing operation, and Barbara LoMonaco, our Webmaster and Chicken Soup for the Soul Editor, for invaluable assistance in maintaining our story database and proofreading this manuscript. We would also like to thank Chicken Soup for the Soul Editors Madeline Clapps and Valerie Howlett for invaluable assistance in putting this book together.

We owe special thanks to Amy's children, Michael and Ella Damiano, for providing the inspiration for this book, and for helping us to solicit stories. We would never have received such high quality submissions without their work for us on the Internet.

As always, we thank our Creative Director and book producer, Brian Taylor at Pneuma Books, for his brilliant vision for our covers and interiors. Finally, none of this would be possible without the business and creative leadership of our CEO, Bill Rouhana, and our president, Bob Jacobs.

Chicken Soup for the Soul

for the Soul

Empty Nesters

101 Stories about Surviving and Thriving When the Kids Leave Home

Jack Canfield,
Mark Victor Hansen,
Carol McAdoo Rehme,
Patricia Cena Evans

This book provides support during a very emotional but exciting time for parents — sending their children off to college, new homes, or careers. It's a must-read for parents grappling with their own bittersweet new freedom. These heartfelt stories about gazing at surprisingly clean bedrooms, starting new careers, rediscovering spouses, and handling the continuing, and often humorous, needs of children, even while they are away at college or ensconced in their own apartments, will inspire, support, and amuse parents. They'll nod their heads, cry a little, and laugh a lot, as they recognize themselves and their almost grown-up children in these stories.

978-1-935096-22-1

Check out our great books about

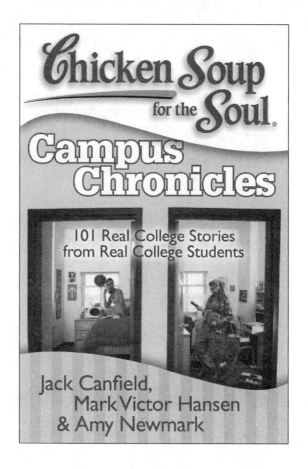

College life can be fun, stressful, exciting, and educational in many ways. Campus Chronicles is a book for any current or prospective college student who wants to know what really goes on in the dorms and in the classroom. Story topics range from the academic, like studying abroad and picking majors, to partying and life choices. Read about other college students' spring breaks, personal growth, relationships with family and significant others, Greek life, transferring schools, money woes, and alternative paths. Campus Chronicles is about growing up, making choices, learning lessons, and making the best of your last years as a student.

978-1-935096-34-4

THE
COLLEGE YEARS

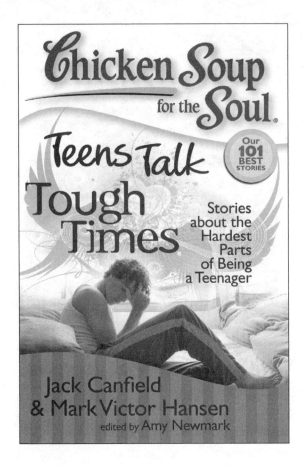

Chicken Soup for the Soul®

Teens Talk Tough Times

Our 101 BEST STORIES

Stories about the Hardest Parts of Being a Teenager

Jack Canfield
& Mark Victor Hansen
edited by Amy Newmark

Being a teenager is difficult even under idyllic circumstances. But when bad things happen, the challenges of being a teenager can be overwhelming, leading to self-destructive behavior, eating disorders, substance abuse, and other challenges. In addition, many teens are faced with illness, car accidents, loss of loved ones, divorces, or other upheavals. This book includes 101 of our best stories about the toughest teenage times — and how to overcome them.

978-1-935096-03-0

*C*heck out our great books for

Chicken Soup for the Soul

CHRISTIAN Teen Talk

Our 101 BEST STORIES

Christian Teens Share Their Stories of Support, Inspiration and Growing Up

Jack Canfield
& Mark Victor Hansen
edited by Amy Newmark

Devout Christian teens care about their connection and relationship with God, but they are also experiencing all the ups and downs of teenage life. This book provides support to teens who care about their faith but are trying to navigate their teenage years. This book includes 101 heartfelt, true stories about love, compassion, loss, forgiveness, friends, school, and faith. It also covers tough issues such as self-destructive behavior, substance abuse, teen pregnancy, and divorce.

978-1-935096-12-2

TEENS!

Resources

W e are often asked about resources for college applicants and their parents. Many of the test preparation services and the SAT/ACT/AP preparation books and college guides are extremely helpful and we think they make a worthwhile investment.

In addition, we loved a free website called:

CollegeConfidential.com

It was a great resource during the application process, and again during the painful wait to hear the answers. We also found it a great support system for kids on the waitlist.

We were so excited when College Confidential loved this book and gave us their endorsement, and we wanted to make sure that you all know about their wonderful website since we found it so helpful. We hope it will make your lives a little easier too!